ADVANCE PRAISE FOR *THE WORKBOOK FOR TEST*

"We all know what it feels like to be at our best. The problem is that the experience can be erratic or unpredictable. Often, our performance is not at its peak when it really needs to be—especially when we're in high-pressure or high- stakes situations. I have seen Ben Bernstein help scores of students achieve peak performance when it counts. Nowhere is this truer than under the circumstances of being tested. *The Workbook for Test Success* is an astonishing rendition of what it is like to be coached personally by Dr. Bernstein. His strategy for helping students remain calm, confident, and focused by bringing physical, mental and even spiritual forces to bear in high-pressure performance-testing situations offers a transformative life strategy. It is one aimed not only at bringing out the best, but also doing so reliably and consistently."

Charles N. Bertolami, D.D.S, D.Med.Sc.
Dean, New York University School of Dentistry

"What I needed was a game plan because experience alone was not enough. After failing a professional examination on the first try, I sought help and found answers through Dr. B's methods. I sat for the exam again and aced it by following the suggestions in this workbook. Embracing the test-taking strategies allowed me to shrewdly apply my knowledge come 'game time.'"

Dianne Burns, Forensic Scientist

"Dr. Bernstein's techniques are invaluable because they help the student to access, process and retrieve the right information in a timely manner. In this way, the student is able to perform according to his or her potential: capable, in charge, and successful."

Toby Mickelson, Educator, learning specialist, parent

"Kaplan, Princeton Review and College Board take note: Ben Bernstein is adding a major piece to the test prep puzzle. *The Workbook for Test Success* is the must-have companion to every test prep book on the market."

Sandra and Ian Griffin, authors of
Step Into College Booklets: 118 Tips on Succeeding on Standardized Tests
*and **110 Tips for Getting into the College of Your Choice.***

"I was really afraid of the SAT until I started working with Dr. B's method. He showed me how important it is to be calm, confident and focused, not just on the test but while I was studying. My SAT scores were much better than I ever imagined they could be."

Peter Nguyen, High school senior

"This workbook helped me think about what one can actually *do* about making the most of what is becoming a more and more ubiquitous aspect of our lives from age 5-25. Bernstein has put together, out of a lifetime of work in the field, wonderful ideas for tackling testing—and making us all more naturally good at it."

*Deborah Meier, author of **In Schools We Trust** and **The Power of Their Ideas**, MacArthur Fellow*
Award winner and vice chair emeritus of The Coalition of Essential Schools.

"Dr. B's methodology gave me a tool box so I could be calm, confident, and focused during high-anxiety exam situations. Using Dr. B's model I went from saying 'I want to' to knowing 'how to.' He helped me unleash the connection between my ability and how I performed on tests. Before working with Dr. B's model I was unable to demonstrate my knowledge of the material during exams. Now I am a successful and skilled test taker."

Steven Markson, College student

"Dr. Bernstein's advice is simple, effective and downright magical. This book will help parents learn how to support their student— no matter how test-phobic— through the gauntlet of standardized testing of middle school, high school, college, and beyond. I have seen Dr. Bernstein's clear, practical tips help students overcome anxiety and athletes sustain their focus and determination. Use this workbook for lifelong support through the stresses of performance anxiety."

Catherine Hunter, Head of School, San Francisco Friends School

"At last, an educator who understands the difference between coaching and teaching. Dr. B presents test prep support in a logical, loving and totally accessible way. Anyone can benefit from understanding how and why they fear various exams, and then utilize that same self-knowledge to become more successful with all of life's tests. I have witnessed Dr. B's remarkable work with students, and I am thrilled that he is now sharing his coaching methods in this delightful workbook! I can't wait to use it as I guide students through the college admissions process."

Sharon Cravanas
Director of College Counseling KIPP King Collegiate High School
College Admissions Consultant with College Board
Former Director of College Counseling, Head Royce School

"I am forever grateful to Dr. B for providing me the tools I needed to pass the California Bar exam. After four failed attempts, it wasn't until all three aspects of my life—mind, body and spirit— were completely balanced that I was able to pass. I continue to utilize Dr. B's visualization techniques while preparing for challenging trials in court."

Karen Sheehy, Esq., Public Defender

"Ben Bernstein's workbook is a great help for anyone who has suffered from being too nervous when taking a test. This workbook will also be a boon for those who seek to appreciate the psychology of performing; be it in sport, the arts, business or in school. I have observed Dr. B to be a very engaging and creative teacher who sends his students home with clear ideas and practical techniques."

Alison Rhodius, Ph.D.,
Professor, Research Director for Sport Psychology
John F. Kennedy University

"Dr. B's workbook is a wonderful resource for test takers. His approach to test success cleverly reveals a healthy way of living as much as it recommends a methodology to prepare for a test situation. His concise and accurate analysis of test stress, his tools, self-assessment surveys, physical and psychological exercises and his guidance for mastering the testing experience are very helpful and effective. Dr. B's strategy reflects the cutting edge in positive psychology, mindfulness, and the body-mind connection. This workbook will improve the reader's test performance and lead him or her to operate, calmly, confidently and focused within the zone of optimal functioning."

Gilbert H. Newman, Ph.D.
Director of Clinical Training, The Wright Institute

"Dr. Bernstein has captured the true essence of successful test-taking. In so doing, he has given students and teachers the keys to unlock the doors that lead to higher scores and enhanced self-esteem."

Daisy Newman
Director, Young Musicians Program
University of California at Berkeley

"While I was initially somewhat skeptical of this approach, I found it to be incredibly helpful. Committing time and energy to this process allowed me to realize my full potential and achieve results that met or exceeded my practice test scores. I often find myself using these techniques before other tests, major presentations and job interviews."

Elliot Whitman, MBA Student, The Wharton School

"Doing well on college admission tests requires a bundle of knowledge, unwavering self-confidence and the developed skill of relaxing under pressure. Check out Dr. Ben Bernstein on the latter."

*Richard W. Moll, author of **Playing the Selective College Admissions Game** and*
***The Public Ivys**; former Dean of Admissions at Bowdoin College, Vassar College*
and University of California at Santa Cruz.

"Before I used Dr. B's method I thought there was something wrong with me. Now I know what to do when I feel anxious. This Workbook is good for anyone, even if you already do well on tests."

Rebecca Nuñez, High school senior

"As a director of a youth development center, I often ask myself and staff how can we inspire under-performers to want to succeed. This workbook really helped my staff work through clear steps to empower our students to set goals and attain them. *The Workbook for Test Success* is a wonderful guide for everyone, regardless of whether you are taking or administering tests or simply encouraging yourself or others to do well. If you're looking for simple tools and exercises to do well in life, Dr. B's workbook offers important, easy strategies to do it. *The Workbook* offers so much more than test-taking tips. In every chapter, there are strategies for everyone to live life better. The lessons learned from this book will last my staff and kids a lifetime. Dr. Bernstein has provided a simple yet effective method to improve everyone's performance when tested by those life challenges that make us most anxious. It's a wonderfully insightful book and one that I will refer back to until it's messages are ingrained in me."

Anthony M. Brown, M.S.
Executive Director, Heart of Los Angeles Youth Center

"Dr. B coached me to use effective test taking techniques and master the DAT. But the techniques are much more than that. They also make me a better person, one in-tune with my wants and needs and the people and environment that surrounds me. Now in my third year of professional training, Dr. B's techniques have been invaluable, proving their effectiveness again and again. I'm confident that I will continue to use these techniques throughout my career allowing me to be a focused, proficient and successful practitioner."

Michael Erhard
UCLA School of Dentistry

"I have utilized Ben Bernstein's test-prep techniques in my summer programs for first-generation and low-income students, and they have been very effective. Many students later reported how useful the techniques were not only for preparing for exams, but for personal use as well. Dr. Bernstein has a well-proven method that is very effective and comfortable for students to adopt. He also challenges students to reach deep inside to address the fears they possess to overcome the lack of proper test-taking skills. Any student should be able to utilize this workbook to excel on standardized exams."

Charles J. Alexander, Ph.D.
Associate Vice Provost for Student Diversity
Director of Academic Advancement Program, UCLA

"Reading Ben Bernstein's ***The Workbook for Test Success*** is like having a wise, patient, coach at your right hand, ready to answer your questions, telling you what you need to know when you need to know it. I heartily recommend ***The Workbook*** to everyone who is preparing to take a test, or helping someone to prepare. Indeed, Dr. B's three-legged stool model of being calm, confident and focused is an excellent way to approach any test in the deepest sense."

The Rev. Lewis C. Johnson
Episcopal Vicar and Psychotherapist

"I never understood why tests caused me such anxiety until I took Dr. B's performance coaching course. His techniques added the final touch to intense preparation, translating to significantly higher scores the second time I took the DAT. Dr. B's workbook teaches you what Kaplan and Princeton Review can't—how to *optimize your potential* for test taking by delving into the source of your anxiety. He gave me the tools to be calm, confident and focused— tools I use not only on test days, but in all aspects of my life."

Joy Magtanong-Madrid
University of the Pacific School of Dentistry

"I was always scared of tests and I never did well on them. It was really frustrating. Dr. B coached me and showed me what to do. I did it and it worked. Now I don't panic when I take tests and I do much better on them."

Stephanie Chung, high school student

"I have found Dr. Bernstein's program to be wise, engaging, and profoundly effective. For me, the most powerful and important aspect of Dr. Bernstein's program is the effect it has on the *experience* of the learner in the course of test-taking. It turns one's attention away from non-productive thoughts about external consequences and toward what one has learned. It provides the means to connect thoroughly with what one knows. It allows students to be thoughtful and even creative under test conditions."

Charles A. Ahern, Ph.D., Neuropsychologist
Clinical Director, Educational Therapy Program, Holy Names College

"Through successes and setbacks I use Dr. B's methods to perform at my highest ability. I am confident that his approach will continue to help me blaze trails and lead me to the most positive destinations in the future."

Ian M. Thomson, Fellow, Princeton-in-Asia Program

The Workbook for Test Success

How To Be Calm, Confident and Focused on Any Test

by
Ben Bernstein, Ph.D.
Performance Coach

SPARK AVENUE

EMERYVILLE, CALIFORNIA

The Workbook For Test Success:
How to Be Calm, Confident and Focused on Any Test

Spark Avenue
P.O. Box 99373
Emeryville, CA 94662

http://www.WorkbookForTestSuccess.com

Library of Congress Control Number: 2009911569

Bernstein, Ben
    The Workbook for Test Success:
    How to Be Calm, Confident and Focused on any Test

Summary: "A training program for test takers to reduce test anxiety, improve self-confidence, and eliminate distraction; thus improving test performance. A companion to every content-oriented test preparation book." -Provided by publisher.

ISBN 9780981995908

1.Test preparation. 2. Education. 3. Self-help. 4. Psychology. 5. Teacher resource. 6. Parent resource.

Cover design by Dave Innis www.innisanimation.com
Book design by Marianne Wilma Wyss www.wyssdesign.com
Illustrations by Adam Burleigh www.blue-rabbit.co.uk
Author photo © Marcia Lieberman www.marcialieberman.com

Printed in the United States of America

10 9 8 7 6 5 4 3 2

The Workbook
for Test Success

To my teachers,
with gratitude

May I fulfill their hope and my promise.

TABLE OF CONTENTS

HOW DID HE DO IT?

For the last thirty years I have been coaching people to success. My clients include students, athletes, doctors, actors, business executives and opera singers. Some of my clients win Pulitzer Prizes, some Academy Awards, some get into the best medical, dental and law schools and some sing at the Metropolitan Opera.

Yes, they are talented, skillful and work tirelessly. But the real secret to their success is not just how hard they work or whom they know. I work with them on the inner skills they need to succeed. What does that mean?

I coach them to be calm, confident and focused.

On November 4, 2008, 66 million people elected Barack Obama the 44th president of the United States.

How did he, a young man with a brief resume, make this dream come true?

All the pundits weigh in: "He's smart." "He's savvy." "He put together a great team." "He raised a phenomenal amount of money." All true, but not the whole truth. Through my eyes as a performance coach I see something more fundamental.

Obama has all three traits that I discuss in this workbook. He is calm, confident and focused, and that makes people trust him and believe in him. He never loses his cool, he never seems dejected or bitter at a loss, and it certainly doesn't make him lose steam and he is never off-message. Obama's story is especially amazing when you take in the challenges he had to overcome—an African American with little money, virtually no experience on the international stage, and with the middle name Hussein.

Calm, confident and focused. To many this combination seems elusive and mystical, improbable to achieve. Not so. Barack Obama wanted the presidency and on the path to achieving his goal he had to pass many tests. He passed them all with these invaluable traits.

Not everyone wants to be president. But anyone can learn to be calm, confident and focused. We all have that potential.

You too can cultivate these qualities. You too can succeed at even the most difficult tests.

Let me show you how.

WHO SHOULD USE THIS WORKBOOK?

If you are a high school, college or graduate student who hates to take tests, this workbook is for you. The material here will help you if

✳ You feel anxious before or during tests.

✳ You lack self-confidence about your ability to perform well.

✳ You find it hard to stay focused when you study or take a test.

✳ You study a lot but your scores don't reflect the effort you put in.

✳ You want to raise your scores on standardized tests (SAT, ACT, MCAT, LSAT, etc.)

Even if you like taking tests (some people do!) and perform well on them, you can probably raise your test scores by following the program in this workbook.

If you are already out of school but have to take a professional licensing or a qualifying exam (bar exams, state boards, a test for a specific job or a driver's license), this workbook will help you improve your performance.

If you are a parent and your child hates tests or is not performing up to potential this workbook will help you. Presented here is a comprehensive program for understanding what's going on with your child and what to do about it. You will learn how to support good test performance without becoming stressed out yourself. Read, and use, the entire workbook and refer especially to Chapter Nine, Help for Parents.

If you are a teacher you can use this workbook to understand why some capable students do not perform well on tests. By familiarizing yourself with the coaching program in these pages you can use the tools presented to help your students improve their test scores. You will also learn how to reduce your own stress about tests and testing. I recommend you read the entire workbook, which ends with Chapter Ten, "For Teachers."

If you are a school administrator or an educational policy maker this workbook will give you insight into what makes for good teaching and learning and what contributes to good test performance.

If you are a counselor, advisor or psychotherapist this workbook will help you appreciate the difficulties of under-performing students. It also provides a plan of action in working with them.

The program I present here is the product of my forty years as a teacher and psychologist. It builds on what I have learned in my own personal development and in my work with thousands of students, teachers and clients. I offer a model for improving test performance by addressing the true platform for success: being calm, confident and focused through the test preparation period and during the test itself.

Test stress is rampant in our culture. It makes everyone nervous and hopelessly competitive. It is destructive. It turns young people off to learning because it puts the focus on results rather than process, and because so much—from college admissions to teachers' salaries—hinges on test scores.

But testing is inevitable—and necessary—and tests are not going away any time soon. You may hate tests, but you still have to deal with them. "Hate" is a strong feeling. It is filled with passion. Hating something can make you fight it or drive you away from it. But if you have to take tests, which we all do in our lives, fighting with them or running away from them is not going to help you. You want to channel that powerful energy so you can achieve your dreams.

My aim in writing this workbook is not to convince you to like tests. You don't have to like tests to do well on them. I will show you how to deal with them so that all your hard work will pay off and you can have a successful test taking experience.

Chapter One

Getting Started

HOW THIS WORKBOOK CAN HELP YOU

As you use this workbook, I will be your performance coach.

When people come to me I figure out why they are under-performing and then coach them to achieve better results. If a high school student is scoring low on her SATs, or a graduate student needs to raise his GRE scores, I give them the tools for raising their scores.

Providing *tools* is a vital part of my job as a coach. Think of the workbook you are holding as a toolbox. It has what you need to fix your problems with testing. In the following pages I will give you the nine essential tools you need to improve your test performance.

But a shiny new toolbox with powerful tools is not enough. You have to know *when* to use them. There's a right moment to use each tool in this workbook. I will coach you to develop your awareness of that moment. When your awareness is keen, the tools become indispensable. Say you read a question and the answer doesn't come immediately. It looks too hard. You think, "I'll never get this," and you start imagining the worst: *failure.* Once you refine your awareness you'll immediately recognize that your confidence is slipping and you'll use the right tools to recover it. The people who have trouble with tests become more and more anxious and the mounting tension paralyzes them. Awareness is another word for *paying attention.* Imagine driving down a road with signs that say *Danger ahead!* But you don't see them. The signs become bigger and maybe you see them but don't take them seriously. What happens? You crash. When you read the signs (that's your awareness) and manipulate the car accordingly (those are the tools) you can look forward to a safe, pleasant journey. As your coach, I will work with you throughout this workbook to cultivate your awareness and to use the tools. You need both. As an old song goes, "You can't have one without the other." If you have the greatest tools but lack the awareness of when to use them, the tools are useless; likewise if you are aware that you need tools but don't have any, you can't change anything. This workbook will give you both.

WHAT DO YOU HATE ABOUT TESTS?

*Imagine yourself saying: "**I hate tests because…**" (check all that apply)*

❏ 1. They make me nervous.

❏ 2. No matter how much I prepare I can't do well.

❏ 3. It's hard for me to study.

❏ 4. Tests are stupid.

❏ 5. I throw up every time I have to take a test.

❏ 6. I believe everyone else is smarter than I am.

❏ 7. My mind keeps wandering when I am taking a test.

❏ 8. I don't think tests measure what I really know.

❏ 9. I can't sleep before a test.

❏ 10. I am not good at memorizing.

❏ 11. My parents put too much pressure on me to do well.

❏ 12. This country is test crazy.

❏ 13. Tests stress me out.

❏ 14. If I hit a wall during a test I fall apart and everything goes downhill.

❏ 15. I don't really care about them but everyone else does.

❏ 16. After the test I don't remember anything, so what's the point?

❏ 17. My stomach is in knots every time I take a test.

❏ 18. My sister/brother/mother/father was really good at taking tests, but I'm not.

❏ 19. Tests count for too high a percentage of my grade.

❏ 20. Tests are too impersonal.

❏ 21. My mind is always racing before a test.

❏ 22. I never do well on tests.

❏ 23. Everyone else places too much importance on tests.

❏ 24. Tests don't give me the chance to show what I really know.

❏ 25. There's a secret to doing well on tests and I don't know it.

We'll look at what you checked off in a moment. But before we go on I want you to know that there are two ways to use this workbook: you can work through it chapter-by- chapter, cover-to-cover, or you can troubleshoot.

Chapter-by-chapter. You have already started. Keep reading and work through each exercise as you go along. By reading through the entire workbook, you will receive a comprehensive training in improving your performance on tests. I recommend you use the workbook this way. You've invested the money; you might as well receive the full return on your investment.

Troubleshooting. Maybe you don't have the time to read the whole workbook. Maybe you are about to take a test and you need help *right now*. In that case, I recommend you carefully read chapters 1-3 and then, referencing the items you checked above, turn to the relevant chapter.

If you checked:	*Go directly to chapter:*
1, 5, 9, 13, 17, 21	4
2, 6, 10, 14, 18, 22	5
3, 7, 11, 15, 19, 23	6
4, 8, 12, 16, 20, 24	7
25	Every chapter

THE MAJOR ISSUE: TEST STRESS

To obtain anything these days—from a driver's license to a doctor's license, from citizenship papers to a college degree—you have to take a test. And standing in the way of passing the test—for many people, from all walks of life—is test stress.

Stress is a kind of pressure, strain and demand. A low amount of stress is not a problem, and in fact, some stress is a necessary and helpful part of life. However, when the amount of stress overwhelms your ability to cope, you feel tense, frustrated, overwhelmed, and often fatigued. Test stress presents its own brand of discomfort. Before, during, and after a test, a very specific dynamic occurs for each individual.

When you are sitting in a classroom during the final countdown before the test is handed out, a number of things are running through your mind. First and foremost, you feel pressured to perform well; you are bringing all of your studying and knowledge to bear at this one time and place, and you have to make a success of it. You know that in a matter of minutes you will have to practice instant recall and quick reasoning. You must answer all these questions in a limited period of time. You realize that forcing your mind to act in a speedy way will hurt your performance. In the past, that tension prompted you to provide the wrong answers, to leave answers out, and to fail to understand some of the questions. You are quite aware, as you look around, that you're in direct competition with everyone else in the room, and you feel isolated in your own anxiety. There is a vague sense of the consequences that await you if you fail: the blow to your self-image, and the negative impact on your future and on your confidence when you take other tests down the line.

And this is only a description of what is happening in the room. What about before the test? Whether you are in high school, college or graduate school, you will never find yourself with an unlimited amount of time to memorize, or even fully comprehend, all the material given to you, and sometimes it just seems like too much for your inner hard drive to hold. I've heard people say, "There's just no more storage space." The sad thing is that sometimes you actually begin to enjoy the material; you want to grasp it at a deeper level and find the answers to real questions. But there's no time for that. You can only keep shoveling in the information.

Of course when you are preparing for a test, you can't put the rest of your life on hold. You still have to answer the phone, walk the dog, do the laundry, and occasionally eat. I say "occasionally" because it is not uncommon for test stress to make people lose their appetite, not to mention sleep. Others sleep too much because the very tension of having to perform at their best makes them want to drop out or zone out as a way to find some relief. When you are in the midst of test anxiety, you know that you've been through it many times before, yet it never seems to get any better. Each time you face the pressure, it seems like the end of the world. And each time, you feel like you're the only one who suffers this way. *Other people probably think this is a breeze. I'll never understand this material. No one else finds it so hard.* The negative thoughts can snowball into outright panic.

Maybe when the test is over, you're finally treated to a welcome sense of relief, but that may last only a few seconds. Most people walk out of the classroom obsessing over their performance. *Question twenty-three. Did I read that right? Did it mean something completely different than what I thought?* This is a useless activity, of course, and it just reinforces your sense of helplessness because you can't go back and re-do it. Your assessment is probably not even accurate because most people don't really remember their answers very well. Anxiety distracts them.

Nevertheless, in your mind you play and replay taking the test, wishing in vain that you could do it again and do it better. Nervously, you ask others how they did, but because people tend to either over-rate or under-rate their performance, you never get an accurate picture. Next you start damage control. You begin to strategize how you'll do things differently next time. You'll start studying sooner, and unplug the phone, and be nicer to the teacher, and improve your study habits, and pray to God, and give money to charity. Maybe you're one of those people who wail to anyone who will listen to how poorly you did so you can gain sympathy and understanding. Some people, when they go home after a test, feel so bad that they just shut down. In their isolation, catastrophic thoughts flood in. They start planning for the worst. *I'll just have to drop out of school. There's nothing else I can do. Then I'll have to move to another state because I'll never be able to pass the state exam here.*

Does any of this sound like you? If so, you are one of millions who go through this drama on a daily basis. And test taking is on the rise. Every year, Americans take more and more tests: SATs, APs, GREs, MCATs, LSATs, standardized state exams for children, and professional licensing exams for adults. The list goes on. Testing is steadily and relentlessly covering more ground and becoming a more popular way to assess who should be "accepted"—who will be offered jobs, promotions and licenses, and who will be granted entrance to a good college or grad school. More and more, tests are used as a determinant of salaries, a measure of your ability and ultimately your position in the world.

To feed our cultural obsession with taking more tests and receiving higher scores, a worldwide, multi-billion industry has emerged that promotes and sells books, CDs, websites and personal coaches, all to help people prepare to take tests. Test preparation is truly a growth industry. It is literally booming.

Unfortunately, far from reducing test stress, the test prep industry makes it worse because all of the materials sold do not help people with the stress involved in taking tests, they only help with memorization. Books, courses, coaches and websites are all directed at one thing: *results*. The industry simply has overlooked the whole *process* of making the journey, from the initial stages of studying through the taking of the test, more satisfying and empowering. The big test preparers like Kaplan, Princeton Review and the College Board don't give the test taker tools to make the process less punishing and anxiety provoking.

Why is this important? Because when you take a test, the way you feel about yourself inside the exam room and how able you are to stay grounded and present, largely determine how successful you will be. Understand that the *quality* of the experience of test taking directly affects the *results*.

The reason for this is simple: stress affects performance. This is well known in many fields, especially in sports. Athletes need a certain amount of stress to charge them up so they can perform at their best. But if the stress crosses a certain line—either too much stress or too little—it starts hurting their ability to do well. This concept is known as the "zone of optimal functioning."

This workbook is about you, and the tools you need to perform at your best.

The amount of stress needed to produce optimal performance, the amount considered healthful, is different for each person. Some people have to feel extremely worked up to jump-start themselves to perform well. Others will feel jangled and nervous with that much stress, and it will destroy their concentration. For each person there is a zone of optimal functioning where the level of stress is just right. They are stimulated just enough to be creative and energized, to solve problems rationally, and to achieve a sense of self-satisfaction in their performance. Their adrenaline is not pumping too hard, nor are they lethargic, so they are able to progress at a good rate.

This workbook is designed to show you how to find and stay in your zone of optimal functioning. Through reading the examples and doing the exercises, you will learn how to control stress rather than let it control you. While it's unrealistic to think you won't have any stress when you're taking a test, you need to know how to keep your stress at an optimal level so that it charges you up and keeps you at the top of your game rather than wears you out and runs you into the ground.

STRESS AND PERFORMANCE

The relationship between stress and performance is one of the most thoroughly researched phenomena in the field of psychology. A hundred years ago two psychologists were the first to study it and produced the *Yerkes-Dodson Curve*, which looks like this:

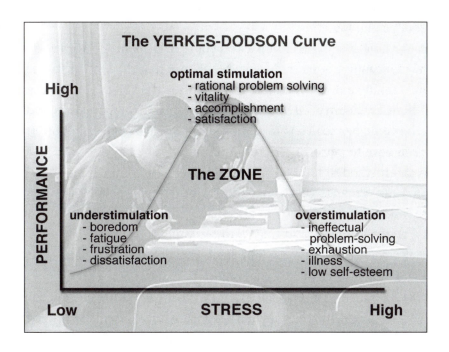

As you can see, when your stress escalates to the point of discomfort, your effectiveness diminishes. When there's too much stress, you leave "the optimal zone." The result is your problem-solving skills contract and your self-esteem and confidence decline. You have trouble staying focused so you feel tense, sometimes to the point of feeling sick or exhausted. At this point, your temper is short, fuses blow and your performance goes down the tubes. This relationship between stress and performance holds true whether you are performing in a play, or playing a baseball game, or delivering a speech. And it kicks in every time you have to take a test. What is a test if not a performance? To most people, a *performance* suggests something that happens on a stage or an athletic field. But its definition is broader than that. A performance is "the act of carrying out something; an execution or an action." That's what an academic test is: it's more than learning the material. It is the act of carrying out, showing, and proving what you know. Performance involves learning how to be fully present in the moment, right there at test time. It doesn't matter how well you tested last week, or how well you will do tomorrow; the only thing that counts is how you perform *now*.

As far as tests go, knowing and performing are not the same thing. Knowing refers to the comprehension of content. Performing refers to what you *do* with what you know. The primary complaint I hear from clients is that they study hard to learn what they're supposed to know, yet they cannot perform when it's time to take the test. The bottom line is that you have to *know* the material and you have to *deliver* the material you know.

Because stress has a direct impact on your performance, it is essential that you learn how to recognize it and reduce it. Make sure that the level of stress you experience when taking a test is not destructive. This is the key to your success. But the test-prep industry doesn't tell you that. The myth they perpetuate is that the only way to achieve higher scores is to learn more stuff. Yet knowing more stuff is not enough. You have to perform well. Up till now, no one has devised a clear, simple, and powerful method to teach people to do that.

I am a performance coach. My job is not to teach people how to memorize more, study better, or cram in more information. My job is to show you how to carry on in a test environment so that nothing impedes your performance. *My focus is on performance under pressure.* I will teach you to recognize stress when it starts building and then use specific tools to reduce it, on the spot. That's the way you can stay in your "zone" and perform better every time. My clients include a wide range of "performers." I coach high school kids taking SATs, young adults taking LSATs MCATs, DATs, GREs and finals, graduate students defending their doctoral dissertations, and lawyers taking the bar. I coach musicians, athletes and actors—people who face performance tests on a daily basis. I coach professionals in technical jobs, doctors, dentists, lawyers and nurses. I also coach creative people: writers and actors who have gone on to win major awards and prizes.

In working with these people, I have seen again and again how stress affects performance. Sadly, I've watched the adventure of learning turn into a paralysis of shame when a bright high school student crumbled under the weight of intense competition and forgot what she knew on her calculus AP. I have seen a mountain of time, energy and money bite the dust when an intelligent young lawyer failed the bar exam after his fourth try and gave up hope. I saw how the fear of rejection made it impossible for a singer to share her gift with an audience.

On the other hand, I have also seen how people can overcome their handicap. I watched a student's low SAT scores rise dramatically once he learned how to calm down during the test. I saw the utter joy of a rower when she finally learned how to focus her energy throughout the entire race. I was particularly moved when I watched two parents build their son's self-esteem instead of tearing it down, by relaxing their completely unrealistic expectations of him. Happily, everyone watched his SAT II scores improve.

When people come to me for performance coaching, my first thought is: What does this person need to perform at his or her best? Of course they have to learn the subject matter—I never make light of that—but as we have seen, that is only part of the picture. Subject matter is always changing. You might have a test on algebra, chemistry, law, history, medieval literature or some combination of them when finals come along. But there is one thing that doesn't change, one constant at the center of every test, no matter what the subject, no matter what the setting. That constant is *you,* the individual. It might be a driving test or a diving test. Whatever the test is for, you are the one who is taking it. The question you have to ask yourself is: "What can I learn about myself that will help me perform better in any situation? How can I take control of this process?" Unfortunately, neither the school system, nor the test prep books, nor the courses, address you as the test taker. They address only the object of study, not the subject. The common use of the word *subject* is the material being studied, but in reality, the subject is you.

You can use the tools on any test, any time, anywhere.

When I say, "the constant is you," I mean that *you* are what is certain and continual in all of your test situations. Certainty refers to something that stays the same in spite of outer conditions. Imagine what it would be like to have this certainty in yourself when you take a test, the firm faith in success under any circumstances. You might feel rushed, you might be tired, or you might be under extreme pressure to achieve a high score. You might break a pencil or lose your place. During an oral exam you might be answering questions facing people who look at you like you know nothing. Whatever the challenge, whatever the environment, performance coaching can teach you how to be constant in yourself so you can perform at your best.

LIFE IS A TEST

While I was writing this, there was a knock on my door. It was Joe Rizzo, an older man who came to fix our chimney. He asked me what I do for a living, and I told him simply that I coach people who take tests. He shook his head. "Life is hard," he said, pointing his finger and jabbing it into the air. "Hard. You have to work for everything. You know what the problem is today? Everyone wants his tummy rubbed. They want things done for them. Whatever you get in life, you have to work hard for. Life is a test."

He's right. Life is a test.

Everything I have written about so far has been about tests in an exam room with an instructor and other students. But as you might have gleaned by now, what

I've been saying is also applicable to all of the challenges life throws at you. Over the years, clients invariably have told me that they've been able to apply the performance tools I taught them, not only to school tests, but also to life's tests. No matter what kind of job you have or what age you are, you are confronted with new obstacles every day. You have to overcome them, and you're often expected to do that with sterling results. That is a test. Will you or won't you perform well? The added bonus to the tools in this workbook is that you can take them with you wherever you go.

Just as in the exam room, the content of life's little tests vary. You might have to ask someone on a date, give a speech, fire an employee, or host an important function. Once again, the constant is you. You're the one who has to perform. So although you may have picked up this workbook to get by on classroom tests, you will be able to take what you learn here out into the world because many of these lessons apply as well to life as they do to school.

Have you ever wondered what the purpose of your life is? Common answers are "success," "happiness" or "satisfaction." While these are all worthwhile goals, isn't it more accurate to say: *The purpose of your life is to face every challenge, every test, as a chance for you to become the person you are meant to be. Life is a test for you to become your highest self.*

When you want a flower to grow in your garden, you go to the nursery and buy a packet of seeds. You can see exactly what you're going to end up with because there is a beautiful color picture of the fully-grown flower on the front of the packet. But when you open it, what do you find? Tiny black lumps that look like mouse droppings. Does that discourage you? No, because you know what these seeds are meant to become. You set up the environment for the seeds to grow. You prepare the soil. You plant the seed, and then make sure you give it the right amount of sunlight and water. When that tiny seedling finally sprouts, it is delicate, and you protect it and care for it until it grows into the flower it is meant to be.

I believe that somewhere inside you there is a seed packet with your picture on it, a picture of the fully realized you. It's not easy to grow this flower. There are challenges all along the way. But when you face them, you learn from them and you grow with them. Through this process, you grow into the flower in full bloom. Flowers cannot become fully realized unless they push their way up through the soil and compete for sun and space with other plants. Our conditions aren't much different. We have to find our way in the world, and all along we face tests of physical illness, mental troubles, financial reversals, unfulfilled expectations and loss.

Though we cannot choose most of the tests we face in life, we can choose how we're going to face them. Are we going to have a miserable experience, crumble under the pressure, run away, or avoid challenges altogether? Or are we going to find the strength and inner resources to rise to the challenges and fully actualize our potential? That's the term psychologists use for becoming the person you are meant to be. Facing tests in the right way will give you this opportunity. When you face the tests of life, learn from them and grow with them, you become that person. The tests of life require you to call on the inner resources residing deep inside you. By doing that, you come to know yourself and to develop your innate capacities. That is what we mean by actualizing your potential, and being tested presents you with the opportunities to do it. Tests are like a challenging teacher or friend; if you maintain a good relationship with them, many of your best qualities will emerge.

Fortunately, we don't have to reinvent the wheel here. There are exquisite role models who have preceded us and can show us how to face the vicissitudes of life in a meaningful way. These are the teachers and masters, saints and sages, the divinely inspired women and men who dedicated their lives to finding meaning and purpose through their struggles. Jesus on the cross, Buddha under the bodhi tree, Moses in the desert, Mohammed in the cave. Each faced the tests that life handed them, and they mastered the ability to learn and grow and become fully realized beings. We may not all be sages and saints, but we all face tests on a regular basis, and some of them are severe and daunting. Do we have the strength to overcome, the fortitude to persevere, the humor to see things in a lighter way? With these capacities, it is possible to do more than just get by. We can do something inspiring with our lives. Great beings create a memorable path through life's tests. Because ultimately, that's what life is—a path with tests at every bend in the road. Every test is there to help us grow and to fully become the people we are meant to be.

ONE MORE THOUGHT

You may have noticed that the title of this book isn't **Dr. B's Bag of Magic Tricks**. There's no kit with a top hat and a wand that you wave over your head and then *Presto!* You can now sail through tests without studying and without concentrating. My job as a coach is to show you what to do. Your job is to do it. For some people, that's not an easy thing. It isn't that the information is hard or the message indirect. The material presented here is very direct and clear. The problem is that they don't particularly want to work for a solution to their problem. They want someone else to solve their problems for them. Perhaps they're hoping this workbook will do it.

Over the years, I have discovered that there are two groups of people: those who are ready to work for change and those who want a quick fix. The latter often come into my office cramped with anxiety over an upcoming test. After the first session, they are filled with hope and enthusiasm. They come to the second session all pumped up saying, "This is great, I get it." But several weeks later they call or e-mail, moaning in a most painful way, "Oh, Dr. B, I'm still so stressed out! I haven't done any of the exercises you gave me. Do you have any more tips?"

Yes, I do have lots of "tips," but what good will they do if the person won't follow them anymore than they worked with my original tips? If you want the results, you have to follow the coaching. Ultimately, you have to become your own coach. There's no way around it. And if you do, the rewards are great. I have watched high school seniors raise their SAT scores by 200 to 300 points. I've seen doctors ace strenuous licensing exams. Outside the classroom, I've watched as athletes win games and musicians succeed at auditions. And in the other arenas of life that we don't ordinarily call a test environment, people who practice being calm, confident and focused overcome challenges and become their personal best.

Learn to be your own coach. Practice being calm, confident and focused.

In facing the challenges, they learn life's most important lesson: be present. You know that phrase they use at raffles? "You have to be present to win." The same is true of life. Only by being present can we develop the awareness that we're veering off track, and then get back on track. How many times in your life have you had to admit that you *screwed up* because you didn't *show up?*

There is a real correlation between awareness and excellence, but awareness doesn't happen accidentally. Usually, our minds are wandering far from home, leap-frogging from the past into the future, oblivious to what's in front of us. To cultivate awareness and achieve your highest potential, you have to train yourself.

Taking tests in a classroom, much as we may hate it, actually has a silver lining. It trains us to bring our awareness to bear on the present moment and to practice being calm, confident and focused. When you learn how to master yourself in the tense environment of test taking, you will feel empowered to take those skills out of the classroom and into the rest of your life. You will have taught yourself to be strong, responsible and embodied when confronted with a difficult and challenging task. You can use that knowledge anywhere you go.

As long as you are willing to do the work to become a successful test taker, I can coach you through the process.

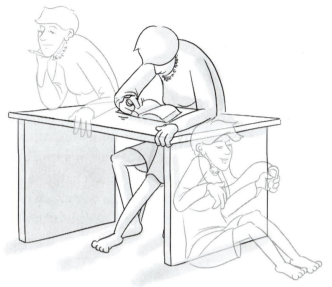

Chapter Two

Disconnection

When I begin working with a client, the first question I always ask is, "What do you think causes your test stress?" Here are some of the things people tell me:

* ✳ "I have too much to study."

* ✳ "I don't have enough time."

* ✳ "My parents put a lot of pressure on me to get good grades."

* ✳ "I don't work well under deadlines."

* ✳ "My sister is the smart one in the family, not me."

* ✳ "If I don't receive a high score, I won't be accepted by a good college."

* ✳ "This stuff is just too hard to understand."

✳ "There are too many other things are going on in my life."

✳ "Tests just make me nervous."

When you hear statements like these, you're probably thinking, "Yep, that just about covers all the bases." But what if I told you those weren't the bases? What if I said none of those "reasons" is actually the *cause* of test stress?

We all seem to think that test stress comes from too little time, complicated subject matter, exorbitant expectations, unfavorable comparisons with others, and so on. I know it looks as if these conditions are the source of your problem, but they aren't. These are merely part and parcel of test taking. They include the clock, the subject matter, the test questions, what your parents would like you to achieve, and the reward or punishment (raising your allowance or losing your scholarship) based on your grade. You may take a test under some of these conditions, under all of them, or under conditions that seem unique to your life. It doesn't matter because conditions in and of themselves do not cause stress. If they did, everyone who operated in the test environment under the same conditions would react exactly the same way and succumb to stress. As you'll see, this is not the case. Many people have the ability to successfully manage the test conditions.

I can hear you thinking, "But all of those things really *do* cause a lot of tension." There's no question about it, tests *are* stressful. As you'll see, I have a different theory about what causes stress. It starts with looking at what you are doing when you face a test.

YOUR REACTION IS STRESSFUL

I've had people tell me that the word "test" stands their nerves on end, but *test,* after all, is nothing but a four-letter word—four little letters of type on a page. T-E-S-T. It does not *cause* a bad reaction in you. Neither does the clock on the wall ticking time away. Nor do multiple choices on a page staring up at you. Nor does the teacher sitting in front of the room. All of these things are conditions that exist outside of your skin. They are never within your control, and we all know that if you had your way, they wouldn't be there at all. These conditions don't really affect you, however, until you let them get under your skin. That's when you transform them from external factors to internal problems.

In any situation you will have a reaction to outside events, and it will either be pleasant, unpleasant or neutral. That's the range. When your reaction is unpleasant, that's what we call stress because it causes you to reject what's happening. The string of thoughts goes something like this: *I don't like what's going on. Something is wrong. I want this situation to change. I want it to go away.* The first clue that an outside event is causing a stress reaction is that all of a sudden, you cannot relax and you want things to be different. You can't accept this moment just as it is. Whenever something *has* to change or you won't be happy, that is the experience of stress.

Not everyone has an unpleasant reaction to the same events. Imagine two people taking the same test, Sally is sitting at a desk on the left and Judy at a desk on the right. Sally is sure she is going fail. Her body is tense, she's doubting herself and she can't stay on task. Judy, on the other hand, is working through each question, one at a time, in a calm, confident and focused way.

Many people taking a test will identify with Sally. They are nervous. They exhibit physical symptoms (headache, stomachache, stiff neck), they are attacked by self-doubt, and they can barely keep their mind on the page. The result is they fail or receive poor scores that don't match up with their ability or effort.

Or maybe their scores turn out to be respectable in spite of the strains upon them. But there's hidden damage. They may do well, but they suffer far too much. Taking tests causes them a great deal of anguish and anxiety, yet they still manage to be fairly successful on test after test. They don't do anything about their discomfort because they don't think that it can change. When I ask about the possibility of improving the experience, they shrug their shoulders and say, "That's just the way it is. Tests are a pain. I hate them, but I do all right."

So there are two categories of people like Sally: either they're miserable and they fail or they're miserable and they succeed. It's good to succeed, but the process doesn't have to be as insufferable as sitting on a pack of thumbtacks.

Now let's talk about Judy. Those who identify with this individual are not agitated at test time. Somehow, they are much calmer, they believe in themselves, and they are able to stay on task. The taking of the test, the amount of time they have to take it, and the expectations upon them to do well—*none* of these factors triggers a negative reaction. Their scores are good to excellent without all the drama.

Ask yourself, "What am I doing to make myself feel so stressed out?"

Here's the important question: what are *you* doing that causes you to feel so much stress?

THE THREE BASIC STRESS REACTIONS

If you are suffering from test stress, you are doing one or more of the following:

* ✳ You are physically tense.

* You are thinking negatively about yourself and your performance.

* You are becoming distracted when you are studying or when you are taking the test.

In the last chapter, I said that stress is a pressure, strain or demand. These definitions match up perfectly with the above list. When you grow physically tense, when you think negatively about your performance, or when you are distracted from completing the task at hand, you are putting unnecessary pressure, strain and demands upon yourself. You know this is happening because you feel like you're being punished or threatened. You may also feel exhausted, uncomfortable and panicked. The physical tension, the negative thoughts and the distractions—these are all burdens you are placing on yourself, and they negatively impact your performance. In other words, you are making test taking much harder than it has to be.

To further understand what I'm talking about, let's look at Mike, a college sophomore who has a great deal of difficulty taking tests. The game we're playing here is "What's Wrong with This Picture?" As you imagine Mike in the following sequence, see if you can figure out what he is feeling, thinking and doing that causes him so many problems.

WHAT'S WRONG WITH THIS PICTURE?

In each part of the following sequence something Mike is doing is getting in the way of his performance. Can you tell what it is? As you read the unfolding story in the left hand column, cover up the right column until you can answer "What's wrong with this picture?" Then look to see if you figured it out.

The scenario	What's wrong with this picture?
1. Mike is in class, at his desk, listening to the teacher. The teacher announces "We're going to have a test next Friday." Mike thinks, *Oh my God, there is no way I'll be ready by then.*	1. Mike is sinking into negative thinking. Negative thinking will cause a self-fulfilling prophecy. He probably won't be ready by test-time.

2. Mike is in the library. His books and notes are all spread out in a mess; he's on his cell phone, talking away to a buddy. "I got wasted last night. Did you see that girl who wanted my phone number?"	2. Mike is not focused. He should be studying, but he ends up distracting himself from the books by talking on the phone.
3. It's the middle of the night. Mike is at home drinking a carafe of coffee. There are big dark circles under his eyes, his books and papers are scattered all over the place. *I should have eaten dinner. No time for that. Gotta get more coffee and stay alert. Where are my cigarettes?*	3. Mike is not taking care of his body so that it will support him. He's drinking too much coffee and not getting enough sleep. He's not physically rested enough to study well and to take the test. His habits are wearing him down.
4. Mike is slumped over his desk. He's despairing, *I can't remember a thing I've studied. I'm no good at this.*	4. Mike's confidence is slipping by the minute. His negative thinking is causing low self-esteem and is becoming a distraction.
5. Mike is sitting in the exam room now. The test is in front of him, but he's looking at the ceiling. *As soon as school is out, I'm heading for the beach. The surf should be great today.*	5. Mike's mind is littered with diversions. He's not keeping his attention on the questions. Instead, he's thinking about things that have nothing to do with the test. He's not being present to the task at hand — the test.
6. Mike is sitting with the pencil poised in his hand to mark off a multiple choice answer, but inside he's imagining that he's standing on the ledge of a tall building ready to jump. *My life is over. I'll never get into law school now. I'll end up flipping burgers and my girlfriend will leave me.*	6. Mike's panic is exploding into catastrophic thinking. Negative thought patterns are taking over.

Tests do not have to be a nightmare. Mike is making his life miserable. The first step is to recognize that you are causing yourself problems so that you can identify them and learn how to fix them.

DISCONNECTING FROM YOURSELF

All of Mike's behaviors fall under the three basic categories of stress reactions:

1. Becoming physically tense
2. Thinking negatively
3. Being continually distracted

What do all of these behaviors have in common? Simply put, they all involve pushing away from the test. I call it *disconnecting*. That's what is hurting Mike, and that's what is hurting your test performance.

Since disconnecting is an important concept that threads through this entire workbook and is an integral part of my performance model, I'm going tell you what I mean by disconnection and then show you how it actually causes test stress.

First, think about the word *disconnection*. What images come to mind?

Here are some that occur to me:

Telephone line going dead
Pulling a plug out of a socket
Head popping off a body
Wheel coming off a car

The word *disconnect* is made up of two parts. The Latin origin of *dis* means, "separate, move apart, go in different directions." *Connect* means to "fasten or tie together." So to *dis*-connect means to pull apart something that is already together. What is the result? Disruption. Disharmony. Disarray. If you're talking on your cell phone and suddenly you can't hear the other person, the transmission has been severed. There is no more communication. If you're reading a book and someone trips over the lamp cord and yanks the plug out of the wall, the light goes out. If you are running the bath water and a pipe outside bursts, the water shuts off. When disconnection takes place out in the world, things cease to function.

Now let's look at what happens *inside* of you when you disconnect from yourself. What does that look and feel like?

First, you have to understand that you are a whole person, one package made up of three interrelated systems called the body, mind and spirit. Since being disconnected means being separated from the whole, being disconnected inside of you means that the body, mind and spirit are detached from one another. It can also mean that there is a disconnection within any one or more of the three systems.

To put it more simply, when you are faced with a test maybe you tense up. Maybe you become afraid and tell yourself you can't handle it. Maybe you find it impossible to keep your mind on the material. You want to escape, to run away. This is disconnecting. It has a purpose. It is a way of coping with a difficult situation. You want to get out of there!

But why and how does this cause stress? To show you that, we have to briefly examine the body, mind and spirit under the magnifying glass of our awareness.

The Body

The body is your physical container: your flesh and bones, blood and guts, membranes and muscles. To function at peak capacity, it needs ongoing nourishment, proper exercise, enough rest, and a modicum of self-care (a shower and teeth brushing as needed). When you disconnect from your body, you dissociate from it. In a way, you leave it, you lose awareness of it, or you stop giving it what it needs. You eat poorly or not at all, you don't exercise enough, you catch a little sleep when you can.

When you treat your body this way, you are not taking care of your physical container. It's like driving a car and letting the gas or oil tank go empty. The car eventually will stop or will seize up and break down. When you let your body's gas tank run on empty, it breaks down too, and even if it doesn't stop altogether, it certainly becomes less efficient. You feel tired, sick, anxious or depressed as a result. And all of this occurs because you are losing awareness of your body and its fundamental link to how your mind and spirit function. Most people think that only their mind is taking a test. In fact, their whole body is part of the experience, and if it isn't running efficiently, neither will the other two systems.

Jasmine is a perfect example of this. She is a bright, high-achieving high school senior. Even though her intelligence and aptitude were high, her SAT scores were quite low and certainly didn't reflect her true capacity. Before her first appointment with me, her mother told me over the phone, "Jasmine freezes every time she even hears the word *test*." When I met with Jasmine and her parents, sure enough, every time someone said the word I could see her stop breathing for a beat. After this happened a dozen times and she looked increasingly anxious, I asked her if she was aware that she was stopping her breath.

"No," she answered. "Why? Is that important?"

Here is what I told her. "When you hear the word *test* and you stop your breath, you are disconnecting from your body. Bodies need oxygen, and you're not giving it what it needs in that moment. Your brain immediately goes into high alert. Bells ring, lights pulse, and you practically see a neon sign flashing *Danger!*"

It was clear to me, listening to them speak, that Jasmine and her parents believed that her stress came simply from hearing the word *test*. Many of you may believe that too. But remember, that word is just a phonetic combination of letters. It's a condition, a trigger, but it doesn't *create* the stress. The feeling of stress inside Jasmine was coming from what she was *doing in reaction to the word*—stopping her breath. She was pulling the plug on her energy source, oxygen. As we saw with the reading light, pulling the plug *is* disconnecting. Jasmine's supply line—her connection—to an element that is absolutely essential to being calm and having a sense of well-being, was severed.

The body is meant to be healthy and whole; good, steady breathing is essential to that unity. When we disconnect within our bodies, we are splitting up the wholeness and causing disharmony within the entire system. Why is this stressful? Because when you stop your breath, you place your body under a strain. Your brain isn't getting the oxygen it needs to survive. Your heart has to pump harder and you feel a rush of adrenaline. Glucocorticoids, the chemicals your body manufactures when it's in danger, start coursing through you, putting your nervous system into a state of high arousal. Your body is having a stress reaction, and whether you are directly conscious of it or not, you feel it. In this particular example, holding the breath caused the disconnection. In Chapter Four we will examine other ways in which people dissociate in their bodies and how this causes test stress.

When your body is agitated you can't think clearly. Calm yourself down.

The Mind

Mind is a big word. In general, it means the sum total of our consciousness, what we perceive, what we think, what we believe. One of the things the mind does is talk to itself in the form of thoughts. It does this a lot, all the time, in fact, when we're awake. It's like having a talk-radio station on with no "off" switch. There is a continuous chatter going on inside each one of us, commenting on everything we see, think and feel. *This is green, that's big. She's funny, he's a jerk. They don't like me. Who cares? I care,* and on and on and on. The commentary also covers what everyone else is doing, but in this workbook, we're going to concentrate on *how you talk to yourself about yourself.* There is a good reason for this: that is the part of your mind that can either help or hinder you when you are taking a test. You are, after all, performing, and your mind is, in a way, either your supporter or your critic. Is it bringing out the best or the worst in you?

Jake is a recently graduated dental student who came to me for performance coaching after failing his state's licensing exam twice. He complained, "This test is so hard. No matter how much I study I can't learn all the material. Whenever I think about the test I feel like I'm falling into a black hole. I try to study harder but basically I think I don't have what it takes. I'll never pass this exam."

Jake's internal dialog was riddled with negativity. "I can't learn all the material. I just don't have what it takes it be a dentist." It wasn't really the amount of material or the fact that he failed the test before that was causing his tension. Those problems might have been triggers, and they might have influenced his performance—but they weren't the *cause* of his stress. The source was the negative messages he kept feeding himself about himself, messages churned out by his own mind.

Why is this stressful? When you say to yourself, *I'm not good enough and I will never succeed*, you are removing your inner support system. In math terms, negative means subtracting, making into a minus, taking away from. Negative self-statements are no different. They take away your inner support at the moment you most need it: when you are taking a test and your capacities should be at their peak. When you are disconnecting from your mind in this way, you are being disloyal to yourself. You are, in effect, a traitor to yourself. You're giving up in the heat of battle, pulling away and jumping ship. What you need at such a time are positive, self-affirming messages but you're getting the opposite.

A negative mind stresses you out. A confident mind is your ally.

Negative messages like these are not the truth; they are distortions, because these kinds of statements tend to be global and blown out of proportion. *I'll never succeed. I can't take tests. I don't have what it takes.* While there's always room for healthy self-criticism, these overly dramatic statements distort the real picture. They suggest that something is wrong with you, that you are defective, a certified loser and you might as well give up, none of which would bear up under the evidence (you got this far, didn't you?). Distortion is one way that we disconnect in our minds. We make grossly negative self-statements, we imagine the worst, and then, of course, we want to bolt.

When you feed yourself negative messages, your mind is working against you instead of helping you. You're under all this pressure to perform with no help from this important system. Your mind is sending out a stream of negative statements and pictures: you see yourself failing the test; you hear your parents yelling at you or standing there with a look of profound disappointment on their faces; you imagine all of your classmates passing with flying colors and going on to illustrious careers while you're left behind. You see your teachers feeling very frustrated. What are most people afraid of when they're chastising themselves in this way? They're afraid of looking stupid. They want to avoid this at all costs.

When this mental process snowballs, it almost guarantees a poor performance, which means that you probably *will* fail. And this, in turn, sets you up for failing again—a truly vicious cycle. In Chapter Five, I will describe in detail how your mind becomes embroiled in this dynamic and I will give you the tools to correct it.

The Spirit

The next part of yourself that this workbook addresses is your spirit. "Spirit" is a loaded, often misunderstood word. Depending on your experience it could have negative connotations like being required to attend weekly religious services, or heavy moralizing about what is "good" and "bad."

As a performance psychologist, I think of spirit in a different way. In this workbook, I am speaking about spirit as the part that directs us to become what we're meant to be in life. To me it is the highest self, a person's heart and soul. It's the part that moved me to become a psychologist, my wife a novelist, my college roommate a minister, my next-door neighbor a devoted mother. Spirit defines and drives us to pursue our authentic goals and it supports us in taking actions that are consistent with those goals. Simply put, when you are connected in your spirit, then your actions lead you to your goals. When you are disconnected in spirit, you either don't have goals that are important to you, or your actions lead you away from them. A disconnection from the spirit causes people to be distracted.

Stay connected to your spirit. Keep moving towards your goal.

Laura is a competent biochemist who was facing a different sort of test. She was completing a laboratory research project and racing to submit a grant proposal before a rapidly approaching deadline. However, she had a problem: "I start off the day knowing exactly what I need to accomplish. But then I get to the office and instead of getting to work I start checking my e-mail and things go rapidly downhill from there. Then come the phone calls, the appointments, lunch and exercise, and before I know it, the day is shot. I haven't accomplished anything substantial on my project."

The e-mail, phone messages, junk mail—all the little tasks we have to take care of these days—they are not causing Laura's stress. She experiences them as annoying nuisances stealing her time from her, but she is the one who is allowing herself to be distracted from her real goal. Some people, for instance, make a decision to spend fifteen minutes on day on e-mail, and no more. They don't let distractions keep them from the important work. For Laura, they do. What is the price she pays? She becomes disengaged from her spirit—her driving force—which is directing her to be an excellent biochemist, complete her research, and finish her grant application. The health of your spirit depends on a continuity of actions that lead to accomplishing the goals of your highest self. When you break that continuity, when you pull the plug on your goals, you create stress. Let's not forget that stress causes the feeling that something is wrong and as long as it is wrong, you cannot relax. All the while Laura is letting herself be preoccupied with nonessential tasks, and she's feeling anxious. Work is piling up, she's overwhelmed, and she knows she's wasting her time. The sign of a disconnection in spirit is being distracted. The stress that it causes debilitates performance. How it does this is the subject of Chapter Six.

In a test situation, when you disconnect, you are pulling away from the test. *I don't want to be here. I'd rather be any place but here.* The problem is that you have to be there if you want to accomplish your goals, goals that are important and will make a valuable contribution to your life and to the lives of those around you. Since you cannot *not* take the test, you may as well stop fighting it and be there. Really be there. By continually trying to run away from taking the test, you are making the whole experience odious and repellent. The test isn't going to go away. Disconnecting from yourself in a vain attempt to disappear in spirit, even if you can't physically remove yourself, doesn't work. The more you disconnect from your spirit, the higher your stress will be. You're going to feel worse and worse, and your performance will suffer.

ANALYZING DISCONNECTION

The following is the story of a client of mine. It illustrates perfectly how disconnection works in the body, mind and spirit.

Recently, a psychologist referred one of her long-term patients to me. Marianne, a woman in her late forties, was a clinical social worker. She was facing a professional state-licensing exam and prior to the referral, she had failed it twice. By the time she came in to see me, she was terrified that history was going to repeat itself. The experience of failure had had such an impact on her that she vowed that if she failed again, she was going to quit her profession and take up another one, or move out of the state altogether. This woman did not fit the profile of a loser. She was a bright, competent person with two advanced degrees and fifteen years of professional experience in social work.

This is Marianne's description of her two previous experiences with taking the licensing exam:

"I don't even remember what happened during the first test. All I can recall is walking into the room. The rest of it is a big blur. The second exam was a little better, but not much. I remember that my body felt like stone. I looked at the test and thought, *There's no way I can do this. I'll never get anything right.* I found it impossible to think about the answers and recall anything I had studied. I just wanted to run out of there."

Let's analyze Marianne's story. Her statements are in the left hand column below. The analysis and the form of disconnection she is experiencing are in the right hand column.

"My body felt like stone."	Disconnection in the body
"I never get anything right."	Disconnection in the mind
"I just wanted to run out of there."	Disconnection in the spirit

As Marianne and I worked together, she learned to be aware of what was happening whenever she started disconnecting in her body, mind or spirit. She learned to use the same tools that I am going to give you in this workbook. And she applied them. Even so, she challenged me and tested herself. Twice before the exam, she grew very sick, she had severe dips in self-confidence, and she had to endure physical tension. But she never gave up. She kept following the coaching and refused to remain stuck in fear and anxiety. When the day came, she marched in and took the test.

She passed!

What did Marianne do to make this possible? How did she break through her substantial obstacles and dissolve her difficulties over taking tests? Marianne didn't take a magic potion; she simply cultivated an awareness of that moment when she began to disconnect in her body, mind and spirit, and then she practiced using the tools to reconnect. Instead of running away from the test, she taught herself to stay connected. In so doing, she brought her stress levels way down, which had a remarkable impact on her performance.

In the next chapter we'll look at how you disconnect. Your self-analysis will be the first important step to raising your test scores.

Chapter Three

The Three-Legged Stool

Picture this: you walk into a classroom to take a test. People all around you are fidgety and nervous, gnawing their fingernails and chewing their pencils, but you stretch your legs out comfortably and think, *I can handle this. Bring it on.* You open the test booklet and start answering the first question, then move onto the second and then the third. The fourth is a tough one, but you are still relaxed because your mantra is, *I know how to stay on course. I can work out the answer.* You surge on like this from one question to the next like a fearless lion. You're not mousing your way along, you're pouncing.

Do you think this is a fantasy? It's not. You can do it. You just need to learn how.

The secret is learning how to reduce the stress in your body, mind and spirit and to keep it at an optimal level throughout the exam. Think about what throws you off during a test. Are you rigid as a wooden plank or hyped up like a jumping bean? Either way, your body is not calm. You need it to be in a quiet, *unagitated* state so you can sit still long enough to do the work. Your mind cannot be undermining you by broadcasting alert warnings. Thoughts like *Loser on the loose!* will not boost your performance or pump up your faith in yourself during the hard questions. And your spirit cannot desert you by becoming distracted when you need it to help you stay on task and spur you on from start to finish. You have to take that test whether you like it or not, and wishing you were someplace else is not the kind of attitude that will pivot your attention toward your goal. In fact, thinking "I just want this to be over" only distracts your attention from the task at hand. It increases stress because it pulls you away from answering the questions in the allotted time.

Remember what I said before. Stress is not really caused by what is happening to you from the outside; it comes from the reaction you're having on the inside. The answer to physical tension, negative self-messages and fractured attention is to learn how to reconnect within yourself. This is how you lower your stress. This is how you stay in the game from start to finish and do your very best, no matter how rough it gets.

The steps that will ensure your success, whether you are taking a history quiz or defending your doctoral dissertation, are learning to be calm, confident and focused. Successful test takers embody these three characteristics. Everything inside is pulling for success.

When you take a test, all of you is there in the room—body, mind and spirit—and all three have to cooperate fully. That's your team. When a team **When your body, mind and spirit work together you have a winning team.** works toward one goal, each team member has to pull his own weight or he will let the team down. On a baseball team, for example, the outfield coordinates with the infield, the catcher works with the pitcher, the guys on base are all alert to each other's moves. But if the pitcher ignores the messages of the catcher or the third baseman takes his eye off the ball thinking the shortstop should catch it, they're not going to have a winning team. It will fragment and fall apart.

Your body, mind and spirit are your personal team. If any one of them is absent or weak you can't maximize your full potential. But if they work together, each operating at top capacity, you'll hit home runs. Every member of your team must fully participate when you face a test in order for you to reach your optimal zone. Any disconnection seriously undermines the whole team's efforts.

Once you learn how to work with your three team members you will notice immediately when you are disconnecting inside. More important, you'll know how to get yourself back into the test-taking performance mode. The secret of success, quite simply, is staying fully connected so that all the members of your personal team mutually reinforce each other's strengths. People who flourish on tests know how to play the game. By staying connected, they keep all parts of themselves working in concert. In each of the next three chapters, I will show you specifically how to stay connected in body, mind and spirit every time you take a test.

If you're thinking, *Is that all there is? If I stay calm, confident and focused I can pass my tests without studying for them?* The answer is: of course not. You have to study the material and study well if you want to succeed. But *how* you study and prepare will have a direct impact on your test performance. If, while you're studying, you are tensing up your body, broadcasting negative messages with your mind, or becoming distracted from your higher goals, you can't prepare well, let alone score high. Can you be successful in an athletic competition if, when you are getting ready for it, one of your team members doesn't show up at practice? You can't. Teams practice strategic moves together right up until game time. Like them, you can practice getting your body, mind and spirit working together from the day you start studying right through the last question of the test. Success doesn't happen only at the finish line. It's a path. You're on it, step by step, from beginning to end.

A MODEL FOR EVERY TEST

Practicing all three together—being calm, confident and focused—creates a dynamic, forceful unity. These three elements form a natural triad, and a triad is a powerful figure. It's the fundamental structure of harmony in music. In geometry, a three-legged configuration is the sturdiest of structures, much more stable than one that is four-legged. The three-pointed figure always stays a triangle, unlike a square that can be pushed into a parallelogram, or a circle that can be squished into an oval. This unity of three is a potent structure. It shows up in music, in religious traditions and in symbols, and it comprises the totality of who you are: body, mind and spirit.

When I work with clients, I hold up a three-legged stool when I introduce them to the idea that to improve their performance they need a calm body, a confident mind, and a focused spirit.

The three-legged stool, a structure that is ages old, is one of the sturdiest, most durable and long-lasting constructions ever produced. In the past, people used it for milking cows and sitting around fireplaces. This structure forms a three-point foundation that resists toppling. Visualize one, and then imagine that each leg represents a different part of you. One leg is your body, one is your mind, and the third is your spirit. All three together make up the totality of who you are. They are all part of the same unified structure called "you."

Each leg also represents what's necessary to reduce stress and improve performance.

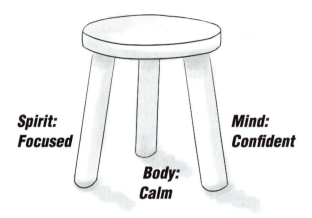

Spirit:
Focused

Mind:
Confident

Body:
Calm

When all three legs of the stool are equally strong, it is remarkably robust, so strong, in fact, that a baby elephant can rest its full weight on it. When your body, mind and spirit are sturdy and stable, you have a powerful platform on which to build your optimal performance. All your parts—your team members—are contributing to the integrity and potentiality of the whole.

Life is full of unavoidable challenges, and you need a strong foundation to meet them successfully. If you were taking a trip across the ocean, you would want a ship that will stand up to a storm. If you are going camping, you want a tent that will stand up to the wind and rain. When you're taking a test, you want be sure you can depend on your own internal structure to withstand the challenge of difficult questions. You need to trust that your "inner team" will be dependable in the face of anything the test throws at you. A strong foundation of body, mind and spirit makes up your three-legged stool, a platform that will support you.

But what happens if one of the legs is weak or short? The stool wobbles and loses its stability. Any leg that is weak imposes a strain on the entire system, which places excess pressure on the other two. What happens if that baby elephant tries to stand on a stool with one fragile leg? The whole thing collapses and the elephant falls on its rear end. You operate the same way. You need each leg of your stool to do its job and for all three to be equally strong. If one leg is weak, it will pull the other two down with it.

A perfect illustration of this point is the story of Alicia, a college senior. She was applying to medical school and was about to take her MCATs. Although she usually was calm and confident enough when *taking* tests, Alicia often found herself distracted when *preparing* for them. Instead of hitting the books, she went to parties. Instead of applying herself and going over past exams, she watched late-night TV. Her habitual pattern was to cram at the last minute and enter the classroom somewhat prepared, but not completely ready. For the MCATs, however, that strategy wasn't going to work. It was too big and too important, and it required sustained focus while preparing for it over a long period of time. As the date for the test drew nearer, Alicia became noticeably tense, and she started losing her long-held belief that she could pass any test no matter how much time she wasted beforehand. This time, the fact that she was so ill-prepared ate away at her confidence and it unnerved her.

The "weak leg" of Alicia's stool was her Focus/spirit, and it undermined the other two legs. By the time test day came around, her whole system was disturbed. She was physically anxious and she was lacking confidence. Her inability to focus and study had caused a weakness that her mind and body could not overcome. In other words, the weakest leg debilitated the other two. No three-legged stool can rest on only one or two legs. To pass the MCATs, Alicia had to work hard in the one area where she wasn't pulling her weight.

The good news is that this process is dynamic: when you strengthen any one component, it reinforces the other two. The first time around, Alicia scored poorly on her MCATs and then came in for coaching so she wouldn't repeat the performance a second time. We identified Focus as the aspect she most had to work on, and she learned how to do it: she made a study schedule, she set specific goals for herself, she rewarded herself for reaching those goals, and she reminded herself on a daily basis how crucial it was to attain a high score on these tests. With a low score she would literally have to choose a new career. This was high motivation for a young woman like Alicia, and she was diligent in aligning her actions with her goals. She found that as she reinforced the one weak leg, the other legs reacted accordingly. When she went to take the test for the second time she was more relaxed and she had more faith in herself. Her score went way up, and she was accepted into medical school.

One weak "leg" can disturb your whole system.

When your performance is off, you sometimes can be so thrown by it (especially if you are expecting to do much better), that you can't immediately identify which leg is the weak one. The beauty of the triad is that each leg is connected to the others. Whichever leg you begin with, you are immediately linked with the other two. It doesn't matter where you begin. This isn't a hierarchical model where you have to start at point A and move to point B, then go from there to C. You start where you can, and then move on. Just because the paradigm is called "calm, confident and focused," doesn't mean you have to work it in that order.

Alicia, for instance, worked on her Focus/spirit leg first. Once she was focused, she started to calm down. Another client, Steve, who was a high school soccer player, used the Confidence tools first. Feeling good about himself paved the way to relaxing his body and placing his attention on the task. Everyone is different, and every person will have his or her own entry point in working the model and using the tools.

What does your three-legged stool look like? I have designed a self-diagnostic tool to help you take a snapshot of yours. The Bernstein Performance Inventory (BPI) will give you a reading on which of your legs is the weakest and which is the strongest in most test situations. The BPI is made up of nine questions and takes five minutes to complete. By diagnosing yourself, you will find out which leg has been holding you back. You'll identify what your problem area is and where to apply your attention.

THE BERNSTEIN PERFORMANCE INVENTORY (BPI)

Recall a recent situation in which you had to perform in a particular time and place. Identify one that was difficult or challenging for you. It can include taking an examination, learning to ski in front of an instructor, or singing before an audience for the first time.

Visualize the details of the event, remembering the situation as clearly as you can. What happened and how did you feel about it? In a few words, describe on the line below what the context was for having to perform (SAT, GRE, musical audition, athletic competition, etc.) and how you felt about it:

_____

Below are nine statements. Read each one and circle the appropriate number to the right of the statement to indicate how you felt during this performance situation.

Before the test began:

	Not at all	A little bit	Somewhat	A lot
1. I felt calm and relaxed.	0	1	2	3
2. I was confident in my abilities.	0	1	2	3
3. I was able to focus on the task and do what I needed to do.	0	1	2	3

⇨

As the test proceeded:

	Not at all	A little bit	Somewhat	A lot
4. I stayed calm the whole time.	0	1	2	3
5. I remained confident for the duration.	0	1	2	3
6. I retained my focus all the way through.	0	1	2	3
7. If I started feeling nervous, I knew how to calm down.	0	1	2	3
8. If my confidence slipped, I was able to retrieve it.	0	1	2	3
9. If I lost my focus, I knew how to get back on track.	0	1	2	3

SCORING YOUR BPI

To determine your overall scores, total up your answers as follows:

After you have added your scores, fill in the following diagram with your totals:

Calm
Total your answers for
questions #1, 4, 7 _____

Confidence
Total your answers for
questions #2, 5, 8 _____

Focus
Total your answers for
questions #3, 6, 9 _____

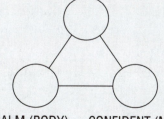

FOCUSED (SPIRIT)

CALM (BODY)   CONFIDENT (MIND)

HOW TO INTERPRET YOUR RESULTS

As you can see, the above diagram looks like a three-legged stool. Examining the numbers in each of the three circles will tell you what your relative strengths and weaknesses are. Since the highest score you can achieve in any one "leg" is nine, any number less than nine shows that you need to reinforce that leg.

To show you how scores are interpreted and where you can go from there, let me walk you through the example of one of my clients.

Sam was a high school senior who was under-performing on his AP history test. His BPI scores were: Calm, 2; Confident, 4; Focused, 7. What do these numbers tell us about Sam? Obviously, his strongest leg was Focus, his weakest was Calm, and Confident was somewhere in between. After listening to Sam tell his own story about how he approaches history tests, his BPI scores will make sense to you.

"I might not be a genius, but in general I'm a pretty good student. I mean, I keep on top of my studies and I'm not a slacker. I do all my assignments and turn them in on time, which is a lot more than I can say for most of my classmates. Also, when it's exam time, I don't wait and cram just before the deadline. But unlike all the other tests I have to take, before history tests, and sometimes right in the middle of them, I just get these scary thoughts like, 'You're totally not capable of dealing with this. There's just too much stuff.' Thoughts like these bug me, but they don't really waylay me from doing the job. I can kind of ignore them. What does get in the way is that I feel really nervous. My heart starts pounding, my legs and arms feel weak, and my stomach is in knots. Sometimes I even feel like I can't breathe. These physical symptoms I can't ignore. They usually start right before the test, and on a bad day, they stay that way through the whole hour. When it's really intense, I can barely think."

Here's what Sam's scores on the BPI looked like:

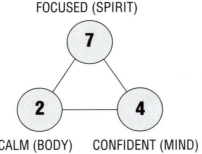

FOCUSED (SPIRIT)

7

2   4

CALM (BODY)   CONFIDENT (MIND)

Sam's score on Focus was 7 out of a possible 9. That's to be expected since he reported that he did all his assignments and kept up a decent study schedule. That means he was connected to his spirit, his driving force, and had no trouble staying on track. His Confidence score, at 4, was a little shakier. He was, from time to time, beset by negative thinking that undermined his belief in his abilities. Somehow he managed to shake those thoughts off and retain his self-assurance. But he was never able to conquer a pure case of nerves. His inability to stay calm in the face of an impending test was his weakest leg. His score of 2 in the Calm leg attests to his difficulties. By his own words we can tell that he was dissociating from his body, which caused him to become more and more physically tense, which in turn made him feel ungrounded. Naturally, the fact that his heart was pounding and he had trouble breathing became a significant distraction. It made it harder to keep connecting to the task at hand. This, in turn, affected his confidence. As his confidence level slipped, he found it harder to rebound. What we can see from this example is how the weakness in this one leg—Calm—put a strain on the entire structure and kept him from achieving the grade he should have gotten, considering how hard he studied.

Strengthen any one leg and you strengthen the other two.

Sam's strongest leg was his ability to stay focused on a goal, so I gave him a new goal to focus on: to learn to become calm in the face of a history test. In no time at all, he learned the three tools for calming down. As the physical tension began to dissolve, we noticed that his ability to focus grew even stronger than it had been before. Naturally, this gave his confidence a huge boost because he had been able to conquer this beast that had caused so much agitation and strain. He grew ever more sure of himself as he was able to remember the material and think through test questions without physical tension overwhelming him.

Remember: working on any one of the legs links you to the other two and makes your whole system stronger.

YOUR SCORES GIVE YOU A STARTING POINT

What does your three-legged stool look like? Which is your strongest leg? Which is your weakest? Recognize that you are not comparing yourself to another person—just to yourself. These scores tell you what *you* need to strengthen in order to reduce your test stress and improve your performance.

As you do this you may be thinking, *Hey, wait a minute Dr. B! My scores aren't accurate. They say that I'm not very confident. But that's not true! I'm usually very sure of myself.*

The BPI is not a definitive statement on how you are in every aspect of your life. It is meant to help you examine how you perform under pressure. Another thing to consider is whether your BPI scores accurately represent how you are in *most* test situations. Sometimes when people take the BPI, the situation that comes to mind is some horror story about a test that isn't really typical of their usual performance. Consequently, their BPI scores aren't representative of most of the tests they take. Look at your scores and ask yourself if they are a reflection of how you perform most of the time on tests. If you find that your BPI scores don't reflect your overall performance, then re-take the inventory based on what you are usually like in stressful situations to obtain a more accurate reading.

Before we go on, look at your scores again. What do you most need to strengthen? Being calm? Remaining confident? Or staying focused?

In the next three chapters, we will take on each leg of the stool. You can begin by working on your shortest leg (your weakest score), by going straight to the chapter that covers it. But you can also start with your strongest score since some people benefit the most by working from their strength. You can also read sequentially through the next three chapters. This model is not a rigid structure that you have to squeeze yourself into. Its beauty is that wherever you begin, you will end up encompassing the whole. Even if you scored high in one particular leg, it's still important to check out the tools in that chapter because you can always grow stronger. If you happened to score low on all three, that is only showing you that you have room to grow in all three areas.

The end goal of the next three chapters is to teach you how to become calm, confident and focused on every test, whether inside the classroom or outside it, so that you will always have a sturdy, stable platform and be ready to perform at your best.

Chapter Four

How to Calm Down

Last September a bright high school senior named Jamal came to see me. Anxiously, he asked me to help him raise his SAT scores by 200 points so the college of his choice would accept him. He had one last chance to take the test. After that, he was at the mercy of whichever college would take him. Why had he performed poorly?

"Because on the last SAT test," Jamal told me, "I grew more and more nervous as the time went on. I couldn't remember the information I studied so I started thinking 'What hope is there?' After I scraped by on three questions in a row, I hit a wall. I just froze up."

As Jamal spoke, his right leg bounced up and down rapidly, his shoulders tensed and rose almost to his ears, and his speech accelerated like a car with a jammed gas pedal. Several times while he spoke, he held his breath. "Just *talking* about the test makes me nervous," he said anxiously, a comment which of course was unnecessary since his whole body communicated it. "I feel like I'm flipping out right now. This is what happened to me on the SAT."

It was a natural mistake: Jamal believed that remembering the test was making him nervous. In fact, *all the nervous things he was doing with his body* were causing his anxiety: bouncing his legs, tensing his shoulders, holding his breath. His *body* made his mind nervous, not his memories. When I told him this he looked at me like I was from another planet. "My *brain* is taking the test," he shot back, "not my body. I *always* sit like this. What does all that have to do with my SAT scores?"

This is very common misconception. Most people think that only their mind is working on an exam. That's where the information is stored, right?

Not quite.

Since your body is one of the three key players on your team, *all* of your body is in the room and engaged when you take a test. If you want to perform at your best, then all of you, not just your brain, has to be fully present and supporting the process.

An agitated body creates a jumpy feeling of impatience and it makes you want to run away. Physical tension can quickly shut down your ability to remember what you have studied and if you are expected to produce this information for a test, you are immediately thrust into a state of anxiety. The feeling grows. Soon, you feel like you are losing control. The result: poor performance, perhaps failure.

On the other hand, a calm body can significantly improve your ability to think, to recall information, to answer questions properly, and to make good use of the time available.

When I observe students taking tests, I see so much nervous body language—hunched backs, tight shoulders, bobbing knees, facial grimaces, taut fists, and constricted breathing. Test takers are often completely unaware of what their bodies are doing and how profoundly that is affecting their performance. Frankly, it's amazing that so many students even make it to the end of tests without having panic attacks.

If your body is agitated, then your performance will suffer.

Tensing during a test creates stress. Adrenaline surges through your gut, your blood pressure shoots up and your entire system goes on alert. Your brain screams *Danger!*—as if a tiger is chasing you. A torrent of stress hormones unleashes into your bloodstream. It becomes increasingly hard to focus and think. Looking at the test questions makes you panic because suddenly you just can't answer them. It looks as if those questions are causing your anxiety, but questions are just printed words on paper. They aren't doing anything *to* you. Your stress is mounting and your performance is suffering because you are disconnecting from your own body. You are not aware of what your body is doing, but it's spinning out of control. You may even feel like you want to flee, but you can't. You have to sit there and force yourself to answer the questions.

How can you possibly perform well in the face of all that tension, when you want to run away but can't? These are all forms of disconnection. Remember: disconnection causes stress and too much stress causes poor performance.

It's the same for any type of performance. If a basketball player is sitting on the bench waiting to go into the game and she keeps tensing her body, when the coach finally sends her out on the court she will be nervous right from the start. She'll miss shots she ought to be making and she'll be out of sync with her teammates. It doesn't matter how hard she practiced. She needs to stay loose on and off the court. If a piano player's fingers lock in the middle of a piece, they can't float effortlessly over the keys. Again, it doesn't matter how well he knows the music.

In all these cases, the performers disconnected from their bodies. Remember the three-legged stool? Disconnection in one leg immediately hobbles the other two. When you lose the feeling of calm in your body, it precipitates negative thoughts (in your mind) and you'll easily become distracted and lose heart (in your spirit). Stress can build very rapidly and when it grows past a certain point, your performance will suffer. Guaranteed.

To improve your test performance you have to reduce the stress in your body. Simply put, when you take a test you want your body to be *calm*. The rest of this chapter will show you how to do that.

AWARENESS FIRST

To keep your body in a calm state you need to learn two things:

* How to recognize when you are *not* calm.

* How to use specific tools to calm yourself down.

In this section we will work on your awareness of your body. We'll pay attention to how your body feels when you are anxiously anticipating a stressful event (like a test tomorrow), or when you are mid-way through the test itself.

If you're like most people, you are not too aware of your body throughout the day, unless you're in pain or you feel sick. A sore throat, a stomachache, a cold, a fever and a toothache call attention to themselves. But until the discomfort reaches an uncomfortable level, we tend to minimize or even ignore the early signs. *It's nothing. It will go away.* We don't become aware until the pain is virtually shouting at us. *My tooth is killing me!* That's when we do something about it.

For certain people this doesn't hold true—people who use their bodies all the time—a dancer, a swimmer, or a singer. They *have* to pay close attention and not ignore any signs that all is not well, and then attend to them because their jobs depend on it, often in front of a crowd. The upside is that they are connected to what goes on in their bodies. Most of us don't have that threat hanging over us. The problem we have is that when we ignore the signs of disconnection, it causes stress to build. But ultimately, we face the same failure. If we have a test to take, it behooves us to increase our body awareness—when are we *not* calm—so we know how to deal with it at critical times.

Let's start with this question: what signs and symptoms in your body tell you that *you* are not calm?

I know when I'm not calm because …
(Check all that apply)

❏ My chest feels tight.

❏ I have a headache or feel one coming on.

❏ My shoulders ache.

❏ My neck feels stiff.

❏ I stop breathing.

❏ My stomach hurts.

❏ My heart beats rapidly.

❏ My muscles ache.

❏ I start sweating.

❏ My skin feels prickly.

❏ I feel tense all over.

❏ I feel like I'm gasping for air.

❏ My feet curl up.

❏ My legs cramp.

❏ I make fists with my hands.

❏ I feel like I want to run away.

❏ My mind starts racing.

❏ I start talking too fast.

❏ I bite my nails.

❏ My nerves are jittery.

❏ My eyes ache.

❏ My voice rises.

❏ I feel generally uncomfortable.

Perhaps you checked off one, perhaps ten. Everyone is different, so consider what other symptoms may be true for you.

People often ask me, "But why is it necessary to be aware first?" Think about it this way. When you are driving a car and you see sign that says **STOP,** it is telling you exactly what you need to do: put your foot on the brake and stop the car. If you disregard the sign and keep going, you are risking your own life and that of others. The physical signs of tension in your body are like a stop sign sending you a message.

Pay attention to uncomfortable feelings in your body.

It is your body's way of signaling you that you are disconnected, which is useful to know because it tells you that you need to re-connect to your body and calm down. If you don't pay attention to these signs, you are going to crash.

Awareness of when you are *not* calm is the first step in the process of reconnecting with your body.

THE THREE WAYS WE DISCONNECT PHYSICALLY

It doesn't matter how many or how few items you checked above. Becoming aware of what is going on with your body when you are not calm is a big step in the right direction. Besides, there are only three basic ways we human beings lose our sense of calm. Each of your responses, on the checklist, is related to one of these:

✳ We stop breathing or we breath irregularly.

✳ We become ungrounded.

✳ We shut down in one or more of our five senses.

As I explain each way of disconnecting, think how it characterizes you.

Irregular Breathing

The most frequent way we disconnect from our bodies is by holding the breath or breathing irregularly.

When I observe students taking tests, I see this familiar scenario: the exam proctor hands out the test booklets and then instructs everyone to open to the first page and begin the test. If you listen carefully, the next thing you hear will be a collective "gulp" of air. Then silence. That means most of the test takers are holding their breath.

Why is this significant? Because holding your breath immediately causes stress. Without breath your brain is deprived of oxygen. It starts sounding an alarm: YOU ARE DYING! This is a fact: if your brain really were cut off from oxygen permanently, it would die. The automatic reaction to a loss of oxygen broadcasts an emergency signal. This isn't conscious. It's instinctive. Your anxiety level is directly affected by how you breathe. Stop breathing, and your anxiety level immediately shoots up.

But there is another connection between your breath and your ability to think clearly and logically when you are taking a test. Breath is intimately connected to your thinking. A shortage of breath causes a fear reaction, which disturbs an orderly thought process.

When your breath has stopped or it is irregular, chances are that your thoughts are jumping around and you are worrying about the future (*What's going to happen…?*) or you are dwelling on the past (*If only I had…*) When your breath is steady and regular, and you are able to be in the present moment, then your brain is free to deal with the task at hand. Conscious attention to the breath puts you firmly here, now. And that's just where you have to be when you take a test. You must deal with the question in front of you, right now. It doesn't matter what you did yesterday (past) or what you're going to do tomorrow (future), you have to think and answer test questions *now*, in the present. This is hard to do if your thinking is restless, if you're anxious about what's going to happen, or if you're endlessly replaying what already went wrong. The remedy to this situation is not *mind* control. It's *breath* control. With regular, steady breathing you can be in the present and give your full attention to the question in front of you. Your thinking will be clearer. You will be calm.

The way you breathe mediates your anxiety level.

Problems with the breath show up in three ways, all of which pull you right out of the present and cause anxiety to mount rapidly. Which pattern describes how you breathe in a stressful test situation?

1. You hold your breath.

2. You breathe in short, shallow, little bird-like breaths.

3. You breathe erratically—you gasp, you hold your breath, you breathe only a little.

If you are not aware of your breathing habits, try observing yourself over the next day or so. For twenty-four hours, check in with your body and ask yourself, *How am I breathing?* You might be surprised to discover that sometimes you have stopped breathing or that your breath is very shallow or erratic. If you start feeling anxious—about an upcoming test or a speech you have to give—immediately pay close attention to your breath. Chances are it has stopped, or is shallow or irregular.

I recommend that you keep a record of your observations in the *Awareness Log: Calm* (see page 191). Use the log as you work through this chapter and record when you become aware of your breath. Using it will help you train yourself to be more aware of your unconscious breathing habits, which is the first step to changing these habits.

Turn to the log now and begin recording your observations of how and when you disconnect by not breathing in a steady, deep way.

Becoming Ungrounded

The next way that we disconnect in our bodies that causes anxiety is by losing our awareness of and contact with the ground.

There is a great, settling, connecting force on earth and it's called *gravity*. Gravity holds us to the earth and keeps everything from spinning away and out of control. We've all seen the pictures of astronauts floating around. They're in a zero-gravity environment. It looks like fun, but here on earth, it would make us feel shaky and tenuous. We feel most secure when we are in contact with the earth, and we become *un*grounded when we pull away from the earth, often without even realizing it. Let's examine the two ways we become ungrounded.

When I find myself deep in thought about some challenge—say I'm about to talk to an audience of a thousand people—my thoughts may become anxious, *I should have prepared more. Maybe I won't remember everything I have to say. Am I going to start sweating? Will they like me?* I begin to notice that I am definitely *not* feeling the chair I'm sitting on, nor am I feeling the floor under my feet. This is what I mean by "becoming ungrounded."

Why is this noteworthy? When I'm ungrounded, I literally lose touch with the ground. I'm trying to run away from the present moment. When I pull my awareness back into the present, however, I feel the chair supporting me. When I consciously place my feet squarely on the floor, I feel that supporting me too. Immediately the anxiety lessens, even though the situation hasn't changed. I am still about to speak to a large group of people, but my attitude toward it has changed. I have physically *re-connected* to where I am *right now* and what I have to do *now*. Grounding, quite simply, has a profound calming effect on the body and mind, giving you an enhanced ability to fulfill your spirit and perform.

The second way we become ungrounded is by holding physical tension. When you tense a part of your body you are, quite literally, pulling away from the force of gravity. Joseph, a 45-year-old surgeon, failed his professional board certification exam three times. As he talked about the test I noticed his jaw becoming more and more rigid. When I called his attention to this he was surprised. "Hmmm, I've often felt tired in my jaw after I finish doing a surgery but didn't know why. But how is that related to failing my test?" Because as he disconnected from his body through tension, he felt more and more stress, which increased the likelihood of making an error. I asked him to imagine an Olympic diver tensing up in the middle of a dive, or a dancer tightening as she executes a *pas de change*. As a performer disconnects from her body, the tension rises and she has less control of how she uses it. She can't follow through with the performance. During Joe's certification exam, or in the OR performing surgery, he tenses his jaw. He is not letting the calming, settling force of gravity work for him. Gravity, by definition, allows the body to relax, and that calmness improves performance.

When your muscles stay tensed you are disconnected from the present.

When you are tense somewhere in your body you are, quite literally, "holding on." Think of life as an ongoing flow of events that moves through you and around you. If you are holding on somewhere—your shoulders, your jaw, or your hands—you are disconnecting from the ongoing flow.

It's like taking a ride in a boat on a river, but the boat isn't moving along with the river's current because it is tied to the dock. The present is not a static point; it's a series of moments in a sequential flow. Physical tension keeps you out of that flow. When you are tense you are holding onto yourself, disconnected from the movement of things around you. As we learned earlier, physical tension is also "*anti-grounding*." You're pulling up and away from the ground, from the force of gravity that offers an ongoing connection to the present.

Chances are that in the past you haven't paid a whole lot of attention to being grounded, but now you need to cultivate your awareness of it so that you learn to re-ground and stay calm. Observe how you become ungrounded as you study for a test and use your *Awareness Log* to keep a record of your observations. Especially observe yourself during a test because that is the environment that especially unseats us.

To help you identify the areas in your body where you habitually hold tension, look at the *Tension Map* that follows. Then ask yourself, "Where do I usually feel tension when I'm studying or when I'm taking a test?" Anywhere you are holding tension—anywhere that you are disconnecting—can be transformed and become a place of connection and calm relaxation instead—but only if you're aware of it first.

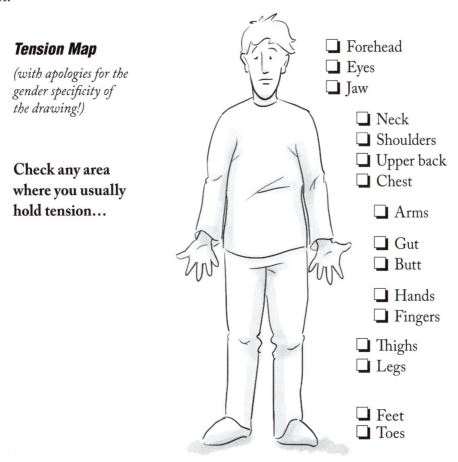

Tension Map

(with apologies for the gender specificity of the drawing!)

Check any area where you usually hold tension…

❑ Forehead
❑ Eyes
❑ Jaw

❑ Neck
❑ Shoulders
❑ Upper back
❑ Chest

❑ Arms

❑ Gut
❑ Butt

❑ Hands
❑ Fingers

❑ Thighs
❑ Legs

❑ Feet
❑ Toes

It is often useful to observe other people too. The next time you are on the bus, in the market, or standing in line at the bank just look around. We do not live in a relaxed society. You will see people with their shoulders hunched, or holding one of their hands in a tight fist, or making deep worried furrows in their forehead, marking the obvious places on the *Tension Map*. You can almost tell what they're feeling; all you have to do is remember what you felt like when you were tense in the same areas of your body while studying in the library for a three-hour stretch.

In addition to the usual areas of tension (upper back, neck, jaw) there are also not-so-obvious places—in the toes, the tongue, behind the eyes, in the arches of the feet, to name a few. As you become more familiar with the obvious places where you store tension, you will start becoming aware of the deeper, more subtle places. Once you are able to observe your entire body, you can use the tools for calming down to establish a peaceful atmosphere throughout the entire test-taking period.

Now that you see how much you are affected by tension, it's time to cultivate your awareness of how and when it arises in your body by using the *Awareness Log*.

Shutting Down the Senses

The third way we disconnect in our bodies is by shutting down one or more of our five senses.

Sarah is an accomplished pianist working for a major opera company. A sensitive soul, she is also a consummate professional. She prides herself on being exceptionally well prepared for every job, but one day she had to step up and perform without the usual time to prepare. A colleague had taken ill, and Sarah was called in at the last moment to play for a run-through of Verdi's opera, *Il Trovatore*. She may have had some familiarity with the musical score, but it had been years since she'd looked at it, and there wasn't enough time to review it thoroughly. At the rehearsal, she grew increasingly nervous about being unprepared. "We started working on a scene," she recalled, "where the music is very difficult to play. I froze up. I became totally fixated on the notes. I wasn't listening to the singers or watching the conductor. Worse, I wasn't hearing the music."

We can hear from Sarah's own words ("I froze up") that she disconnected in the first two ways described in this chapter. She stopped her breath and she was caught up in physical tension. But there was one more thing she said that was a clue, "I wasn't listening to the singers or watching the conductor... I wasn't hearing the music."

Sarah shut down in her senses.

The five senses are the gateways to our awareness. We see, smell, hear, taste and touch the world. When we shut down in one or more of our five senses we disconnect physically to what is around us. When we say, "He's out of touch" we usually mean the person is disconnected from reality. This means that the person who is out of touch is not in *contact*, through his senses, with what is going on around him right now. If he is not in touch with the present through his senses, he is literally disconnected from the world. Performance is all about how you manipulate and interact with the world, so you can see how this puts you at a disadvantage.

I noticed this when I was eating lunch the other day. All I was thinking about was an upcoming meeting at 3:00 pm. I was not tasting the food that was passing my lips. I forked the bite of potato salad into my mouth and swallowed it, but the physical, connected act of sensing the flavors, textures and temperature of the food was absent. When I finally shifted my awareness, I put my attention on the sensory experiences of taste, smell and sight. My stress instantly decreased several notches because I was connected, again, to the present, not fretting about the impending event. Finally, I enjoyed the meal even though I still had the difficult meeting a little later. The meeting would either go well or not. "Right now," I thought, "I am eating."

The expression "Come to your senses!" has real import here. When you open up your senses you are connecting to what is going on right here, right now. And test performance always takes place in the now.

The other two ways of disconnecting (breathing and grounding) were fairly straightforward as far as tests are concerned. But being connected through the senses is a little tricky because being too open can also distract you. You don't necessarily want to let your attention focus on your hearing in a big exam room where people are sighing heavily, or focus on your sense of sight when the person next to you is squirming with anxiety or picking his nose. The object of your senses is not an asset if it is upsetting, disturbing or frustrating. You want to use your senses selectively when you take a test so that you help, instead of hinder, your performance. In the next section I'll show you how to do that. Right now, all you have to do is become more aware of when you are shutting down in your senses. Use the *Awareness Log* to bring your attention to all five.

Use your five senses to stay in the moment.

Refining Your Awareness

Before moving on to the three tools for calming down, I would like you to refine your awareness of how and when you disconnect from your body. Below is a chart that summarizes what we have done in this chapter. Read through the chart and think about the questions it is asking you, then answer what you can. If you can't answer all of the questions right now that's fine. You might need to do some observation first so you can collect what we psychologists call "baseline data" on yourself with your *Awareness Log*.

Remember, the more you cultivate your awareness of the ways in which you disconnect from your body the more quickly you will be able to catch the stress well before it builds. In other words, you will reconnect right away and actually *reduce* the stress. It won't have a chance to reach the point of having a negative impact on your performance. Even better, it will be at just the right level (remember the Yerkes-Dodson Curve?) so that you can perform at your best.

As you fill in the chart remember a test you recently took or imagine one you are about to take.

AWARENESS INVENTORY: BODY

When I am in a stressful situation such as taking a test, I notice the following things in my body.

Check all that apply in each category.

BREATHING	❏ I hold my breath. ❏ My breathing becomes very shallow. ❏ I breathe erratically (I gasp, I stop breathing, I take small breaths).
GROUNDING	❏ I'm not aware of the floor or of the chair I'm sitting on. ❏ My feet are coming off of the ground. ❏ I feel tension in my (name body parts): _____ _____
SENSING	I tend to close down (i.e. I'm not aware of) my sense of (check as many that apply)… ❏ Touch ❏ Smell ❏ Taste ❏ Sight ❏ Hearing

---

Remember, awareness means *paying attention to what's going on inside of you.* As you study for a test or take one you may realize that you are doing all sorts of unhelpful things with your body that you probably didn't notice before. The difference now is that you are going to *pay attention* and treat the symptoms in your body as road signs to help you stop and reconnect.

The more aware you are, the more effectively you can use the tools I'm about to give you.

THE THREE TOOLS FOR CALMING DOWN

Now you are ready to learn the three tools for calming down. These tools will help you to reduce quickly any stress building up in your body. The tools are easy to learn and effective. If you worked through the last section on awareness you already have a jump start on them.

TOOL #1: Calming Down by Breathing

It should come as no surprise that breathing is the first tool. Let's work on this together.

* ✳ Take a good deep breath. Inhale … breathe in through your nose.

* ✳ Exhale…breathe out through your mouth.

* ✳ Do it again … inhale … exhale.

Notice *where* the breath is going. When I ask people to "take a good deep breath" almost everyone puffs up their lungs and upper chest. This is not a *deep* breath. A breath that raises your shoulders and expands your chest does not calm you down; it actually amps you up. I call it a "fight or flight breath" because it prepares you to do battle or to run away. This kind of breathing feels like fear. It's what the body does when it's reacting to danger. Imagine you are walking in a jungle and suddenly a ferocious tiger is facing you, baring its teeth. Fear courses through your body. When you take a big gulp of air while facing a tiger, it goes to your upper chest. Either you're going to face the danger or you're going to run away from it. Either way, this is a survival breath and its purpose is not to relax you.

Take a calming breath. Breathe deeply down. Inhale, exhale. Keep a steady rhythm going.

A calming breath, on the other hand, goes to a different and deeper place —your belly, which is why Tool #1 is a calming *belly* breath.

EXERCISE: The Belly Breath

To start with, sit comfortably in a chair with your back well supported.

Place your body in an open position—uncross your arms and your legs. (If your arms or legs are crisscrossed you will restrict your airflow.)

Rest your palms on your thighs and place both feet on the floor.

Now place your hands on top of your navel and let your belly just relax. This means don't hold your belly in. (Resist any temptation here to suck in your stomach so you can look thin.) Let your belly hang out and relax.

First, exhale through your mouth … Now breathe in through your nose, but don't suck in your belly. Let it stay expanded. You will feel the breath seep into your lungs as you breathe in, but your chest won't be heaving up and down. Both belly and chest will be calm as your breath keeps dropping down into your lower belly.

Slowly, **breathe** in and out three times in this open, expanded position, chest relaxed and belly wide.

If you want to deepen your breath even more, reach your hands around you and place your palm and fingers on both sides of your lower back right along the hips. Now, breathe deeply down and feel your bottom back ribs very gently expand as you do this. This is a small, subtle movement. You have to be quiet and tuned in to feel it, but as you sense this gentle movement of your ribs you will notice your calmness deepening.

Now, inhale again, deeply down into your belly and lower back.

Slowly exhale … let the breath out gently.

Breathe in and out like this three times.

Feel yourself calming down. Don't force the breath in and out and don't hyperventilate.

At this point you might start yawning or feel sleepy. Many people have this reaction. Recently, a bright, athletic, 17-year-old girl came to me for SAT coaching. As she talked about herself she was so charged with energy she could hardly sit still. With lightning speed she rattled off an incredibly long list of activities in which she was involved. I couldn't help but notice that she hardly took a nanosecond to breathe. We started working on deepening and regularizing her breath. In less than five minutes she started yawning. A lot. Then she actually fell asleep! Her system was so tightly wound and deprived of oxygen, so needing to *rest*, that given the first opportunity to calm down she conked out. So, if you are yawning, are sleepy, or feel light-headed as you start paying attention to and deepening your breath, know that this is actually a *good* sign. Your body is calming down. It is telling you that it is not used to breathing deeply and regularly, and it needs some rest!

The way to deep belly breathing is to work slowly, gently and determinedly on cultivating your breath. It may feel a little strange at first and all that oxygen might make you may feel a bit light-headed. Your system simply isn't used to taking real breaths. It's used to short, choppy, mini-breaths. After a while though, deep, steady breathing will feel like the most natural, calming thing in the world.

Putting Breathing into Action

The next time you notice that you are not calm, treat the anxious feelings like a road sign. If your stomach is churning, or you start sweating, or your legs are shaking, your body is sending you a message: "You need to calm down." This is your awareness kicking in. The first thing to ask yourself is, "How am I breathing?" because it is the most primary. You've probably stopped breathing or your breath has become very shallow or irregular. Do the exercise above and you will feel yourself calming down immediately.

Once you have started breathing deeply and regularly say, "Thank you" inside. Why do this? Because the awareness you just received that you were not breathing is a gift. It is a realization to be grateful for. Whether you believe your awareness comes from a God, a Goddess, a Higher Power, your Highest Self, Nature, the Universe, or Life, the very fact that it is coming to you at all is like a present. Gratitude acknowledges the giver and encourages future giving. Imagine receiving a wonderful gift from someone and not saying thank you. The giver wouldn't feel like being generous again, "Well, she didn't say 'Thank you' last time." Expressing gratitude invites more of what you're grateful for to come your way.

What most people do when they notice that they are "breathing wrong" is to beat themselves up, *I can't believe I'm still doing that! When am I gonna learn?* They don't appreciate the awareness at all. This kind of critical response is not allowed! I urge you to try saying "Thank you" every time you become aware of anything that you are trying to change in yourself. Gratitude is the opposite of criticism and it spreads an atmosphere of kindness and compassion—exactly the right atmosphere for inner growth.

Breathing deeply and then saying "Thank you" reduces feelings of stress, and you actually improve the possibility of attaining your goal of higher test scores because you are cultivating a helpful relationship with the powers of change. When you breathe deeply and regularly you are giving your brain, blood and body the oxygen it needs to perform optimally. Even if you don't believe in a God, Goddess or Higher Power, expressing gratitude still cultivates a better relationship with your own consciousness and highest self (the best person you can be).

TOOL #2: Calming Down by Grounding

Susan is about to take the GRE. She is sitting in a room full of other college seniors. Everyone is fidgeting. You can smell the anxiety in the air. Susan herself is perched on the edge of her chair, one foot coiled around the leg, her other foot is lifting off of the ground, knee and leg bouncing. She is definitely *not* calm. What is wrong with this picture?

Susan is very ungrounded.

Feel Supported by the Floor and Chair

Becoming grounded has two parts. The first part is feeling supported by the floor and the chair. To have this experience, do the following simple exercise as you continue reading:

 EXERCISE: Grounding Yourself

Start by sitting comfortably, upright, in a chair.

Uncross your arms and your legs.

Place your feet flat on the floor.

Breathe down to your belly.

Now, feel the floor under your feet.

Feel the floor supporting your feet.

Now feel your body sitting on the chair. Feel your legs and butt and back touching the chair. If the chair has arm rests, feel your arms being supported by them.

Feel your whole body being supported by the floor and the chair.

This is the first part of **grounding**. Continue it for one minute and enjoy the feeling that comes over you.

Did you remember to breathe? Most people, when they start learning how to ground themselves, often stop breathing! Don't let that happen. You can use two tools simutaneously just by keeping your breath deep and steady as you ground yourself by feeling the support of the floor and chair.

The combination of breathing and grounding is very powerful, and goes a long way toward connecting you to your own body, calming yourself down and staying present.

Releasing Physical Tension

The second part of grounding is letting go of physical tension. Let's look at Susan again, a little further into the test. Now her shoulders are hiked way up and her brow is deeply furrowed. Her left hand is making a fist and her right hand is tightly squeezing the pencil. All of this is *physical tension*. When you hold tension in your body you are actually pulling away from gravity, which is a great settling force. Gravity draws everything in us to the earth. When you tighten muscles in your legs, neck, back or forehead, you are pulling away from the earth, *un*grounding yourself.

In the awareness section of this chapter you identified the areas in your body where you hold tension. Now, let's use the tool of grounding to release that tension. Another name for grounding is *letting go*. This means just what it says. Let go of—release—wherever you are holding tension. Let gravity work. Let the tension flow out of you and into the ground. Practice this by tightly clenching an object in your hand. Start with something soft like a small stuffed animal, an old tennis ball, or a bunched up T-shirt. Now clench it really tightly and heighten that tension. Squeeze it even more tightly. Good. Now let go. Relax your hand muscles. The object will drop to the ground. Feel the wave of calm pass through your whole body.

To practice letting go in your body, try an exercise called the "Tension/Release Scan."

 EXERCISE: Tension/Release Scan

Sit comfortably in a chair, arms and legs uncrossed.

Tighten the muscles in your left foot and leg.

Now, with an exhale, release the leg muscles.

Tighten the muscles in your right foot and leg.

With an out-breath, release them.

Tighten the muscles in your belly.

Breathe out and release.

Tighten the muscles in your left hand and arm.

Breathe out and release.

Tighten the muscles in your right hand and arm.

Breathe out and release.

Tighten your chest and shoulders.

Breathe out and release.

Tighten your neck muscles.

Breathe out and release.

Tighten your jaw muscles.

Breathe out and release.

Tighten your whole face.

Breathe out and release.

Tighten your whole body.

Breathe out and release.

After this exercise, locate the area in your body where you store the most tension. Is it your jaw? Your lower back? Your legs? Wherever it is, feel the tension there, hold it and even heighten it for five seconds. Now, on an out breath, let it go.

Release the tension into the ground. At the same time feel yourself supported by the floor and chair (the first form of grounding). Doing this expertly sets you well on the way to calming *down*. That phrase has more meaning now, doesn't it?

TOOL #3: Sensing

The third tool for calming yourself is **sensing**. It is easy to turn on *one* of your five senses—seeing, hearing, touching, tasting or smelling—when you become aware that you are anxious. As you make the connection through your senses to the world around you, you will start feeling more calm in your body.

What is the relationship between opening your senses and calming down? This tool is a little more complicated than the first two, so stay with my explanation below and you will reap great rewards.

Your senses connect you to the world. They tell you what you are looking at, listening to, tasting, touching or smelling. Without your senses you wouldn't know where you were or what was happening around you. You would feel very disconnected, which would be frightening. A well-known psychology experiment proved this. When people were placed in a pitch-black, soundproof room they immediately became disoriented. Soon they grew severely anxious. Why? They had no reference points to anything familiar. They were cut-off and adrift, disconnected from any sensory input. Sensory input is connection, how we make contact with our world. Since stress is a function of disconnection, it makes logical and practical sense that to reduce stress, anxiety and tension, you want to increase your connection, this time, through your senses.

Let's start with your sense of sight. Opticians notice that when we are anxious, our sight tends to be compromised, as is reflected in the phrase, "He has tunnel vision." Commonly, we use the phrase to describe a person who is not taking in the whole picture. We might say "John has tunnel vision when it comes to politics" because John is unable or unwilling to see the other side's position. We conclude, "John is cut off." Contrast this to a person who has a broader perspective, "Jane has a balanced approach to negotiating. She has a wider view." Jane may well have a position she feels passionately about, but her view of the overall situation is larger than the perspective of someone who can only see one side.

The narrow or expanded view isn't just an attitudinal state; it's an actual visual connection through the sense of sight. When you open up your sense of sight you can actually reduce stress in your system. This is true for the other senses as well. When you do so you will feel more calm.

Let's work on your sense of sight by starting with the following simple exercise. It is meant to open up your sense of sight by expanding your peripheral vision.

EXERCISE: Tapping Into the Big Picture

Sit comfortably and look straight ahead of you.

Keeping your head still, move both of your eyes all the way to the left, and see how much you can see.

Bring your eyes back to center. Breathe.

Now move your eyes all the way to the right. See as much as you can see to the right.

Bring them back to center. Breathe.

Now look up as high as you can. See as much as you can above you.

Now bring your eyes back to center. Breathe.

And now look down, all the way down.

And back to center.

Breathe.

Now, looking straight ahead of you. You have just expanded your vision in four directions. Notice how much more you can see now than you were aware of before you started this exercise.

Breathe, ground, and feel the calm throughout your body.

Why would expanding your vision be a calming experience? The short answer is that when you are able to relax your eyes, you calm your whole body down because you have opened your peripheral vision and tapped into your parasympathetic nervous system. It all has to do with how the human nervous system works.

Your nervous system has two branches, the sympathetic and the parasympathetic, and each branch serves a different and complementary function. The sympathetic nervous system regulates arousal; it amps you up and keeps you alert. The parasympathetic system regulates relaxation; it calms you down. When a perceived danger is lurking, your sympathetic nervous system kicks in, sounding an alarm and sending warning signals to the brain: *Danger! Watch out!* Adrenaline flows. Blood starts pumping. Your gut tightens. Your breath shortens. The "fight or flight" response takes over and you either attack the oncoming threat or you run away from it. In contrast, when the danger is passed, your body needs to settle, to be quiet, to rest. That's when the parasympathetic system takes over. We need both systems because they balance one another. If we were on alert all the time (sympathetic) we'd be freaked out, and if we were relaxed all the time (parasympathetic) we'd be flaked out.

How does all of this relate to your eyes and to calming down?

Our sense of vision has two parts, the central vision and the peripheral vision, and each part is hardwired to a different branch of your nervous system. You use your central vision, which is connected to your sympathetic nervous system, to identify what is coming toward you or what is right in front of you. Whether you are staring at a ferocious mountain lion or reading a road sign, when your central vision is turned on, your system is at least somewhat aroused. On the other hand, when you are taking in "the big picture" and your peripheral vision, which is wired to your parasympathetic nervous system, is turned on, you are calming down.

This takes on immediate significance for test takers, since tests require reading, which almost exclusively uses the central vision. Thus, a high, ongoing demand is being placed on your sympathetic nervous system, putting you in a continuous state of arousal. No wonder students report feeling "fried" after they have hit the books for a long time. When they use their eyes for detailed focus (as in reading), they are actually amping themselves up without even realizing it. Uninterrupted reading for long periods of time is an intense stress-inducing activity. If you have ever felt more edgy while reading a test booklet, or when taking a test on a computer, you may believe that the test questions are "making you" nervous. But actually the problem is the strain you are putting on your sympathetic nervous system. You need to give your eyes a break. If you're studying for a test or taking one, you have to rest your eyes occasionally and let your parasympathetic nervous system take over, balance you out, and calm you down. That's what you did in the last exercise.

Resting your eyes every so often helps you stay calm.

What we have just done with your eyes you also can do with one or another of your senses, though a bit differently with each one. Open up your sense of smell and taste when you are at the dinner table. Most of us race through our meals. We eat as if we are making a pit stop at the gas station—*"Fill 'er up!"*— hurrying rather than really savoring the food. The next time you are eating a meal, take the time to taste the different flavors, feel the variety of textures as you chew, and smell the subtle aromas. This is how many Europeans dine. They enjoy their food and the occasion of sharing a meal with others.

Work on your sense of hearing by opening up to the sounds immediately around you (maybe those being made by your own body first). Then hear the sounds in the room, then the sounds just outside of the room and then the sounds outside of the building and beyond.

Work on your sense of touch by feeling the different textures of your clothes next to your body. How does your shirt or blouse feel next to your arms and chest? What does the fabric of your trousers feel like next to your legs? If you are holding a pen or pencil feel its weight and firmness in your hands. (As you are doing this continue to breathe and ground yourself.)

Connecting with your senses is an effective way of staying in the present and not being swept into tension and anxiety. Your senses are always available and are the handiest tools you have to connect you to the here and now. It is remarkable to me how unaware people are of what is right around them, and how infrequently they actually use their senses to help themselves feel calm.

This tool—sensing—can help you particularly when you are preparing for a test or thinking about one. We start fretting about what we don't know, or imagine failing; all kinds of other negative scenarios shoot us into the future or yank us back to the past and work us up. Are you worked *up?* Right. So calm *down.* Connect through your senses. Right here, right now. Breathe. Be grounded. Do it. It works.

When You Are Taking a Test

Please don't tell me, "I don't have time to breathe on the test." Recently, one student tried that out on me. I paused and looked at him. "No time to breathe?" I think what he meant was, "I don't have time to pay attention to my breath and to use the calming tools." My response? You're breathing all the time anyway. You might as well learn to *use* your breath to help you pass a test. It might take a few seconds away from a test question, but it will make a big difference in how you perform overall.

However, if you really think you can't afford to do the other exercises in this chapter, at least do this very effective exercise, which I call "The Wedge," which is like pressing the "restart" button. It gives you a new spurt of attention and energy, and it takes only a few seconds to learn, and even less to use once you are practiced at it.

EXERCISE: The Wedge

As you exhale, close your eyes and let them rest.

Feel the breath go down the front of your body and into the floor.

Now breathe in, feeling the breath coming up the back of your body and up to the top of your head.

When it reaches the top of your head, open your eyes.

The Wedge is great because it combines all three calming tools—breathing, grounding and sensing. Some students who used The Wedge consistently through taking the SAT improved their scores 100 to 200 points.

Consistency is the key: decide that you are going to use the calming tools (breathing, at least) after every 5, 10 or 20 questions. If you study using old exam questions, practice this routine during study time and then carry it into the exam itself.

Another student confronted me after a class in which we worked on these calming tools. She was quite ticked off. "I've *done* the breathing thing," she said, meaning, "That didn't work. *Now* what?"

There is no other now or what. Breathing is a life-long activity, and yet it takes time to become practiced at being more *aware* of your breath. It takes time to increase body awareness and to consciously use the tools to stay calm and present. You are reversing old habits of a lifetime, so be patient with yourself. If you have trouble remembering to prompt your awareness I encourage you to use my CD, "*Dr. B's Gentle Prompts for Calming Down.*" It is a CD you can download to your iPod or MP3 player and use while you are studying. On it you will hear my voice prompting you at varying intervals to breathe and ground and sense. The more you hear these reminders, the more your system is being trained to remind yourself.

Be patient with yourself. Staying calm takes practice.

Breathe, ground and sense.

That's all you need to do. Your body is the physical foundation for your power. Embody yourself. Do it, and keep doing it. For the rest of your life.

QUICK CHECK: Calm

When you are studying for a test...

Become aware

❑ Are you tense in some part of your body? (shoulders? stomach? jaw?)

❑ Are you having anxious thoughts?

❑ Are you holding your breath?

Use the tools

❑ **Breathe** deeply down to your belly and lower back three times. Breathe in through your nose and out through your mouth.

❑ **Ground** yourself (feet on the floor, butt and back in the chair).

❑ **Open your senses** (see the colors, feel the fabrics, hear the sounds).

Stay in this state for a few minutes.

Return to studying, staying connected in your body.

When you are taking a test...

Become aware

❑ Notice when you are not calm (jittery, physical tension, thoughts racing).

Use the tools

❑ **Breathe** deeply down to your belly and lower back three times. Breathe in through your nose and out through your mouth.

❑ **Ground** yourself (feel your feet on the floor, your butt and back in the chair). Release tension.

❑ **Open your senses** (feel the fabric of your clothing next to your skin; relax your eyes).

Return to the test items, staying connected in your body.

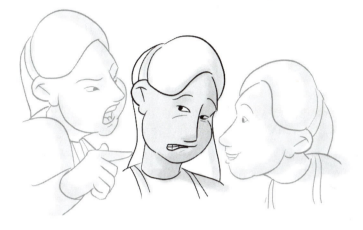

Chapter Five

How to be Confident

ALL TIED UP IN "NOTS"?

Sophie, a college sophomore, was struggling to talk through her tears. "On every test I take, the same thing happens. After a couple of minutes I have trouble remembering what I studied. As the material slips further away, the questions become harder to answer. I think I don't know anything. I feel like I'm drowning. I just want to give up." Sophie's voice was saturated with frustration, particularly because she prepares so thoroughly each time. Even her friends, knowing how hard she studies, seek out her advice on potentially tricky test items before exams. When she ended up with a C- on her history final (far from the B+ she wanted and felt she deserved), she was understandably disappointed and upset, "Compared to how hard I work at this, my friends hardly study at all," she said, tears welling up. "They hang out, they cram at the last minute, they don't even *understand* some of the material. And then they get better grades than I do! It's not fair! I just freak out."

When I asked Sophie to explain what she meant by "freak out," she described the intense static going on in her mind while she attempts to answer the questions. "I keep thinking, *I don't understand the question … I didn't study the right things … I don't remember anything … I'm not going to get this answer right … My scholarship won't be renewed.*" Her voice trailed off. She looked discouraged and dejected as she whispered, "It's a mess."

Sophie was describing one of the worst experiences a test taker can have: losing self-confidence during the test. When you are trying to figure out an answer and your mind starts broadcasting negative thoughts, *I don't know this… I can't work it out… I'm so stupid*, you're all tied up in negativity—in "nots": *I'm* not *remembering anything. I'm* not *going to pass. I'm* not *smart enough.* Of course, all this negativity makes you feel horrible about yourself. The self-doubt kicks up dust-loads of fear—that you're going to fail, of what will happen if you don't perform well, and fear of what others will think of you if you do poorly. The anxiety and self-doubt quickly turn into a self-fulfilling prophecy. Suddenly, you can't remember what you studied, you aren't sure about your own reasoning and judgment, and the answers to the questions elude you completely. With all this negativity, your stress level soars and your performance suffers, no matter how well prepared you are.

If you want your performance to show off all the hard work you put in, you need confidence—positive feelings about yourself. You have to believe that you have what it takes to succeed, that you *are* smart enough, that you *do* understand the material, and that you *can* figure out an answer. It's the same self-fulfilling prophecy I mentioned just above, but this time in a positive direction. When you believe in yourself you are much more likely to perform well.

Self-confidence seems mysterious to many people. They think you either have it or you don't. The lucky ones do, but it's mysterious where they get all that confidence. Were they born with it? Was it their upbringing? Is it something they ate? To me, it isn't mysterious at all. In this chapter I'm going to show you that you're not helpless. You will see where it comes from and how to find it in yourself. I'll also train you how to retrieve it quickly when you feel it slipping away.

CONFIDENCE: IT'S ALL IN YOUR MIND

How does confidence fit into our model of the three-legged stool? One of the legs stands for your mind. Your self-confidence is determined in large part by what is going on in your mind. *Mind* is a big word and the definitions for it vary depending on who is talking about it. Ask a philosopher, a systems analyst, a psychologist and a clergyman to define "mind" and you will hear four different explanations.

Most people think the mind is a big filing cabinet or hard drive where information is stuffed in and stored. When it's time to take a test, you just go to the storage cabinet, pull up the file, and then spit back the information. As a performance psychologist and your coach, I have a different notion.

To me, the mind is a chatterbox, a personal talk-radio station constantly broadcasting a steady stream of thoughts that compare, encourage, criticize, evaluate and judge everything inside and outside of you. *She's beautiful. This food is terrible. He's an idiot. I love steak. I hate broccoli.*

When it comes to your test performance, your mind broadcasts an ongoing, often contradictory monologue about yourself: *I'm good at history. I'm terrible at geometry. I always do well on these things. I'll never pass. I understand this question. I have no idea what the right answer is. I'm going to end up with a bad grade.* And on it goes.

When your mind produces positive, affirming, encouraging thoughts like *I can do this, I've got what it takes, I'll make it through,* you feel confident. You have faith in yourself. You believe you will succeed. You move ahead, feeling good about yourself. But if your mind is broadcasting negative self-statements, *I'm not smart enough, I'll never make it, I'm a loser,* then you are swamped in self-doubt. You don't trust yourself. This is utterly distracting, and the deficit of confidence can seriously hurt your ability to perform well and score high.

> **Train your mind to be your steady, loyal supporter.**

In this chapter, I'm going to train you to make your mind work for you. First, we will examine what confidence actually is. Next we will look at how your mind affects your performance positively and negatively. And finally I'll show you how to strengthen your mind so it is positive and working for you even in the most challenging test situations.

WHAT *IS* CONFIDENCE?

The word *confidence* is made up of two Latin roots: *con*, meaning "with," and *fidelis*, which means "faith" or "trust." A confident person has faith in herself and trusts that she can accomplish the task.

Fidelis has an additional meaning, and that is *loyalty*. We can interpret this to mean that a confident person is also *loyal* to herself. When she's taking a test and the questions are hard she doesn't jump ship. She believes she can work it out and stays with the process right to the end.

If you struggle with self-confidence, you probably have the opposite feeling when you take tests. When the going gets rough you feel like you want to bolt. *I can't do this, I'm out of here*. When you glance around the exam room it looks to you like everyone else is fully engaged. *They can do it, what's the matter with me?* I can tell you, after working with thousands of test takers over the last thirty years, you are projecting onto them a sense of security they probably don't have. Many other test takers in that room are also fiercely battling negative self-talk. They feel overwhelmed by the test and they wish they were anywhere else but there. They may look still and focused, just as you might look like that to them, but inside they also feel like running away.

Wanting to bolt creates a problem because it means your attention isn't fully present. It's on its way out the door, you might say. Your mind, like your body and your spirit, is a key player on your "Team of Three." Your mind has to play its part so that you can win. Whenever you perform—whether it's on a test, on a ball field, in a theater or a concert hall—you need your mind to stand by you, to support and encourage you through thick and thin, *not* turn against you and undermine the process. When your mind is yelling, "Let me out of here!" it is a way of abandoning you, which we can certainly call a form of disloyalty. You have to train it to be loyal, to have faith in your ability and to trust that you can do the job well.

NEGATIVITY AND DISCONNECTION

Your self-evaluating, talk-radio mind has two sides, positive and negative. On the positive side you are broadcasting approving and encouraging messages about yourself: *I can do it. I've got what it takes. I am smart enough.* When it's negative, you are sending out disapproving, discouraging, self-defeating messages: *I can't possibly succeed. I don't know what I'm doing. I'm not going to make it.*

In mathematics, a negative sign is a minus symbol; it is subtracting, taking away. It lessens the whole. When you are saying negative things about yourself, your mind is subtracting from who you are; it is taking away the possibility that you will be wildly successful. In other words, you are minus-ing yourself. You are disconnecting from the positive side of your mind, the one that wants to support you on your path to be the best you can. A negative mind persists in yanking you off the path into the gutter.

> "I can't... I don't... I'm not..." Negative thoughts make you anxious.

The more you say negative things about yourself (the more you disconnect from the positive side of your mind), the more your stress will build. Remember our basic formula: *stress is a function of disconnection*. You will feel increasingly disturbed and worried, you will forget what you've studied, and you won't trust your own judgment, making you prone to error. Clearly, your performance will be severely compromised.

Liza, who was preparing to take the LSAT exam for entry into law school, suffered from this negativity. In spite of being a bright, compassionate young woman, with an exceptionally high GPA, Liza came undone every time she sat down to study for this all-important test. So much was riding on her LSAT scores. If they were high, she would fulfill a childhood dream, receive a scholarship, and qualify for law school. High scores would prove that all the time and money she spent on prep courses actually paid off and they weren't a waste of valuable resources.

As Liza spoke, I noticed that her hands shook and her voice quivered, which indicated to me that she was agitated, so I immediately thought it best to give her the three tools for calming down. I taught her how to monitor and regulate her breath, to keep herself grounded and to open her senses, just as I did with you in the last chapter. Though she experienced some relief after we did this in the first session, a few days later she telephoned me, disappointed. She said that the relief the tools had provided her was only temporary. "I'm still stressed out," she added, sounding exhausted.

For our second session, I asked Liza to bring her LSAT prep book with its practice questions. I wanted to observe her while she was answering questions. As she began the process, I watched her dutifully use the calming tools by breathing and grounding herself. Yet a minute into the practice test she started shaking her head, wiping her brow and fidgeting in her seat. She looked pained and worried. She made another attempt to use the calming tools, but her head-shaking and brow-wiping escalated so quickly that she looked like she was clearly in crisis. Concerned for her well-being, I told her to stop. "What's happening?" I asked. She turned and looked at me with a very painful expression and shook her head. "I can't do this. I'm not smart enough for this test. I always wanted to be an attorney, but I guess I don't have what it takes."

Being a lawyer had been Liza's dream since childhood. For many years she worked exceptionally hard to achieve that dream, but her disparaging self-talk was causing a major disconnection from her positive, true self. She was not being loyal to who she was and she certainly wasn't aware that her negative thinking was pulling her away from her goal, nor that it was the true cause of her stress. With all of that disconnection, how could she possibly perform well? Her three-legged stool was tilting all over the place. Once Liza was able to learn and use the tools for remaining confident, she stayed with the process throughout the test and her LSAT scores went up, dramatically.

FEELING ALONE

When you think ill of yourself, you are not only disconnected from anything positive inside of you, but also from people around you who might offer support. Perhaps you are afraid if you tell others what you are really feeling about yourself you will look stupid and weak in their eyes. You believe that no one will really understand what you're going through. After all, everyone else seems really confident, right? Wrong.

No one is confident all the time. But everyone can learn to build confidence.

Sometimes it is natural to feel badly about yourself. No one goes through life feeling totally self-assured at every moment. We all go through periods of losing our confidence. Everyone. But maybe you believe you are the *only* one who thinks he's dumb or a fake, and if anyone else finds out you will be humiliated. Your peers, your teachers and your parents will think less of you. In some cultures, this is called "losing face." It can trigger a host of unpleasant and embarrassing feelings. So you don't say anything. You keep all your pessimistic feelings to yourself.

To avoid the humiliation of being seen, you pull away from others, including people who might support you. But the isolation only causes you to feel even worse about yourself, causing more stress at a critical time when true support from others who care about you could be very helpful. We all need the encouragement that comes from those who are close to us. Without it we agonize silently and feel lost.

Thomas, the 16-year-old son of two lawyers, suffered from this feeling of being all alone. No matter how hard he studied, every time he so much as saw or heard the word *test*, he lost confidence in himself and shut down. In our first session he admitted, "I look at the test questions and go blank." When I asked him why, he shrugged his shoulders and said, "I don't know." That was the best reply he could muster. He was frightened and looked away.

As we started working together I found out that Thomas had an older sister and younger brother who were both high achievers. He was constantly being compared to them by his teachers and by his parents. Although Thomas's parents expressed concern about their son and seemed to want what was best for him, they were actually more preoccupied with their own social image. They didn't like being seen as the parents of a child who couldn't perform well. They hid his difficulties behind a façade that said, "Everything is OK."

But everything was certainly not OK for Thomas. He was a sophomore at a very competitive high school where, it seemed to him, everyone else was extremely competent. He was embarrassed to admit to his teachers, his guidance counselor and certainly to his friends, that he felt stupid. With no one to talk to at school, Thomas felt alone. At home, where his parents didn't discuss this issue openly and wanted to keep up an image, he avoided talking about his problems because he certainly didn't feel that they were open to it. He was stuck.

This is how many people feel when they lose confidence in themselves and in their ability to face tests. They feel isolated and immobilized. While it is true that when you are sitting in an exam room you *are* alone, that doesn't mean you have no support. And you are not really stuck—you just feel stuck. When you are taking a test, your *mind* is there with you and it can act either as your supportive friend, helping your performance along, or your worst critic, seriously undermining your efforts and causing you to stall and even break down. How you use your mind to talk to yourself makes all the difference.

AWARENESS FIRST

Throughout this book I'm training you in a two-step process to raise your test scores.

Step 1: Become aware of the signs that your stress is building because you are disconnecting, and

Step 2: Use specific tools to reconnect yourself, lower your stress level and boost your performance.

In the last chapter we applied this two-step strategy to disconnection in your body. You became aware of the physical signs (tight chest, rapid heartbeat, tense muscles, etc), and then you learned and practiced the three tools to reconnect yourself physically (breathing, grounding and sensing).

In this section we are going to apply the same two-step process to your mind. Let's start with your awareness of what is going on there and examine your negative thoughts about yourself.

The Catalog of Negativity

There are several ways our minds broadcast negativity when we take tests, and they all are disconnections from your positive self. They all undermine self-confidence. As you read the descriptions below, check off which ones characterize your self-talk when you are facing a test:

❏ **1. You doubt yourself.** Your internal monologue is riddled with sentences that begin with the words *I can't... I don't...* and *I'm not.* For example, *I'm going to blow this test because even my own father says I'm no good at math,* or *I always tank playing video games so I know I don't have the hand-eye coordination to get through this driving test.* You are doubting your abilities and are so caught up in a downward spiral, that it is hard to think about anything else, especially the very object of your desires—the right answer.

❏ **2. You believe there is something wrong with you or that you are a bad person.** These thoughts sound like *I'm a mess. I'm a total loser. I must be defective. No one in my family has ever gotten past high school; the O'Connor's just aren't college material,* or *My brother says I was dropped on my head when I was a baby. No one will tell me, but I think it did some permanent damage. That's why I'm always in the lowest third of the class.* You believe that the very fact that you are having these thoughts proves that you are deficient and probably not fixable.

❏ **3. You regret the past.** You are brooding over what you should have done and didn't. *The whole tenth grade was a write-off because I was busy playing with my Nintendo. Now I've ruined my whole life. I'll never catch up,* or *If only I hadn't wrecked my mind reading all the wrong books to prepare for that paper.* You berate yourself about the opportunities you missed.

❏ **4. You imagine the worst (projecting into the future).** Your negativity extends into the indeterminate future. *I know exactly what's going to happen when I go in to take my SATs. Someone will drop a pencil or scratch his ear and it will throw off my concentration, and then I'll get a droopy score and never get into State, just some crappy school—so I should drop out now and take any job I can get.* You feel like you might as well give up.

❏ **5. You feel helpless and alone.** You feel that nothing you can do will change the situation and that no one will help you. *I just don't have a chance against all those kids in the high-powered study groups who egg each other on. All I have is me, and that's not much,* or *Everybody knows how hard I study and then I don't get A's. I look like a loser, and nobody invests in a loser.* You feel lonely and perhaps desperate.

❏ **6. You fear humiliation and retribution.** You imagine a negative reaction from a parent, teacher, or friend if you perform poorly. You hear them saying (or screaming), *You screwed up that test again? What is wrong with you? Even the slow kids passed that one*, or, Father: *Son, when I was your age, I never once brought home a grade like this. How do you explain yourself? What! Silence?* This only makes your negative feelings about yourself worse.

❏ **7. You worry that history will repeat itself.** If you have had trouble on a test in the past you are probably thinking, *I messed up the last GRE royally, so there's no way I can do any better this time. I'd better pick an easier school to get into.*

❏ **8. Your thinking becomes disorganized.** While you are taking the test, you find that it doesn't conform to the way you ordered the material in your mind while studying. All sense of organization becomes unglued and loses any consistent pattern it may have had. Your mind feels like a chaotic mess. *Oh my god, what is this? I've never seen this before! I don't remember anything! I studied all the wrong stuff. My memory is as full of holes as a pound of Swiss cheese!*

❏ **9. You become superstitious**. You start thinking that the everyday little things in life—the socks you wear, the coffee cup you choose, the way you drive to work—have a direct impact on your test performance. *Well, the last time I took the DAT I took a picture of my boyfriend in with me and that relationship didn't work out, whose picture should I take this time?* While this kind of thinking might not seem negative to you, it does indicate that you feel powerless over your performance and that other things are controlling it.

❏ **10. Other possibilities.** Perhaps there is some other way that negativity shows up in your mind. If so, you will have the chance to write it down below, and I would like to hear about it. I am cataloging the different ways people feel badly about themselves. E-mail me directly at DrB@WorkbookForTestSuccess.com and let me know any additions you want to make to the list above for future editions of this book. You will receive a free gift as a thank you!

Your Own Catalog

What is going on in *your* "chatterbox"? This exercise will develop your awareness of the "less-than" messages your mind produces.

 EXERCISE: The Inner Chorus (Negative)

Sit with your feet on the floor and breathe deeply down to your belly.

After you feel quiet, fill in the chart below by following this procedure:

1. For each category below read the question on the right.

2. Close your eyes

3. See the answer on your "inner screen."

4. Open your eyes.

5. Record your answers under each question.

NEGATIVE THINKING	What are your negative, self-doubting thoughts about yourself and your performance? 1. *I can't* _____ 2. *I don't* _____ 3. *I'm not* _____
REGRETTING THE PAST	What are your regrets about how you prepared for the test? 1._____ 2._____ 3._____

IMAGINING THE WORST	What are you afraid will happen if your test performance is below par? 1._____ 2._____ 3._____
FEELING HOPELESS AND HELPLESS	What do you feel hopeless or helpless about in regard to your abilities and performance? 1._____ 2._____ 3._____
FEARING HUMILIATION AND RETRIBUTION	Who will be disappointed or angry if you perform poorly on the test? What will they say or do? 1._____ 2._____ 3._____
WORRYING THAT HISTORY WILL REPEAT ITSELF	What unrewarding experiences have you had with tests in the past that you worry you'll have again? 1._____ 2._____ 3._____
DISORGANIZED THINKING	What happens to your thinking when your thoughts are clouded with negative, self-doubting thoughts? 1._____ 2._____ 3._____

OTHER FORMS OF NEGATIVITY	Are there any other ways *your* mind broadcasts negativity? If so, record them below: 1._____ 2._____ 3._____

The Litany Loop

At the time I was writing this chapter, a new client came in for her first appointment. Joanne had twice failed her state licensing exam to become a psychologist and she was in a panic. If she failed a third time, she would lose her job, which required that she hold a license. As a single mother, simply imagining being unemployed was enough to paralyze her. When I asked Joanne to tell me about the test she said, "I can't hold all the information in my head at once. I mean, I study very hard, but I don't think I can do it. Maybe I'm not really psychologist material."

I can't... I don't... I'm not... Her mind was a catalog of painful self-deprecation that weighed her down after a while. Painful, because she was actually a highly intelligent and capable clinician. Certainly, the licensing exam presented a major hurdle—the amount of information really was formidable, and a lot was riding on the exam—holding onto her job, and her ability to support herself and her two small children. Nevertheless, Joanne's stress didn't actually come from either of these facts; it came from being stuck in a loop of negative thinking that disabled her from being able to perform well. This was truly self-defeating: no matter how hard she tried she was held back and trapped in a cycle of unfavorable thinking that began and ended with her self-nullifying thoughts.

Negative thinking is a self-fulfilling prophecy.

I call this a "litany loop." It's a personal list of fearful outcomes that you repeat over and over again from which there is no escape, and which leads you to fulfill the negative predictions. You tell yourself you aren't good enough to succeed and—surprise—you don't succeed. You believe you can't perform and—you can't perform. You think you don't have a chance and—you don't seize the chances that come your way. This loop has a quasi-religious flavor (the "litany" part) because you keep repeating it over and over again, as if you are devoted to it. How can you possibly do well when your mind, one of the three key players on your team, is downright devoted to being negative about you and your chances?

If your self-confidence is low, the first step in reversing the process is to *become aware of your personal litany loop of negativity.* If it's going on behind a curtain, you can't possibly fight it. I have found that we all have our own list of negative self-statements, our own personal repertoire of *I can't*s, *I don't*s, *and I'm not*s that start spinning whenever we face a challenging test.

There are certain common negative messages that come up most frequently in your mind.

Customizing Your Litany Loop
Look at the longer list you catalogued above, and find the statements that appear most frequently. This is your personal litany loop. In the next section, we'll work with this list as I show you how to use the tools to build your self-confidence.

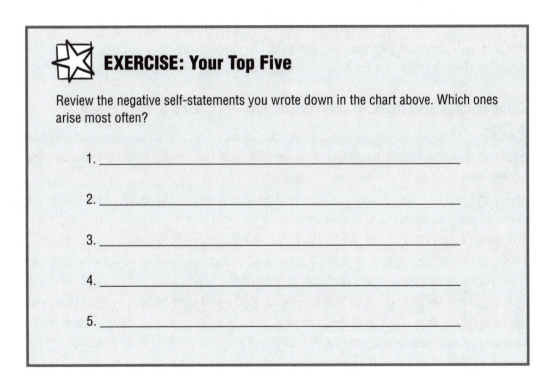

EXERCISE: Your Top Five

Review the negative self-statements you wrote down in the chart above. Which ones arise most often?

1. _____

2. _____

3. _____

4. _____

5. _____

At this point, you have two options.

Option 1. You can keep repeating these sentences, mantra-like, and watch a self-fulfilling prophecy inexorably unfold ("He who believes he will fail, will fail"). This would be akin to going backwards, or at best, standing still and being stuck. Surprisingly, this is what most people default to because it doesn't occur to them that there is an alternative.

Option 2. You can decide, right now, that you want to shift out of this gear-to-nowhere, and learn how to transform these thoughts so your mind can help, not hinder, you.

If you chose Option 1, I can't help you. No one can. You might as well stop reading this book. You are entitled to stay stuck, and don't let anyone tell you differently.

However, since you purchased this workbook, chances are you would like to change your mind about yourself. So I strongly encourage you to pick Option 2 and continue on the road to transformation.

To venture out on this path, you must decide right now that negativity is not going to be your companion. Tell yourself clearly and strongly, "I don't want to be stuck in these self-defeating ideas any longer. When one comes up, I will acknowledge it is there, but I won't play into it. I won't fan its fire by repeating it over and over inside my head. I'll remind myself that my 'less-than' thoughts and bad feelings about myself are road signs telling me that I'm disconnecting. As soon as I become aware of them I'll use the tools to reconnect and build my self-confidence."

Come Back, Come Back, Wherever You Are! —Staying in the Present

One more thought before moving on to the tools. When you are disconnecting in your mind and thinking negatively, you are not only minus-ing yourself, you are also taking yourself out of the present moment.

Let's say you are about to take a big test at the end of the week. You think, *I'll never be able to pull this off.* What time zone are you in when you're thinking that? Are you in the present? No. Most likely you have one leg in the past, based on your previous disastrous experiences with tests, and one leg in the future, projecting forward into a time when you'll probably fail again.

By some sleight-of-mind you are fooling yourself into believing that you can't do something right now just because you couldn't do it in the past. Some awful memory of failure hounds you to this day and you are pasting that event onto this moment. You're looking at this moment through a prism of the past and you literally cannot see that time has gone by. However, you might have studied the subject since then or improved your skills. You have accomplished a few things. You're a different person now. The faulty thinking says that you are the same person who failed that geometry test five years ago. You aren't. You are glomming something negative from your past onto this moment. Or you're predicting the worst possible future for yourself. But this present moment is neither the past nor the future. In this moment you can either go down in flames, or, like the phoenix, you can rise from the ashes. You can let yourself slide into the pit of bad feelings and anxiety, or you can tell yourself, *I have the chance to make things different, right now.* Which direction are you going to choose?

The human mind is famous for flip-flopping from the past to the future, and then back again. Reverse, fast-forward, reverse, fast-forward, reverse, fast-forward. Imagine doing that to your car over and over. You'll strip the gears and the car will be stuck in your driveway. You can't go anywhere. That's what your negative thinking is doing to your mind. It's immobilizing you.

The truth is that the past is gone. The future hasn't happened yet. The present is the moment of action. It is your field of possibility. The following three tools for building your self-confidence are designed to place you firmly in the present.

THE THREE TOOLS FOR BUILDING CONFIDENCE

The tools to build and strengthen confidence were inspired by my dictionary. When I looked up the word *confidence*, I discovered that it was nested in a paragraph that included two other definitions. *CONFIDE*: To impart secrets to someone with trust. To trust wholly or have faith in. *CONFIDANT*: One confided in or entrusted with secrets. A bosom friend.

When I read this I thought, "Brilliant! It is exactly how to kick-start building confidence—*confide in a confidant*." As you will see below, this is the beginning of a roadmap. When you follow it, a positive feeling about yourself is assured.

I am going to give you the three key tools through a series of exercises. With guided imagery, I will ask you to close your eyes and then direct you through a sequence of pictures in your imagination. This is the technique of choice in sports psychology and it is very effective with test takers. Athletes are performing every moment on the field, court or in the pool. Their confidence is being tested all the time. If it starts to falter, they can't afford to stop the action to talk to their coach or call their counselor; they have to re-strengthen immediately. Guided imagery provides the tools. It's the same thing when you are taking a test. If you land on a difficult item and your confidence starts to slip, you need an "inner toolbox" to strengthen your confidence right away. Guided imagery will train you to do that.

TOOL #1: Confide

Here is the first tool for regaining and strengthening your confidence.

EXERCISE: Confide in Your Confidant

Sit in a comfortable position, preferably in a straight-backed chair. Uncross your arms and legs and close your eyes.

Breathe deeply down to your belly.

Feel your feet supported by the floor and your legs, butt and back supported by the chair.

Choose one of the negative self-statements from your litany loop (page 71) and start repeating it over to yourself (e.g. *I can't perform well on this test.*)

See in your mind's eye what you look like when you are thinking the self-defeating thought. How does that affect your posture? Your facial expression?

How do you feel: physically? emotionally? spiritually?

Once you have a clear image of how you look and feel, sweep all of that negativity out to the left.

Now look into a mirror in front of you. At the moment it is empty.

Now someone comes into the mirror, someone you can confide in, someone who has confidence in you, someone you trust. It can be a parent, sibling, a relative, a friend, a teacher or a colleague. It can be someone living or someone who has passed on. It can be a spiritual entity or it can be your highest, best self.

See the image of this person or entity very clearly. This is your confidant.

Tell it about the negativity that is going on in your mind. Don't hold back anything. **Confide** what you are thinking in sentences that start with *I can't, I don't,* or *I'm not.* (*I can't do this. I'm not going to make it. I don't have what it takes.*)

See the confidant receiving everything you have to say without criticizing, evaluating or judging you.

Open your eyes.

Let's explore what just happened.

First, who came into your mirror as your confidant? Here is a short list of those who often appear:

* ✳ My sister
* ✳ My dad
* ✳ My mom
* ✳ My girlfriend (or boyfriend)
* ✳ Jesus
* ✳ Allah
* ✳ God
* ✳ My grandmother who passed away last year
* ✳ My higher self
* ✳ My spirit animal
* ✳ My guardian angel
* ✳ My sixth-grade teacher

This is your confidant, if only for this moment. The next time you use the exercise, the person or entity may change, but trust that this is the best confidant for you to confide in right now.

Sometimes people feel "weird" about who or what appears. Once, when I was doing this exercise with a high-school student and I asked him to see someone in the mirror, tears started flowing from his closed eyes. I stopped the exercise and asked, "What just happened?" He shook his head, "No one is coming into the mirror." He looked sad. I asked, "When you are feeling low, is there anyone you talk to?" He seemed a little embarrassed but after a while admitted that sometimes, when he felt sad, he spoke to his dog, "Popeye." "Good," I said, and I encouraged him to use the image of Popeye in the exercise. It showed me that each of us has someone, or something special to confide in. Don't judge the choice, just trust it.

Why is **confide** the first tool in building confidence? Because when you are holding onto and hiding your bad feelings about yourself, you feel terrible. The feelings become very heavy, and, like quicksand, they suck you into despair. But when you confide them, when you let them out, you move away from this disconnected, lonely place. You unload these feelings about yourself to someone who will not judge or criticize you. That is why we have priests, ministers, rabbis, counselors and therapists to talk with. They are people we can talk to about our bad feelings without being judged. We can finally unload all that negative self-talk.

It might help you to know that there's almost no criticism you can level at yourself that somebody else hasn't thought about themselves too. I taught this tool to a class of student nurses and asked them to write down the negative things they said to their confidants. Then I read the statements, anonymously, to the class. Afterwards one of the students sent me an e-mail: "I felt so much better knowing I'm not the only one who feels bad about herself. I don't feel so weird or different now." I see this all the time in classes when people share. They gain the advantage of knowing they are members of a giant club of people who are, at times, hard on themselves. At some time or other everyone loses self-confidence. Whether your lapse is brief or chronic, it is best to get those feelings off your chest as soon as you can. In order to move on you have to confide. The act of confiding opens the door for something positive to come in and is a big relief. In one of my training workshops a dental hygienist said, "Confiding is like exhaling. When you release what you've been holding on to you can breathe in some fresh air."

> **Acknowledging your negative self-talk is the first step to letting it go.**

Once you've confided, you are ready for the second tool.

TOOL #2: Reflect

Let's continue with the imagery exercise.

 EXERCISE: Receiving the Positive Reflection

Sit comfortably, with your back well-supported.

Breathe deeply and ground yourself.

Close your eyes.

See your confidant in the mirror.

Your confidant, who has just heard your negative thoughts and feelings, now responds. It **reflects** back to you something accurate and positive about yourself in response to what you confided. It speaks to you in sentences that start with, *You can...You do...* and *You are...* Listen to what it is saying to you and receive the positive reflection.

⇨

Thank the confidant for its support (remember *"Thank You"* from the last chapter?).

Breathe in and out.

Open your eyes.

This is the second tool: ***reflect.*** Let's explore it together.

First, what did the image in the mirror reflect back to you? Write down what it said:

_____

_____

_____

Here are some of the things mirrors have reflected back to my clients and students:

* ✳ "Don't give me that! I've seen you do this before."

* ✳ "You are capable, jump in!"

* ✳ "You can figure out what to do if you get stuck."

* ✳ "You have what it takes."

* ✳ "You are able to succeed, you've done it before."

* ✳ "You can do well because you've worked hard."

* ✳ "You do know what you need to know."

* ✳ "You are smart enough."

This tool—**reflect**—is necessary for two reasons.

First, when the mind is stuck in negative feelings we completely forget about our genuinely positive and potentially helpful inner voices. We actually have two voices inside of us: one that is positive and encouraging and one that is negative and hurtful. Why are we always stuck listening to the discouraging voice? Mostly, it's a matter of habit. Though I believe we are all born with the potential to feel good about ourselves, there are, unfortunately, forces that negate and disempower us. In our culture and in our personal lives, they often hold more sway than those that help us build a strong inner confidence and competency. Remember what I said earlier about the media? Turn on the television any time of day or night and it is filled with messages that are basically negative—the reason you need this car, that shampoo, these clothes, that HDTV is that you are *not good enough as you are.* All too often, schools reinforce this negativity with their constant comparison and competition. Rather than nurture the positive they inundate children, teenagers and young adults with the message "You are not good enough." If you keep dwelling on the negative you are bound to feel terrible about yourself. Remember: negative in mathematics is less and zero.

You are *not* less than zero.

You need to have reflected back to yourself the positive things that you may have forgotten or that you don't pay attention to, either not enough or not at all. You need to hear positive, affirming things about yourself so you can feel *empowered.*

The tool of positive reflection is important for another reason. It has to do with what I call "psychic nutrition." When you feed on self-put-downs, inside it's like you are eating all kinds of horrible, non-nutritive garbage. *I can't do this… I'm not like that… I don't have what it takes…* This kind of thinking is totally toxic. Imagine picking up a rotting piece of meat and taking a bite out of it. You will wreak havoc on your digestive system. It's poison! Don't do it! But that is exactly what you *are* doing when you repeat the long litany of why you can't, don't or aren't. Stop shoving the wrong stuff into your mind. Stop the diet of negativity. It will only frighten and hurt you.

You have a strong, confident, positive side. Turn toward it. Hear its message.

I want to emphasize that the mirror is reflecting something that is *accurate and positive about you.* It is not saying, *You're the best in the world. You're a super hero. You can do no wrong.* Those kinds of global statements are mindless ways of pumping yourself up artificially. Accurate and positive means the mirror is specifically zeroing in on something about you that it knows to be true, something already proven, something that you have forgotten because you were stuck feeding on all that negativity.

Hearing and receiving the positive reflection is a big step in correcting your psychic diet. If you want to be happy about yourself and robust in your performance, start feeding yourself positive self-statements. It's like feeding your body healthy soups and salads. Building a diet of positive thoughts about yourself will strengthen you when you face any challenge, particularly tests.

Once you have started correcting your "mental eating habits" you are ready for the last tool to help you build your confidence.

TOOL #3: Envision the Steps to Confidence

Confidence is the faith or trust in yourself that is built on what you *do*—on actions—not just on what you say. The third tool addresses the need for action. Such action must first take place in your mind. In other words, you have to *see* yourself doing what you thought you could not do. With this tool you will envision yourself being successful. You will cultivate an inner image that will help you think and feel better about yourself. You will use your imagination as the springboard to successful action.

Let's continue with our imagery exercise. This is the third tool to build self-confidence.

 EXERCISE: Envisioning the Small, Manageable Steps

Sit comfortably and close your eyes.

Breathe deeply and feel yourself connected to the chair and floor.

You have just confided your negativity in the confidant. The confidant has reflected to you accurate, positive things about yourself, and you have thanked it for that.

Breathe out and let the image of your confidant dissolve.

Now see and feel yourself taking a series of small, manageable steps to correct the original negativity.

Envision each small step in detail. See yourself taking each one successfully. It doesn't matter how small it is—what is important is that it is manageable and that you see yourself taking each one successfully.

Breathe out. Open your eyes.

What is this tool all about, and why is it necessary?

A week ago I received a call from Harry, a 60-year-old man who is starting his third career. He is training to be a therapist by taking all the requisite courses and writing his dissertation. However, he is having trouble with the licensing exam. He failed it twice. He came in very demoralized, his thinking and self-talk were a minefield of negativity. "There is no way I can pass this exam," he said. "There's too much to study for an old guy like me!" We worked on his confidence—obviously the weak leg of his three-legged stool—by using the three tools I have just given to you.

He was able to confide in his confidant (for him, a spiritual entity), and this reflected good, strong positive statements about himself ("Harry, you have passed difficult exams before"), which he was able to receive.

When he came to the third tool, **envision**, envisioning small, manageable steps to correct his negative thinking—Harry was flummoxed. He opened his eyes. He couldn't do it. Everything appeared too big and too hard, like looking up at Mount Everest and thinking, "No way I can conquer *that* sucker." Harry was ready to give up. "There is just too much material," he said.

We worked with this tool so he could identify the small, manageable steps he needed to take while preparing for the exam. Here is what he came up with:

* Set the timer for 30 minutes. Turn off the phone. Read only one section on law and ethics in the test prep book.

* When the timer goes off, take a five-minute break.

* Return to studying for another 30 minutes. Finish law and ethics.

These simple steps helped break down the mass of material into digestible chunks so that he wasn't overwhelmed. A mind that isn't drowning in information is in a far better position to ultimately understand and memorize it.

Harry did the exercise well. He saw himself successfully initiating and completing each step. But at the end of the session Harry still looked discouraged. As we wrapped up he mumbled something about it being "helpful" but he demurred about scheduling another session. "I still feel overwhelmed," he said as he went out the door.

A week later Harry sent me an e-mail saying, "I'm going slowly. One step at a time. It's all a lot easier." He felt a little hopeful. I didn't see him again, but three months later I received another e-mail from him saying he had just passed the test. "It's all because I was able to see myself take one small step at a time," he wrote. Note, Harry didn't see the value of this tool the moment I taught it to him. Only after he practiced it himself was he convinced.

This third tool is not actually about *taking* the steps. That will come up in the next chapter on Focus. This tool is about *envisioning* them, laying the groundwork. In other words, you are engaging your imagination to see yourself successfully taking each individual step in the direction of your goal. This is necessary because everything takes place in the imagination first. Look around you. Everything you see—the table, your chair, the computer, your clothes, the light bulb, this book— all happened in someone's imagination first, long before it became manifest in the physical world. It's the same thing when you have to take a test. First, you must define in your imagination the small, manageable steps to succeed. Then you have to envision yourself taking them, one at a time, with your imagination paving the way. This is how your confidence will gain strength.

You must engage your imagination positively if you are to succeed in a conscious, directed way. You don't want to rely on "luck." (What happens if at test time you aren't lucky?) You want a method that works reliably, especially when the going gets rough and the questions are tricky and your confidence starts to slip. Envisioning yourself successful at every small step will ensure a positive outcome because having a vision of yourself as a success breeds the feeling that you really

> **Pave the way for success by imagining yourself taking small, manageable steps.**

can succeed. What's more, positive images are like deposits in your optimism bank. The more you have saved up, the richer you are, and the more you have to draw on when a test question challenges you.

The other part of this tool that is significant is *small, manageable steps*.

That is because *everything we do is done in small, manageable steps*. Look at how a baby learns to walk. First she turns over, and then, on all fours, starts to crawl. Next she holds on and takes little steps. Finally, she lets go and starts to walk. This is the same process we go through with everything in life, even though we usually don't notice it.

If you have a history of either failing or under-performing on tests and then beating yourself up, you have to change your pattern. This starts in your imagination. You have to see yourself being successful. **Envision** it. Once your imagination is ignited and you see yourself taking each small, manageable step to your goal, then you can open your eyes and move ahead with gusto and enthusiasm.

USING THE CONFIDENCE TOOLS

Build Your Confidence While Studying

Even while studying for a test, you may feel your confidence already starting to slip. Negative self-talk will make you feel anxious, overwhelmed and hopeless, and then you won't want to study. It's so much easier to disconnect. But of course, that will only cause your stress to build and eventually your performance to slide.

To avoid the slide, start each study session using the three tools for building and maintaining confidence. Collect your notes and books, and close your eyes. Check your thinking: are there any negative thoughts? If so, use the first tool, **confide** in your inner confidant—let the thought out. Your confidant will **reflect** back to you something accurate and positive about you. Receive the positive reflection. Then **envision** the small, manageable steps that you can take when you open your eyes to make the study session successful. Open your eyes and get to work.

If, when you are studying, the self-defeating thinking rears up, stop and use the tools. By doing this on a regular, repeated basis you are building your confidence muscles, and the payoff will occur when you take the test. As you study, use the *Awareness Log: Confidence* (page 193) to keep track of your negative self-statements and the tools you use to correct that negativity.

One of the biggest problem students have when studying for tests is that they feel overwhelmed. "There's just too much to take in," is a refrain I often hear. As we saw with Harry's example in the previous section, fixating on the whole is bound to make you nervous (remember Mt. Everest?). In reality you can only take one small step at a time. If you do it successfully, you will reach your goal.

How to Keep Your Confidence Strong During the Test

Any good test will challenge your confidence because it will present you with items you haven't seen before. It's testing you to apply what you do know to something unfamiliar. That's when you need your mind to cheer you on, not crap out on you. Practice using the tools when you study, and they'll be right there when you need them on the test.

Carla's story is a case in point:

"When I took the AP biology exam I came across a question that was different than any I had practiced. I thought, 'I'll never figure this out,' and that flipped me out. I was sure my score was going to be terrible and I wouldn't get into college. Fortunately, I realized I was disconnecting in my mind and body and I calmed myself down and then used the three Confidence tools. As soon as I imagined the small manageable steps I saw a way through the problem. I still don't know if I answered it correctly, but I was able to get through it rather than freak out. This was a big difference for me.

One more helpful exercise before we close out this chapter.

Keep Intruders Out!

Even if you *are* confident, from time to time an "intruder" may come into your mental space to try to disturb and disempower you. An intruder can be a rogue negative thought or feeling that enters your thinking unexpectedly and suddenly. It can take different forms:

* A sinking feeling about how you are doing on the test so far

* A memory of a test you failed or did poorly on

* A worry that you are going to forget the material

* A fear of what will happen if you don't succeed

* A concern over what other people will think of you

Because any one of these intruders can come upon you without warning, they can easily upset you when you need to be at your best. It's very easy to become entangled with the intruder, questioning it and arguing with it. When you are supposed to be thinking through a tough test question, your inner landscape has turned into a war zone, *You can't figure this out!* shouts the negative side. *Of course I can!* yells the positive. *No you can't, ever.—Yes, I can. I can!—It's useless, you are going to fail.—I'm NOT going to fail. Leave me alone!*—And while all of this is going on the clock is ticking and you are losing valuable time. The disconnection—from the test and from yourself—is causing enormous stress. Rather than becoming embroiled in an inner tangle, you need an emergency measure when an intruder barges in on your mental space. You need to get rid of it.

I'm going to coach you through an exercise that will train you to keep your mental space clear of intruders. This exercise is fun and highly effective. It will help you every time a negative thought or image attempts to disturb you. With steady practice, you will become very adept at keeping your space clear and you'll stay confident, strong and powerful.

 EXERCISE: Clearing the Space

Close your eyes.

Breathe in and out three times.

Sense, see and feel, in vivid detail, a place that is really comfortable to you. It can be a room in your home or a place that's been special to you in the past, or you can create your ideal space in your imagination.

See it in all its detail. What is in the space? Is there furniture? Are there walls or is it open? What color is it? Where is the light coming from?

Now see that you have *three powerful tools* to use that will help you clear the space when any intruder enters it. The three tools are:

---

1. A strong **broom**
2. A sturdy **shovel**
3. A powerful **hose**

Make sure you see them vividly and know exactly where they are.

Now, see or feel an intruder coming into your space. It is a negative energy that can take the form of a person, a feeling, a thought, a memory or an image. It might be something you sense but don't necessarily see.

As soon as you are aware that it is there, reach for one of these tools and use it with great determination. Sweep the negativity straight out a door on your left hand side. Pick it up with a shovel and toss it in the trash and toss the trash out to the left. Or turn the water on full power and hose it away from you, again, out to the left. Trust your intuition to tell you exactly which tool you need. Any one of them will leave you feeling purged and clean. (You may even find yourself creating a new tool of your own. That's fine.)

When the space is cleared, return the tool to its place.

Take a deep breath. Inhale…exhale…

Open your eyes.

Imbal, a rather timid dental student, came to me with many fears about her clinical exams—practical tests on a patient while being graded by a faculty member. As we talked we found that her mental space was constantly being intruded upon by negative, disempowering images like the teacher standing next to her, sighing loudly, shaking his head, saying, *How can you even think of being a dentist?* And Imbal became more and more upset, thinking, *I won't finish this exam on time.* Clearly, these intrusive thoughts kept crowding her mind, causing her to disconnect from what she needed to do with the patient and obstructing her ability to do well.

I taught Imbal the exercise to keep intruders out. When she first did it she spontaneously invented her own tool—a powerful vaporizing instrument that totally obliterated *anything* getting in her way. (So much for being timid!) As Imbal used the exercise when any negative image intruded during clinic exams, she was able to stay connected to the patient and her performance improved greatly. Moreover, she realized that there was real strength inside of her waiting to be released. She just needed encouragement and a tool to clear her space and unleash her strength.

I've had clients invent all kinds of tools. Ray guns, spray bottles, mighty, forceful breaths, magic rings. Whatever works. Be creative.

SUMMING UP

To become confident you have to transform your mind. Instead of being stuck in self-defeating thoughts, use the three tools. First, practice letting go of the negative thinking (**confide**) by telling the negative thoughts to your inner confidant. Now you are in a position to receive the positive voice (**reflect**). This will give you the clarity and strenth to move forward. Finally, you **envision** yourself moving ahead successfully by taking small, manageable steps toward confidence.

The three tools help you stay connected to the positive side of your mind so you can be self-supportive and encouraging. Your stress will go down and your performance will go up. This is not rocket science. It's a matter of steady, determined self-effort and practice. You can't use the tools just once and expect, *Presto! Change-o!* you will become a confident person. Like anything good in life, you have to work for it. You become aware that your confidence is starting to slip and correct course. You use the three tools before the stress becomes unmanageable.

As I was writing this chapter, I received a call from Rachel, a social worker who had failed her licensing exam three times. When she showed up at my office she was barely holding herself together. Her face was taut and there were big dark circles under her eyes. After some introductory formalities I said, "I'm going to try an experiment." I looked directly at her and said, "TEST!" She instantly burst into tears. She insisted that she would never pass. She had many superstitious thoughts, "When I'm dressing in the morning I think, *If I wear those shoes, I'm going to fall. But if I wear these, I might pass.*" She felt like she couldn't control anything, not even her own thinking.

> **Use the Confidence tools to train your mind to work for you.**

As we worked through the Confidence tools—with a regular, ongoing dosage of breathing, grounding and sensing—she learned to recognize her self-defeating thoughts and re-direct them. Using the Confidence tools wasn't easy for her, so strong was her habit of disconnecting and feeling badly about herself. But she was determined to pass and she worked hard to dissolve the old habit by putting in place a new, helpful one.

At the time of this writing Rachel is a few weeks away from taking the test. The last e-mail I received from her was positive and forward-looking, "I'm feeling much better. I'm not imagining a catastrophe. I think I can actually pass it."

And, as all of this was going on, Barack Obama ran his campaign for President with the slogan "Yes we can."

No one wins saying, "No I can't."

Rachel carried her strong self into the test and passed.

QUICK CHECK: Confidence

When you are studying for a test...

Become aware

❏ Are you feeding yourself negative self-statements?

❏ Can you identify them? Write them down.

Use the tools

❏ **Confide** your negativity in the confidant.

❏ The confidant will **reflect** your positive qualities back to you. See the reflection.

❏ **Envision** yourself taking small, manageable steps.

❏ Return to studying, staying connected in your positive mind.

When you are taking a test...

Become aware

❏ Notice the negative things you are saying about yourself and that your confidence is slipping.

❏ Breathe, ground and sense (from the chapter on Calm).

Use the tools

❏ **Confide** your negativity about the item you're on to your confidant.

❏ Hear the confidant **reflect** back something accurate and positive about you.

❏ **Envision** the small, manageable steps you have to take right now to answer the question in front of you.

❏ Open your eyes and return to answering the question, staying connected in your positive, supportive mind.

Chapter Six

How to Stay Focused

YOUR GOALS

On February 20, 1998, two billion people around the world were glued to their TV sets, intently watching the final round of the women's figure skating championship at the Winter Olympics in Nagano, Japan. From Milwaukee to Moscow, screens lit up with the image of a 14-year-old American skater from Sugarland, Texas. Tara Lipinski, petite and graceful, leapt, twirled and sailed her way to a gold medal. Following Tara's triumph, her mother told reporters how the seeds had been planted when her daughter, while still in diapers, watched the '86 Winter Olympics. When the competition was over, baby Tara pulled out a Tupperware container, placed it in the middle of the living room, climbed on top, and triumphantly presented herself with a gold medal. At age two, this toddler set herself the goal of becoming a champion. Twelve years later, fifty-thousand cheering fans in the stadium and billions all over the planet witnessed her realize that dream.

How did she get there? Well, to put it succinctly, she had a goal, and she and her family worked for it. Every morning she skated for two and a half hours before school. Her mother sewed costumes and her father drove her across the country for competitions. Nothing was too much in the quest for success. This little girl was, more than anything, focused. She saw her goal and she was willing to do whatever it took to reach it.

That is what the best performers do—they stay focused. Picture an NBA player about to sink a foul shot, standing with his toes to the line. In the midst of screaming fans and glaring lights, he targets his attention onto the basket and scores the point. All top athletes spend years training hard and suffering broken bones and pulled muscles to go for the gold. Athletes offer great examples of focusing because we watch the intensity of their attention live on TV. We cheer when they win and cry when they lose. They show us what it means to stay fully connected to actions and to goals.

This, of course, is true of successful professionals in any field. Consider a brain surgeon who is removing a minuscule, life-threatening lesion from the left frontal lobe of a 6-year-old child. The doctor cannot let her attention wander for a nanosecond since the tiniest lapse could result in her patient never speaking again. When the doctor is finished, five hours later, she informs the anxious parents that the cancer was successfully removed. The couple cries with relief, and the surgeon takes off her gloves knowing that she did her job. What does she have in common with the athlete? She is deeply dedicated to her work. She never loses sight of her goals. Every successful lawyer, dentist, artist, doctor, and business person spends years cultivating his or her skills. Whenever they stumble, which everyone does, they pick themselves up and get back on course. To succeed at the virtually unending series of tests that their work presents, these people have to stay focused.

Focus is the third leg of our performance model—the three-legged stool. Of the three legs, focus is unique because without it you cannot achieve any measure of success. In other words, you will not get anywhere in life. If you aren't calm when taking a test, you can always hold your breath and tough it out. If your confidence is shaky, you can use sheer willpower (or guesswork) to answer most of the questions. But you cannot in any way compensate for being distracted. If your attention isn't one-pointed, your performance will suffer. Without focus, the only way to achieve any measure of success on a test is if a) you're lucky; b) the questions are easy; or c) you happen to know the answers already. If I were in your shoes, I wouldn't chance it. I would learn to focus.

With sustained focus, you can achieve anything.

What do I actually mean by *staying focused*? According to the dictionary, *focus* has a two-pronged definition. As a noun: "the center of interest or activity." Think of the bull's-eye in the very middle of a dartboard. As a verb: "to direct toward a particular point or purpose." Think of throwing the dart directly to this point. In regard to testing, *focus* is also a noun and a verb. There is a goal of scoring well on the test, and there is working toward that goal.

Goals Come from Your Spirit

Being focused is, ultimately and intimately, linked to a very powerful source within you—your spirit. Your goals might engage your body and your mind, but they originate in another part of you. Some people call this their soul, God, Goddess or Higher Power. In this book, I will call it your spirit or highest purpose. Think of spirit as your power generator. It produces the energy that sparks every one of your achievements.

Throughout history, spirit has moved men and women to become great leaders, scientists, poets, musicians and athletes. Mahatma Gandhi envisioned an independent India, and then secured it through a nationwide movement of nonviolence. Marie Curie hypothesized the existence of atomic properties and then discovered their structure. Lord Byron conceived and then wrote sensuous love poetry. Mozart imagined glorious music and then scored stupendous operas. As a kid, Michael Jordan wanted to be a great basketball player, so he cultivated his talent for years, on a daily basis, and ended up sailing through the air as if defying gravity.

Your spirit expresses itself as your deepest goals and as the determination to do whatever it takes to achieve them. Spirit has the same Latin root as the word "inspire." It is *inspirare*, which means to breathe. I always talk about a person's goals as the way in which spirit breathes through him. When people, like those mentioned above, allow this to happen, we say they are inspired. They also happen to be stimulated, animated and invigorated.

This is true for all of us. Think of a time when you had a goal that you were determined to reach and you worked doggedly toward it. Maybe you wanted to learn to ice skate or bake a pie, or ace your chemistry test. Remember what it felt like when you were so highly focused? Chances are you felt enlivened, enthused and satisfied.

When you are focused, you still have to put a great deal of effort into the activity. Focusing doesn't take the work out of work. But there is a payoff, and it doesn't just come at the finish line. During the process, you feel fulfilled because you've got a goal and are fully engaged in achieving it, which means you are satisfying your spirit at every step.

I'm not pulling this stuff out of thin air. There is a historical basis for what I'm saying. For thousands of years, saints and sages have said that spirit is what moved them to great achievements. When the mythologist Joseph Campbell said, "Follow your bliss," what he meant was, "Let your spirit guide your actions." Do you think you have to be a "religious" person to succeed? No, you don't. You just have to understand that your spirit is your driving force and learn how to stay connected to it. Then, whenever you are moving closer to your goal you will feel stronger and your life will be more organized and less chaotic.

The opposite occurs when you are cut off from your spirit. If you don't have a goal, or if your goal is really someone else's, life feels meaningless and aimless. Yet just *having* a goal is not enough; you also need to keep working toward it. If you're repeatedly distracted you'll end up feeling like you're going around in circles. You'll become deflated and discouraged.

Your spirit is your driving force. The more connected you are to it, the more you will realize your dreams.

At this point you may well be wondering, *If focusing feels so right and natural it should be easy to do, right?*

I wouldn't say easy. You have to know how to set your goals and then how to keep working to achieve them. Focused people succeed because they have a path and they stay on it. They are connected to their spirit. Unfocused people wander around and fall by the wayside. Their performance suffers because they keep disconnecting from their spirit. If you want to raise your test scores, the third key member of your body-mind-spirit team has to be fully engaged and connected through the process of studying for a test and actually taking it.

How do you stay connected to your spirit? First you set goals that are important to you. Let's go through the steps.

STEP ONE: Set Your Own Performance Goals

Recently, two anxious parents brought their 16-year-old daughter in for a consultation. Allie was a bright high-school senior, an ace tennis player with a 3.5 GPA. But on her first try at the SAT, her scores were dismal. With her parents present in my office, I asked Allie, "Why are you here?" She responded quickly, "Because my mother wants me to get higher SAT scores."

"Wow," I thought, "that's refreshing—a kid who tells the truth right in front of her parents." When I shot a glance in their direction, I saw that their jaws had dropped. Perhaps this was a little *too* much honesty. Then the kid trumped herself. With a coy smile aimed deliberately at me, she added, "And...I don't want to work for it."

There was a pause. We had just moved from refreshing to cold, hard fact. Now, everyone was wondering how I would respond to *that*. I thought about it for a second, then reached behind my chair and pulled out a small jar filled with gold glitter. I shook it up and down and said, "See this Allie? I call this 'Magic Dust.' Why don't you take it home and sprinkle it on your head every night until your next try at the SAT. Maybe the magic will work and your scores will go up. This way, you can hang out with your friends and watch TV, and you won't have to do any work and maybe you'll still score high on the SAT. Think of the money your parents will save by not bringing you to see me!"

Allie laughed. She got it immediately. There is no magic dust that majestically delivers people to their desired goal. They have to work for it. Not only that, the goal has to be their own, not their mother's or their Uncle Steve's. Although Allie was resistant at first, she was a smart girl and not easily fooled even by her own folly. Instead of staying locked in a fruitless battle with her mother, she realized that going to a good college was *her* goal, and that higher SAT scores were necessary if she was going to end up there. When she identified the greater goal as her own, her spirit kicked in: she felt motivated, she did the work and the next time she took the SAT her scores improved considerably.

Make Sure it's *Your* Goal

Unless a goal is yours, chances are you're not going to work for it. Why should you? It's not what *you* want. If someone else is driving your agenda you might make a half-hearted effort now and then, but only when that person (usually your parent, maybe a teacher) is nagging you. After a while, both of you are going to get tired of this scenario and there will be a breakdown. You will feel resentful, they will be angry; you will lose interest and stop working, they'll pull rank and wallop you with negative consequences. None of this is *fun*. If your primary reason for wanting to do well on a test is to get your parents off your back, you'd better return to the drawing board. *Your* drawing board. You have to want to succeed, for yourself.

> Own your goal. Or else you'll end up struggling with a parent, teacher, coach or yourself.

Make Your Goal Important

When I ask my clients "What do you want to achieve?" and they respond, "I want higher SAT scores," "I want to pass my bar exam," or "I want my driver's license," I follow up with, "Is that all you want?" In other words, passing a test is not a final goal; it's a step to something bigger, to a goal that's more important to your life as a whole. With higher scores on the SAT you have a chance of being accepted at a better college. When you pass your bar exam, you will be able to fulfill your dream of working as an attorney on behalf of welfare mothers. A driver's license gives you the freedom to drive and go wherever you like (assuming you have access to a car!). Reaching your goal usually takes hard work, and if you are going to put in all the effort needed to reach it, the more your goal is connected to the direction of your life, the more you will want to work toward it by succeeding on the tests along the way. Your performance on a test matters to your life: *the quality of your future depends on your present performance*. Passing a test is not a final goal; it's a step to something bigger, to a goal that is more important to your life as a whole.

Think about a test you are about to take and answer this question: why do you want to do well? Make sure your answer links you up to the bigger picture of where you are going and who you want to become. Use the space below to write in your big goal, the one that means a lot to you, the one that shows you where you want to go.

_____

_____

_____

With a highly desirable goal in front of you, putting in the time and effort to study for a test will be easier. The work might be hard, the subject of the class may be boring and the teacher could be uninspired, but you will want to achieve a good grade in that class because you know what's at stake, for *you*.

Consider How You are Going to Get There

Even the best of goals is just a starting point, not a delivery system. Imagining your bright, successful future may charge your jets, but it doesn't tell you specifically how to meet that goal. You've heard the old saying, "A journey of a thousand miles begins with the first step." To reach your big goal you have to take many steps. For example, if you're an undergrad and your big goal is to be a physician, you'll need college-level pre-med courses, including chemistry. Even that single chemistry course requires certain steps: passing your midterms, handing in lab reports, and scoring well on your final. Each of these steps is an action step, a small goal in and of itself.

To ensure success, you need a sequence of action steps that lead you to the big goal. Formulate your action steps in the right way, then facing the challenge will be less daunting *and* you will be moving always in the right direction. Attaining a goal is not like a hostile takeover. You don't say, "I want to go to Princeton," walk into the university president's office and demand a full four-year scholarship. You work your way toward your dream, one action step at a time. In the next two sections I'll show you how to do that.

Divide the Work into Action Steps

For many people, their highest goal seems large and overwhelming. Rather than be sucked into the quicksand of despair, remember: any goal can be broken down into small, controllable chunks. These are your *action steps*. (And yes, they bear a direct relationship to the "small, manageable steps" you envision in the Confidence tools).

Say you have to prepare for a history test on the Middle Ages, the 12th through 14th centuries. It's Saturday afternoon and you have a three-hour stretch ahead of you. What do you do? First, let's hear what Nikki did when she had three hours to study for her bar exam. "I thought I'd be sensible and study at the library where I wouldn't hear my phone ring. My goal was to review all the material, but after taking one look at the stack of books and notes, I froze. It just seemed like too much to take on, and I didn't know where to start. I spent so much time deciding how to proceed that I barely got anything done."

Sound familiar? Hours of study time and all you're doing is shuffling papers. Nikki told me that her goal was to "review the material," but that isn't an action step; it is a goal in and of itself. Staring at that stack of books she must have felt like a climber looking up at the Matterhorn. "How am I ever going to conquer *that*?" The whole idea completely intimidated her. Without specific steps to follow, she was thrown off by her own anxiety.

Let's avoid Nikki's mistake and do it the smart way. Assess the material you have to cover and divide it up into action steps according to the time available to you.

Step 1	12:00	Organize notes according to chapters.
Step 2	12:20	Re-read chapter 1 in depth. Highlight the important points.
Step 3	1:20	Take a short break
Step 4	1:25	Conduct a quick review of chapters 2 and 3, paying special attention to the highlighted sections. Take the quiz at the end of the chapters and score it.
Step 5	2:15	Take a short break.
Step 6	2:20	Read class notes for all three chapters.
Step 7	3:00	End studying for today. Make a plan for what you will do tomorrow.

Action steps break up the process of achieving a goal into increments. Nikki didn't have to burden herself with the concept of "review *all* the material." When she divided the task into small, achievable steps she felt she could do it. It's not overwhelming to take that first step; anyone can manage it. Approaching the work this way would have helped her use both her time and her energy wisely.

Spell Out Your Action Steps: Make Them S.M.A.R.T.

If you need more specific direction in spelling out your action steps, what follows is a time-tested process for doing just that. It's called the SMART formula. When your action steps are SMART, they fulfill these criteria. They are:

S	=	specific
M	=	measurable
A	=	adjustable
R	=	realistic
T	=	time-based

What do these criteria mean?

SPECIFIC
Your goal is precise and well defined.

MEASURABLE
You can gauge whether you've reached it or not.

ADJUSTABLE
You can adapt or modify it if you need to.

REALISTIC
Your goals are attainable given your available time, energy and resources.

TIME-BASED
Whatever goal you set is linked to the clock or calendar.

The whole purpose of this formula is to help you come up with action steps that you can really achieve, that are within the realm of the doable. It takes goal setting out of the "I wish" zone and puts it in the feasible zone. You learn to plot the path to your goals in a way that isn't vague, grandiose or unreachable. Instead, you will take steps that are precise, reasonable and attainable.

A good way to see what *not* to do is to look at Hal. Hal was studying for his biology final. His work throughout the semester was in the C+ range. I gave him the action sheet (below) and he filled out his action steps on the left-hand side. On the right-hand side is my evaluation as to whether the step is SMART or not.

ACTION SHEET FOR HAL

Subject: <u>Biology final</u> **Today's date**: <u>March 10</u> **Test date**: <u>April 4</u>
SMART = **S**pecific/**M**easureable/**A**djustable/**R**ealistic /**T**ime-based

Hal's stated action steps	Is it SMART?
"Review everything."	As stated, this step is too general and not precise. Big, global, general steps make them feel enormous and overwhelming. They tend to paralyze rather than motivate. This step is **not specific.**
"Show what I know."	This is a vague statement that could mean anything. You may know a lot, but it won't necessarily be measured on that test. "Show what I know" is **not measurable.**
"I'll study every single day from 2-5 pm."	While this looks like an admirable action step, it's not realistic. Everyone knows that unexpected events always intrude, even on the best plans. Right now this step is rigid and **not adjustable.** Hal is setting himself up for failure.
"I'm aiming for an A- on the test."	So far Hal's grades in biology have hovered around a C +. It is not his best subject. In fact it's a struggle for him to keep up. Can Hal reach an A-? Not likely. This step is not even a step—it's a goal, and either way, it **not realistic.** Hal is setting himself up for a big disappointment.
"I'll practice with old exams and work on them until I get everything right no matter how long it takes."	This might work if Hal had all the time in the world and nothing else to do but prepare for his biology exam. However, he's got tests in other subjects and has the rest of his daily life to tend to as well. All of it takes time. This step is **not time-based.**

After we talked about his action steps in light of the SMART formula, Hal revised his action sheet. Here's what the new one looked like:

ACTION SHEET FOR HAL (REVISED)

Subject: <u>Biology</u> **Today's date**: <u>March 10</u> **Test date:** <u>April 4</u>
SMART = **S**pecific/**M**easurable/**A**djustable/**R**ealistic /**T**ime-based

Hal's action steps (revised)	Is it SMART?
"Review one chapter per day for each of the next five days."	This action step is **specific.** It spells out in precise terms how much Hal is going to accomplish on each day as he prepares for his exam. By being specific, Hal knows what he needs to do and will be certain when he gets it done.
"On the practice questions, aim for 80 percent correct answers."	Hal is giving himself a clear yardstick for gauging his success. This step is **measurable**. If Hal comes in under this 80 percent he'll be able to analyze his wrong answers and make the necessary corrections. By reaching this percentage of correct answers, Hal is more likely to achieve the score he wants on the test.
"Each day I'll review my calendar and plan to study 2-3 hours during the day. I'll keep that study time in one chunk whenever I can."	This step allows for flexibility. Hal recognizes that he needs to study between two and three hours a day, and he's making this step **adjustable** to accommodate his varied calendar.
"I'll study enough to bring my grade up to a B-."	Hal's performance-to-date in biology has been C+. In this step Hal is pushing to do a little bit better without putting too much pressure on himself. This is **realistic.** He is more likely to achieve this grade than one out of his reach.

"When I practice old exams I'll work on them for one hour and then leave an additional half hour to analyze my answers."	Hal must balance his exam preparation with the rest of his obligations. By creating a **time-based** action step like this one he will be able to accomplish his study objectives and still have room for his other commitments.

For every test you have to take, make your action steps SMART. For one thing, in the face of a staggering amount of material to study, it will keep you sane if you structure your time and set immediate goals that you can actually fulfill. For another, SMART goals will keep your tasks sorted out, clear and above all, manageable.

An important tip: when you put your action steps into words, state what you need *to do*, rather than what you need to *not* do. In other words, make it positive. Negative steps sound punitive and they don't really offer helpful directions. *Don't rush. Don't forget to highlight what will probably be on the test. For God's sake, don't miss anything.* These will push your mind to rebel and say, *Don't tell me what to do!* A positive approach makes you feel better and moves you along in the right direction.

Coaching you to use the SMART formula might feel like just another rule that I'm forcing you to use. Be specific! Be flexible! Be realistic! Most people don't like rules. But I guarantee you that this is not a rule that demands more of you. It is a SMART template designed to make your life easier.

Give Yourself a Break

Before we move onto the next section, where I will show you how to stay focused and achieve your goals, here is a practical pointer that will help you meet the challenge of accomplishing your goals: learn to take regularly scheduled breaks. Students routinely think they ought to be able to study for hours on end and still be alert and attentive. This is unrealistic. The research on cognitive functioning (how a person thinks and learns) shows that optimal study spurts of twenty to forty minutes are the ideal amount of time for understanding and retaining information. So taking a break actually helps your performance. As we discussed in Chapter Four, you must, from time-to-time, engage your parasympathetic nervous system because that calms you down. When you

To sustain top-level performance, every now and then you have to rest your body and mind.

don't take planned, occasional breaks, your sympathetic nervous system—which is all about arousal, anxiety and the fight-or-flight response—zaps you into burnout mode. Studying for two to three hours nonstop, appears *de rigueur* to serious students, but it is usually counterproductive and it can turn into a chronic drain on the person's available energy.

I tell my clients to buy a cheap egg timer from Radio Shack and set it for thirty to forty-five minutes. Work continuously until the timer goes off, then stop and take a five-minute break. Set the timer again and go back to work. After three cycles of this (roughly an hour and a half total) then take a longer break (fifteen minutes). Planning breaks and knowing you are really going to take them is a way of pacing yourself and not burning out. You'll look forward to your breaks as opportunities to relax, to let go. And building the pauses into your study pattern means you don't have to feel guilty about taking breaks. You've done a patch of work and now you deserve a few minutes off. After the break, it feels good to go back to studying knowing that another break will be coming up in a little while.

I have encountered students who don't trust themselves to take breaks because in the past, five minutes led to a half hour, or an hour, or an entire afternoon. After that much time, resistance has set in and they don't want to return to work. They usually say something like, "If I leave my desk and do something else, I'll never go back." Yes, that can happen, but you can train yourself out of that habit. It is essential to take the breaks and learn to return and hit the books again. If you force long, extended study periods on yourself, your efficiency at taking in information will drop off (usually after forty-five minutes). You feel that you are doing all this against your will and you grow tired and resistant and your short breaks will turn into long naps. In the next chapter, I will give you more suggestions about how to take breaks effectively, as well as many other helpful tips. For now, go out and buy an egg timer.

Ready to Move on…

To summarize, formulating a goal that has real meaning for you is the first step in the process of being focused. Detailing a step-by-step plan to achieving it is the second step. Now you know where you're headed and how you will get there. But will you?

DEALING WITH DISTRACTION

At the beginning of the chapter I said that "focus" is a noun and a verb. We've just handled the noun, the point of focus, the goal itself. Now we have to work on the verb—the actions needed to reach the goal. If your action steps are clear, you know what they are. Taking the steps and staying on the path is another matter. You know you have to review a chapter in your history text during your study time tonight. That part of your focus is clear. But what happens when you open the book and actually start working?

I'll tell you what happens: either you do the work and get it done or, if you're like most people, you become distracted. Even with well-defined steps to follow, we all face the problem of distraction. It is the biggest stumbling block to studying and performing well on tests.

Distraction, Distraction, Distraction

On the *Focus* leg of the three-legged stool, distraction is Enemy #1. It derails the momentum of that ongoing stream of actions that are moving you toward your goal. How often have you set out to accomplish something and found that the day has gone by and you spent it doing nonessential little tasks you hadn't planned on and that have nothing to do with your goal? You have a big recital coming up and you haven't practiced for two days. Or, you have to fill out your tax forms, but you end up weeding the garden. Or, you have to study for your SATs, GMATs or French final, but you take your car in for a tune-up instead.

Distractions are a direct manifestation of a disconnection from the spirit. If you look up the word *distraction* in the dictionary, you will find three different meanings with a notable interrelationship:

* An obstacle to attention

* An entertainment that provokes pleased interest and takes you away from worries and vexations

* Mental turmoil, derangement

Doesn't this perfectly cover the process of being distracted? First, your attention is diverted. Second, you kind of like it because now you don't have to deal with the work in front of you. Third, there is a build-up of stress because you've let so much time slip by, so now you are anxious or depressed. What started out as a little blip in your attention span ends up as the content for a therapy session.

Distraction is your enemy and it will defeat you every time if you let it. If distractions are everyone's scourge, how do you conquer them? To put it another, more positive way, how do you stay connected and keep moving toward your goal? Simple. As we saw in the previous chapters on calming down and being confident you have to do two things: 1. Become aware, as soon as you can, that you are disconnecting, in this case, becoming distracted, and 2. Use specific tools to reconnect and put yourself back on track.

CULTIVATE YOUR AWARENESS

The key here is learning to nip this problem in the bud before it morphs into something horrendous. You want to be able to cultivate *awareness* that you are becoming distracted as soon as you begin to veer off track. This is important because many people become distracted and they don't even realize it. Their mind is off and running, and an hour later they wake up and say, "Oh, wait a minute, I've stopped listening to the lecture." Other people know they're distracted, but they're in denial about it. They justify going off track by saying, "But I really *had* to get up from my desk and do the laundry. It wasn't a distraction, it was something that had to be done."

Scott's story is a case in point. He was a first-year medical student who was falling behind. As an undergraduate, his performance had been stellar, but on his final exams at the end of his first term in medical school, his scores dropped way down. At first, the fact that he had put off studying until a couple of days before the test didn't strike him as a problem because in high school he had always gotten away with it. "Now," he admitted, "there is just too much material and I can't leave it all to the end." To his credit, he had created a solid study schedule. But old habits die hard. He kept being distracted from his schedule, yet he was curiously unaware of it and mystified as to why he wasn't getting more done. Here is a transcript from one of our early sessions:

Scott: I planned to study from noon to four and then go to the gym.

Dr. B: Tell me what happened when you sat down to study.

Scott: First, I took out my books and notes. But the papers were a mess so I put them in order.

Dr. B: And that took...

Scott: About a half hour.

Dr. B: And then?

Scott: Then I sharpened my pencils and, oh yeah, I called my girl friend to remind her to buy the meat sauce for the pasta. We were having friends over that night. Then I got a glass of water, used the bathroom, and sat down to study.

Dr. B: About what time was it then?

Scott: I'd say it was 1 o'clock.

Dr. B: What did you do then?

Scott: I opened the book to the first chapter and started in on it.

Dr. B: Sounds good. How long did you do that for?

Scott:	Probably about an hour.
Dr. B:	So you sat there glued to the books for a whole hour?
Scott:	Pretty much. Well, sort of. I had to check on the dog. The vet put a bandage on his foot, so I needed to make sure he was OK. I also felt a little hungry so I got a glass of milk … and a cookie to go with it. Gotta have my cookie!
Dr. B:	Absolutely. But Scott, it sounds like you wanted to study, but a lot of things kept getting in the way.
Scott:	Sort of, but I needed to do all that stuff.
Dr. B:	Oh, I'm not questioning that. I just wonder if you had to do it *right then?* Didn't all of those things, how shall I say, *derail* you?
Scott:	You could say that.
Dr. B:	I just did. *[both laugh]*

When Scott told me how he spent the rest of his study time, I discovered that precious little had actually been spent studying. He checked up on the dog three more times, he and his girlfriend talked at length about what kind of sauce to make for the pasta when it turned out that one of the guests was vegetarian. He went to the bathroom again, and then he raided the refrigerator. The discussion ended with Scott saying "I can't believe how much other stuff I was actually doing! I really thought I was studying."

It might seem unbelievable to you too that Scott gave into all these diversions and that he was blissfully unaware of how unfocused he was, but believe me, in my thirty years of coaching people, I have seen this happen time and again. I have heard every conceivable distracting activity that students engage in when they're supposed to be studying. Here is a list I've compiled. These distractions aren't listed in order of rank, but they will give you some idea of what people are up against.

DR. B's (NEARLY) DEFINITIVE LIST OF DISTRACTING ACTIVITIES

Check all that apply to you …

❏ Watching TV   ❏ Playing video games

❏ Hanging out with friends   ❏ Going to a bar

❏ Picking and clipping my nails ❏ Organizing my desk

- ❏ Cleaning my room
- ❏ Contemplating my life
- ❏ Eating
- ❏ Thinking about eating
- ❏ Talking on the phone
- ❏ Checking my stocks
- ❏ Going out for a drive
- ❏ Surfing the web
- ❏ Listening to music
- ❏ Doing the laundry
- ❏ Messing with my iPod
- ❏ Filing papers
- ❏ Job hunting
- ❏ Shopping online (eBay, etc.)
- ❏ Going to the mall
- ❏ Going to the gym
- ❏ Shooting hoops
- ❏ Playing with my pet
- ❏ Thinking about sex
- ❏ Staring at dead plants
- ❏ Reading a book
- ❏ Complaining
- ❏ Watching re-runs

- ❏ Cleaning the house
- ❏ Shopping
- ❏ Thinking about shopping
- ❏ Opening and looking into the fridge
- ❏ Daydreaming
- ❏ Vacuuming
- ❏ Going to the movies
- ❏ Going to the beach
- ❏ Throwing away old papers
- ❏ Paying bills
- ❏ Cleaning out my wallet
- ❏ Reading papers and magazines
- ❏ Playing Frisbee
- ❏ Checking and answering e-mail
- ❏ Worrying about money
- ❏ Thinking about going to the gym
- ❏ Skateboarding
- ❏ Watering the plants
- ❏ Having sex
- ❏ Picking dead leaves off the plants
- ❏ Making lists
- ❏ Wandering around
- ❏ Sleeping

Now add your own little specialties to the list. Do you need another page? Just kidding.

As you went through the list, you probably found points that made you stop and say to yourself, *Yeah, I did go out to buy food. But I need to. A girl's gotta eat!* I understand—you need to do some of things on the list—but *not* when you're supposed to be studying for a test. If you persist in saying that you cannot avoid these little activities, ask yourself this: "Do I really have to go shopping *right now*? Is it worth sacrificing the security of my future life? Or am I just distracting myself because I don't want to hit the books?"

Often my clients call this "procrastinating" and you would think it was some kind of genetic condition that they were born with and was inherent to their nature. It's not genetic. They weren't born with it. It isn't inherent. And it isn't a disease either, like something you catch from an airborne germ. Procrastination isn't something that is happening *to you*. It is something you *are doing*. Procrastinating, in itself, is an action. It is a fancy word for distracting yourself. You are doing one thing instead of what you should be doing. You are placing your focus on something else instead of on studying. Focusing is all about where you direct your energy and where you train your attention. Procrastinating is about wasting your energy and training your attention on the unimportant.

Learn to recognize that losing connection to your goal by engaging in distractions produces symptoms, the way sniffing and sneezing are symptoms of a cold. When you allow your actions to be diverted from your goal, it shows up as a symptom that you are disconnected from your spirit. That's why it's so important to cultivate awareness that you are being distracted—because it is crucial that you stop and reconnect to your spirit and goals. Let's list some of the symptoms that you can be on the lookout for.

COMMON SYMPTOMS OF BEING DISTRACTED

* The distracting activity suddenly feels a lot more important than studying.

* You feel tired and drained after spending all your energy doing other things.

* You are all jittery because in the back of your mind, you know that test is still looming in front of you.

* Your mind is cluttered with thoughts that start with, *I can't... I don't know how...* and *I'm not sure...*

✳ You aren't only anxious, but you are preoccupied with your anxiety.

✳ You are beginning to lose faith in yourself because, once again, you haven't followed through on what you said you would do.

✳ Other people are nagging you, losing faith in you and questioning your motives.

What are the symptoms that tell you that you have become distracted? List them below:

_____

_____

_____

_____

The awareness that you have grown distracted must come from inside you. If you are waiting for someone else to tell you to get back on track you are depending on an external cue. There are two problems with external cues: first, unless you employ a personal valet or maid, no one is going to be around all the time to monitor you; and second, when someone continually is prodding you (a parent, a teacher, a coach), you are going to feel resistant and angry. No one likes being ordered around.

An *internal* cue, however, is entirely different. It is a thought or emotion of your own that contains the realization, "I'm distracted right now and out of focus. I need to get back on track." And it is essential that you learn to point this out to yourself in a nonjudgmental way because if you put yourself down or talk to yourself in a threatening manner (like an angry parent or a frustrated teacher), then you will feel like you are being punished. *Get back to work or else! If you fail this test, I'm going to be furious. You are such a loser. I can't believe you're not studying.* Sound familiar? If you wouldn't talk to a 5-year-old this way, don't do it to yourself. In other words, start looking at your negative self-talk, as we dealt with in the last chapter, as a distraction.

The following exercise will show you how to cultivate a non-threatening, nonjudgmental awareness that you are disconnecting. It will help you develop the internal cues necessary for sustaining focus.

EXERCISE: Your Symptoms of Being Distracted

Close your eyes. Breathe deeply down to your belly. Feel the chair and the floor supporting you.

Sense and see and feel yourself having a goal and working toward it.

Now, see yourself becoming distracted or derailed into another activity.

What's the feeling you're left with?

Do you feel anxious, frustrated, upset, tense, annoyed, jittery, off track, ineffective, devoid of energy, depressed, lost, insecure or hopeless?

Open your eyes.

As we can see, certain emotions accompany distraction, and once we learn to recognize them, they can inform us of what is going on. It is of vital importance that you develop a keen awareness of your symptoms of distraction during the study phase when you can still make up for lost time. Once you are in the classroom and taking the test, you have no such luxury. The clock is ticking and there is no time to waste. You need to make sure that your "awareness light" starts flashing red as soon as your mind starts to wander so you can rope your attention back in and stay connected to the test.

The chief problem with losing focus on a test is simply that you are losing time, which is flying by whether you are paying attention and answering the questions or not. Once the time is gone, it's gone. And of course, your own perception of lost time creates piercing anxiety, which makes it even harder to focus on the test questions. As all of this occurs, you are becoming more and more disconnected from your spirit. It's as if you have fallen overboard and are drifting out to sea. The boat seems to be moving further away from you as you sink beneath the waves. In addition, when you become distracted on a test you break your own concentration. This usually has a negative outcome since many tests are actually testing your ability to think through a complex issue in a sustained way.

To help you cultivate your awareness of how and when you become distracted and lose focus, use the *Awareness Log: Focus* on page 195. By keeping the log you will see that you lose focus much more often than you realize or would like to admit.

If losing your focus is also a habit in other areas of your life, you can be sure that it will rear its ugly head when you are taking a test. As I said above, part of every test is the challenge to keep your attention in one place during a specified period of time. Those who haven't cultivated an awareness of *how* they lose their attention and what it feels like, will be defeated at test time. The way you know that losing focus has become a habit is if you keep being distracted no matter how much you promise yourself you will change—and if it is showing up on your test scores.

If you repeatedly let pleasant or unpleasant tasks or thoughts divert your attention from studying, or if you continually wait until the last minute to hit the books and then rationalize the detour by saying you don't really have a problem—"This is just my style of working" is the common refrain—then you are in denial. You *do* have a problem. Maybe distractions and procrastination didn't hamper you much in grade school or even high school because you are smart and the material came easily to you, but by the time you reach college, you are playing with the big girls and boys. Now you are facing real competition. By the time you hit graduate training you're in the major leagues. No longer will you be able to get away with, *Don't worry. I can control my behavior. I'll get all my studying done at the last minute.* For those who haven't dealt with their behavior until now, it is probably ingrained. Deed has become habit, and habits have a way of lasting a lifetime. Right into the job market, where goal-oriented, focused people will beat you out every time.

People who are successful on tests, in athletics, or on stage, have practiced staying focused.

By not admitting you have a habit, you are just doing what addicts do: they engage habitually in self-destructive behavior and they are in denial about it. At some point in time you will have to face yourself and your behavior, and take stock and ask yourself, "If I go on like this, am I going to pass my classes? Will I even graduate?" You have to wake up to what you are doing, come clean, and accept the fact that you are distracted from studying on a continual basis and it is working against you.

This, then, is the first step—awareness. You know that you are becoming distracted and you are willing to face it. Unfortunately, that doesn't necessarily mean you want to change. You still need to answer the question: "Do I *really* want to stop distracting myself and start focusing?" Some people answer "no" to that question because being distracted isn't particularly unpleasant for them, in fact, they like it. When I asked one student how she felt whenever her attention was averted from the task at hand, I expected her to tell me it was frustrating. Instead she happily answered that she felt great, "I'd *much* rather play with my cat than study." For her, this was an enjoyable amusement. I felt like saying, "Duh, of course it's more fun to tickle Twinkles than study calculus. That's not the point." But I didn't say that. I simply asked her how she felt an hour before test time when she reflected on how much she had procrastinated rather than study. Her mood dropped precipitously, "I was in a panic, a total mess." And there we have it: it feels good in the moment not to make the effort to concentrate, but the long-term effects can be devastating. Not only did she suffer greatly with anxiety walking into the classroom, but she dreaded facing her parents with poor grades, and she hated disappointing teachers who saw so much potential in her. This student's habits of opting for the pleasant diversion instead of studying was not going to change on its own. She had to transform them.

THE THREE TOOLS FOR STAYING FOCUSED

So here's the good news: if you have such a habit and you are willing to work for a change, you are not stuck with the habit. You can break your old, unhelpful habits, and you can establish new, useful ones. And if you use the tools I am about to give you, you will improve your chances tremendously. Understanding and using these tools do not require an advanced degree in psychology. They may appear simple— and they are. Yet it never ceases to amaze me that people don't do the simple and obvious things to improve themselves. They just continue to engage in the same old unhelpful behaviors and patterns and then think there's some "magic" way to change.

To change, you have to take action. You cannot just sit in a chair, stare at the wall and hope that when you arise, you will be a different person. And you can't take a pill that will cure you of bad habits. And you can't say *Abracadabra!* and watch your old behavior patterns disappear. Your habit is not doing something *to* you. *You* are acting out the habit. So if you want things to be different, you have to act differently.

Remember the old physics principle, a body in motion stays in motion until it is met with an equal and opposite force? Well, it takes an effort equal to the force of the habit to stop its trajectory. You must actually *do* something different, not just try to stop what you have been doing. Simply stopping will leave a void. If you don't do something else instead, the old habits will automatically rear their ugly heads, fill the void, and spring back into action. What you need is a helpful step-by-step process of changing specific behaviors. Through repetition, this beneficial sequence will become your new habit.

You need to train yourself with the following three tools. That's all it takes—three. You simply have to use them consistently and with determination.

TOOL #1: Stop! Look at What You Are Doing

Let's say you are driving from Miami to New York. You are on the freeway and you believe you are making good time. But your car is actually pointed south instead of north. If you don't stop to ask if you're going the right way, you may end up in Little Havana, not Times Square. To make sure this doesn't happen, the first thing you have to do is stop the car.

Now imagine that you are in the middle of a test and you are drifting off. It's Friday afternoon and as soon as the test is over you are headed out to the beach for the weekend. How nice. Suddenly, the proctor announces, "Thirty minutes left," and you are jolted back to reality. How much time have you lost fantasizing about the beach and barbeque? Wouldn't it have been better if you had caught yourself drifting off and said, "Wait a minute! The weekend hasn't started yet. My mind is off in the wrong direction"? When you can do this, you arrest the process of being distracted and stay in the present.

The following exercise will show you how to use the first tool and stop the distracting activity.

 EXERCISE: Stopping the Distraction

Sit comfortably in a chair, making sure your back is reasonably straight and your neck and head are upright. Uncross your arms and legs. Rest your feet on the floor and place your hands gently on top of each leg. Breathe out and close your eyes.

Envision yourself having a goal. Let's say you are taking a test next week, and right now, for the next hour, your goal is to review a particular chapter in an organized and thorough way.

See yourself working toward your goal. You see your books in front of you and you imagine opening one of them and starting to read the required material.

Now see yourself becoming distracted. Quite unexpectedly, the face of a friend you haven't seen in a long time pops onto your mental screen. You think, *I wonder what's going on with him?* Warm feelings about your friend flood you for an instant and you reach for your cell phone.

Now, use the first tool, **STOP!** You see a stop sign, a stoplight, a hand goes up, or an alarm signal goes off. You stop the distracting activity (picking up the phone). As your hand goes toward the phone, you realize, "I'm starting to go off track. I was studying and now, suddenly, I'm starting to make a phone call." The urge to make the call is strong. You haven't seen your friend in so long. But you muster up a little discipline and tell yourself to "Hold it."

Once you have stopped the distraction, ask yourself the question, **"Is this distraction going to help me reach my goal?"** Is calling my friend right now going to help me be better prepared for the test? Clearly, the answer is "No."

Open your eyes.

Sharon, a medical student, learned the value of this tool firsthand during an anatomy final as she told the following story. "The first question on the test threw me and sent me spinning into the worst-case scenario. I thought, 'Oh no, I'll lose my scholarship and never finish medical school!' I was stuck in anxious thoughts for a minute or two before I suddenly realized, 'Hey, I'm distracted by my worrying!' So I immediately used the first tool. I stopped in my tracks. Then I asked myself, 'Will worrying help me ace the test?' Clearly, the answer was no, so I got right back into the test. This happened a few more times, and each time it was easier to catch myself and stop. I didn't let the negative thoughts derail me."

Of course, Sharon wasn't trying this for the first time during the test. She had trained herself to do it when she studied. By the time she was sitting in the classroom with the test in front of her, she knew how to keep herself from being distracted.

This kind of stopping is a discipline that is taught in virtually every spiritual tradition. Why? Because these traditions, especially the ancient ones, have recognized for millennia the tremendous importance of owning your own attention. If you want to meditate, or pray, or become enlightened, or communicate with the great spirits, or understand the meaning of life, or fulfill your highest purpose—all goals of different spiritual paths—you must be able to control your attention. If it is all over the place, you will get nowhere. Unless you make a conscious effort to stop becoming caught up in distractions and change direction, you will sink into a lethargic inertia. It is so easy to default to what is easy and immediately pleasing, to just let our attention traipse around in circles aimlessly. Put another way, it's easier to roll downhill than it is to make an effort to climb the hill. But then time passes and life is almost over, and you have drifted further and further from your goals.

Many spiritual traditions liken being distracted to falling asleep. Stopping is like an alarm clock, ringing, telling you to wake up and reconnect to your higher potential, your highest self. If you cannot stop being enticed by derailing activities, you will just keep drifting. The further away you drift, the harder it is to return to what's important to you. Spiritual teachers know that the only way to reverse the trend is to **stop** first.

No other course is available to you until you stop the distracting course you are on. The first thing substance abusers are told when they enter treatment is that they cannot be helped unless they cease taking the drugs. Until that happens, therapy cannot begin. They can't come in saying, "I need a hit of coke so I can feel good for this session." Of course, we'd all like to feel good when facing something difficult, like rehabilitation or a test, but it doesn't work.

Stop distraction when it arises. Nip it in the bud.

And stopping means *stopping*. It doesn't mean thinking, "I should stop," once you are already off course and into a distraction. If you have a test tomorrow and you should be studying but find yourself on the phone to your sister and are thinking, "I really ought to get off the phone," that's not stopping. You either get off the phone or you don't. People confuse these two all the time—the nagging thought, "I should stop," with actually stopping. To really stop, you have to put the phone down and return to the books.

I describe it to clients this way, "Don't drive up on the curb and into the house." What I mean is, when you are parallel parking and as you are backing up you feel the tires of your car going onto the sidewalk, do you just keep going? Do you then back up across the lawn and crash through the front wall of your house before you finally stop? No. If your car is mounting the curb, that's your first clue to stop. Catch yourself right away before you destroy your house.

But why is it so hard to do this one little thing? Think of stopping as a battle between two parts of yourself: the adult and the child. The adult part understands delayed gratification, the meaning of work, the importance of putting in the time for a test and foregoing pleasures until the studying is done. The child wants instant gratification, playing instead of working, spending time doing fun things, and receiving pleasure now, not later. Children are only interested in what is satisfying right now: eating, playing with toys, sucking on their fingers, hugging Mommy. The child inside you may want a good grade. It might see the value in all the goals the adult has. It just doesn't want to work or sacrifice for them.

Children seem helpless and vulnerable, but make no mistake about it, they are also tyrants. They will make their demands heard even if they have to throw a tantrum. When you're studying for a test, distractions pop up and the child responds because distractions feed the child. If you take the diversions away and try to return to the books, it's like yanking the pacifier out of the little child's mouth. The child doesn't like that. The nipple gave it pleasure. It starts to wail and yell, "Hey, why are you doing that? Give that back to me!" For a person who's supposed to be studying, this presents itself as resistance. "I don't want to stop watching television. This is my favorite show." But it's nothing more than the child crying for the pacifier.

Children are cute and adorable—but you are not a child. One might be living inside of you, but you aren't it. You are a grown person who is about to take a test, and no baby is going to pass that test, get a good job, put a roof over your head or food on your table for the rest of your life. The adult is the one who is expected to perform. Children sit back and expect to be taken care of. Unless you have a nice trust fund waiting for you, you cannot afford to let the child inside of you take over.

Jason is a case in point. He was a high school senior preparing to take the SAT for the third time because he did so poorly on his first two tries. If he didn't improve this time, he still had one more chance, but that was it, so he was under considerable pressure. The perplexing question about Jason was why he consistently answered easy questions with wrong answers. The reason was simply that he read the questions too quickly to comprehend them. All he wanted to do during test time was get it over with so he could play tennis, something he loved and was good at. Instead of teaching himself to read more slowly, he just wanted to practice his ground stroke. He told me in a fairly straightforward way that he still wasn't working with the SAT books because he couldn't stop playing tennis. The child in him seemed always to get its way. I decided to appeal to the adult in him.

Dr. B:	What's your goal Jason?
Jason:	*(all perky)* I want to make lots of money.
Dr. B:	Sounds great. How are you going to do that?
Jason:	Land a terrific job. I want to be a stockbroker.
Dr. B:	Right out of high school?
Jason:	No, dude! I need to go college then business school.
Dr. B:	I see. And how are you going to get into college?
Jason:	*(makes an unhappy face)* I need to get a good SAT score.
Dr. B:	Yes, but if you'd rather play tennis …
Jason:	I can take the SAT again in a couple of months.

Dr. B:	What's going to be different in a couple of months?
Jason:	*(thinking)* Not sure.
Dr. B:	Do you mean you'd rather play tennis now, get another lousy SAT score, and then have to go through this all over again in two months?
Jason:	Well, when you put it that way …

At the end of this exchange Jason couldn't help but see that he might as well stop amusing the child and get on track. Now. Not in some amorphous, but inevitable, future. So far, all he ever did was what he wanted to do, when he wanted to do it. My whole message to Jason was that if he kept going that way he could forget about his future. His child, as they all are, was willful and impulsive. Its needs were clear-cut and immediate. *I want to play tennis. I don't want to study. I want to do what's fun.* If he stayed stuck in this pattern of pleasing the child that is where he would end up—stuck. I could imagine him growing older and becoming an aimless and defeated man, drowning in a swampy miasma of addictive behavior, failed attempts and lost opportunities.

In the step-by-step exercise starting on page 108, we used goal-orientated logic. You asked yourself: *Is this distraction going to help me reach my goal?* Goal-oriented logic works, and I encourage you to use it whenever you're having trouble stopping a distraction. It forces you to take the consequences of your actions seriously. When you really face what will happen if you continue to veer off course, the alternative—stopping the distraction—starts to look a whole lot better. You're teaching the child the value and necessity of delayed gratification. You're saying, "Let's do this right. Then we can do what we want and feel good about ourselves."

To recap, when you become distracted and unfocused use the first tool: **Stop! and ask yourself,** *Is this distraction going to help me reach my goal?*

The answer will be "No!"

Now you are ready for the second tool.

TOOL #2: Listen

Stopping the distraction is only the first tool. You need a second tool that will redirect your actions toward your goal. The following exercise will introduce you to the second tool for staying focused.

EXERCISE: Listening to Your Spirit

Sit comfortably in a chair. Breathe in and out and close your eyes.

Envision yourself having a goal. It can be the same goal you were working on in the last exercise or a different one. Let's say it's to finish studying a chapter.

See yourself working toward your goal. You see yourself reading and memorizing.

Now see yourself becoming distracted. The phone rings. You move toward it.

Now use the first tool, **stop**. You see a stop sign, a stoplight, a hand goes up, or an alarm signal goes off. You stop the distraction. You don't get up from your chair.

Ask yourself the question, **"Is this distraction leading me to my goal?"** The answer is "No." You let the call go to voice mail.

Breathe out.

Now, use the second tool.

Listen to the voice inside that's telling you exactly what you need to do to reconnect with your goal. Perhaps the voice is saying something like, "Go back to the spot you were reading when the phone rang and continue from there."

After you listen to the message, open your eyes.

The second tool is to **Listen and receive a specific inner direction**. Literally, this means to tune into your inner voice, but when you first try listening, what you'll hear are a lot of voices back and forth. You need to think about what your goal is—let's say, preparing well for a test on Thursday—and listen for how to connect to it, stay focused on it and tune out the rest. Something inside you knows exactly what you need to be doing right now to prepare for that test.

Of course, that test isn't the most significant goal in your life, but it is important, and as such it is connected to your highest self—your spirit—which is operating in even the smallest decisions that are made all along the way as you strive to meet your life goal.

Each one of us has this inner voice offering us helpful, explicit directions all the time, and it doesn't just have to be in an academic setting. Joanne has been thinking about an old friend for months, and the voice inside says, *Call him*. Roger is struggling with which dentist to choose, and the voice says, *Pick the one your friends like*.

Marjorie is massaging a client's shoulder and the voice says, *Work deeply in this spot.* This voice is coming from their spirit. It is an inner directive that is always broadcasting, responding to life and giving out clear and helpful instructions.

In that chorus of voices inside our heads, there are bound to be conflicting messages. Sometimes everyone seems to be talking at once. I am well aware that some people do things that are hurtful and destructive, then say that they were listening to their inner voice. In its mildest form, the negative voice promotes bad habits. It tells people to goof off and avoid responsibility. As it grows darker, it represents the call to addiction, urging people to drink, gamble, be sexually unsafe, and take drugs. In its darkest form, it tells people to lie, cheat, steal and kill. This, quite plainly, is the voice of evil.

So how can you tell which one to listen to? You must recognize that out of this chorus, only one is connected to your highest self—your spirit—and it takes discrimination to tell which one. Here's a clue:

The voice of your spirit always guides you towards your highest potential. Trust it.

The voice of your highest self always directs you toward that which is beneficial for you and others, not toward that which causes harm.

Its message guides you in taking the next step, the one that's right in front of you, that will lead you toward your true goals in life. Its voice is connected to the light, telling you how to stay aligned with your highest purpose.

Practically speaking, when you're facing a test, how do you recognize this voice? First, distinguish it from the other voices. Susan, a college sophomore, had to write an essay for a take-home final in her comparative lit class, but she kept being distracted. I asked her to pay attention to all the different voices in her head. She counted seven.

We listed each of them and could see that each was prompting Susan in a different direction.

Voice #	What It Said....	Direction
1	"Write about something easy."	Avoid
2	"Give up, you will never do a good job."	Quit

⇨

3	"Why are you so interested in this anyway?"	Doubt
4	"This is so hard, you don't really want to do it."	Resist
5	"You're not capable of dealing with this difficult material."	Put-down
6	"You are incredible! You can do whatever you set out to do."	Praise
7	"Write down the six most important ideas you must cover."	Act

While none of these voices are "wrong," it is voice #7 you want to listen to because it is offering you a clear direction in the service of your goal.

To prove which is the voice of your spirit, take the scientific approach. Try it out. If this direction serves to bring you back on track then it is the voice of your spirit. If it drives you way from your focus it's not.

After years of coaching people on how to meet their goals, I am convinced that every one of us has this voice and is the benefactor of its signals. Whether we listen to it and follow its direction is another matter altogether.

If you are having trouble grasping what this inner voice is, I'll give you a way of understanding it. Here's what I tell my clients.

First, take the initials to your full name and write them down in big capital letters on a piece of paper. Mine are BBB. What are yours? Write them here:

_____

Next, if you live east of the Mississippi put a **W** in front of your initials, and if you live west of the Mississippi put a **K** in front.

What do you get?

For me, I'm **KBBB** in California and **WBBB** in New York.

What does that sound like?

You're right. It's a radio station. It's your own *personal* radio station.

That is "the voice." It is your own private frequency, being broadcast to you, inside of you and no one else, 24-7-365, and always there to guide you. The mind is like a radio that is constantly switching back and forth between stations. When you turn it on, you'll hear a lot of voices from the various stations, but only one of them is your own personal radio station that broadcasts from your spirit.

You too have your own voice-of-your-spirit radio station, and when you set your dial squarely on your own frequency, you receive a good clear signal that tells you how to stay focused on what's important in your life, right now. It might be major—telling you to check with your doctor immediately about that uncomfortable feeling in your chest, or minor—prompting you to choose an elective for next semester. Usually, people think about higher self as the part of themselves that deals with the mega-questions in life like, "Why am I here? What is the meaning of it all?" But life is made up of ordinary activities, and activities are actually choices that will lead you in a certain direction—either toward your highest potential or toward a life of stagnation and downright destruction. That's why it is so important to listen to your inner voice during all the little challenges, choices and tests that come your way. Every decision you make either contributes to your growth or it takes away from your growth.

Your spirit is broadcasting helpful directions 24-7-365. Stay tuned to that station!

People describe the experience of this helpful, growth-producing voice in different ways. Either it calms them down, or they just *know* that what they are being told is the right thing to do, or they feel peaceful because it has put an end to the inner fighting, or they feel empowered because they realize that if they follow the voice they will be successful.

Listening to this voice isn't always easy. Sometimes we treat it like a snooze alarm—we let it wake us up for a moment, and then, as soon as the going gets tough, we fall back asleep and revert to our old ways. Frank was studying for a civil service licensing exam, which he had to pass if he wanted a promotion. His inner voice would tell him to stop surfing the web for his favorite blogs and shopping and get back to hitting the books, but after a while he refused to listen to it. He needed a stronger message, one that would jolt his spirit into action. One day it said, "Frank! If you keep shopping on e-Bay instead of studying, someone else is going to get this promotion and you'll be stuck in the same old dead-end job. Is that what you want?" *This* message he heard. He knuckled down and studied, and he passed the test. Sometimes a garden variety message works—"Don't turn on your cell phone"—and at other times we need something more forceful—"Pay attention to the path you're on or you're going to drive over a cliff!" When you hear a strong, forceful communication whose purpose can only be to get you back on track, you know it connects to your spirit.

I said above that it wasn't necessarily easy to listen to this voice. But why wouldn't you want to? Clearly it has your best interest at heart. One would think we would all be thrilled to have such free guidance. Naturally, each person has his or her own unique resistance to it, but there are three difficulties I have found to be common to almost everyone. The first is *entitlement* and it comes in the form of, "Why can't I just do what I want to do? Why do I have to listen to this if it's telling me to take on hardships or to face a task that is frustrating and difficult?" Second, there is the *need to be in control*. "I don't want to follow your guidance. I want to decide for myself." And the third form of resistance is *apathy*. "Why should I bother," the person says, shrugging his shoulders. "It's useless. I'll never make it anyway."

In all three cases, the person is pushing the voice away and refusing to accept its presence, support and guidance, partly because he doesn't recognize its importance. It's as if Albert Einstein is trying to tell you something about how the universe works, but you just blow him off. What do people do when they don't like what the voice says? They start flipping the dial on the radio trying to find a different station—a "better" message, "This is more palatable. This is something I like doing and it will make me feel good right now." Switching tracks might work with your iPod, but it won't work with your spirit. It is good to know, however, that even if you change stations, your spirit will keep right on broadcasting. You may not be tuned into it, but it will never leave you.

Whenever my clients fall prey to this kind of resistance, I ask them, "Who are you really fighting here?" Invariably they realize that when they fight off listening to "the voice," they are not hurting anyone but themselves. Again, this can relate even to the small things. Late at night sometimes, I'm on my way to bed and haven't brushed my teeth. My inner voice says, "You need to brush and floss," but I respond with, *No, I'm too tired.* The voice tries again, and if I'm really grumpy I say, *Leave me alone! It's just this one time!* But after a few minutes I realize, *Who am I arguing with? Whose teeth are going to rot? If I don't take care of them, who is going to have to sit in the dentist's chair for hours and pay an enormous bill for the privilege?* That's when I listen. It is the question that makes me pay attention.

The point here is this: when you don't listen to the voice of your spirit, you hurt yourself. It doesn't matter if you like what the voice says. It does matter that you hear it and see the inner direction being pointed out to you without arguing with it, making it wrong, or wishing it were different. Just listen. If you really do that one thing, you will recognize its value and appreciate that it is leading you to the right actions.

TOOL #3: Fulfill

Just listening to your inner voice is not enough. You have to follow through by heading in the direction it is telling you to take. In other words, take action in line with your highest self. The third tool then is: ***fulfill your purpose*** by visualizing and then taking action on the message you've just received.

This is how I coach my clients to use this tool. The exercise reviews the first two tools and then introduces the new one:

 EXERCISE: Fulfilling Your Purpose

Close your eyes and breathe in and out three times.

Imagine your goal. You have to finish reading a novel for an English exam. See yourself diligently working toward it. You are highly focused, and you feel enlivened and empowered.

Now you see yourself become distracted by a desire. You're hungry for ice cream. You want to go to the refrigerator. Immediately use the first tool: **Stop!** Look what you're doing. Ask yourself: **Is this action helping me to reach my goal?** Answer: "No."

Now use the second tool: **Listen.** Your inner voice is telling you exactly how to get back on track. What does it say? "Stand up. Give your body one good stretch and go back to Chapter Five.

Now here is the third tool: **Fulfill.** Do what the voice is telling you to do. Act now. Don't give yourself time to resist. Stand up. Stretch your arms above your head, take a deep breath and remember why the goal is important in the larger scheme of things. Now sit down and start reading again. By re-connecting to your bigger goal, you place the desire of inserting something sweet into your mouth in perspective. It's just a momentary desire. A much deeper form of fulfillment will come from heading in the direction in which your spirit is sending you.

We already discussed why people don't follow their inner voice and act out what is in their best interest: sheer resistance. However, there are also reasons why people don't make the effort to follow through on a goal that they already know they want to achieve. One is that they are lured into the easier task of *thinking* about doing something and they never make the transition to actually *doing* it. A famous New Age group leader once told people to "try to pick up a pencil." Naturally, everyone simply picked up the pencil on their desk. Then he said, "No, I didn't tell you to pick it up. I told you to *try* to pick it up." And so everyone sat there and stared at the pencil and tried, without doing. It's the same thing with endlessly thinking about studying, but not studying. In the end, it all boils down to action. You don't score points for thinking about accomplishing a goal. Anyone can do that—lying on the couch, watching cartoons, eating Doritos. You only cross the goal line when you act on your intentions.

Two: people have trouble with this because it means—horror of horrors—change! We are comfortable with our old habits and we love our neat, predictable little world (even though it may be completely unsatisfying). Change can be scary and unpleasant. We get used to following the fluffier thoughts, the ones that tell us to take it easy and not exert ourselves. And the older most of us grow, the more entrenched we get. That's why thoughts are so very, very important – in the end they determine the course of our lives. There is an old saying: "Thought becomes deed. Deed becomes habit. Habit becomes character. Character becomes a lifetime." Be careful what you think because thoughts, which may seem fleeting and meaningless at the time, actually establish pathways in the brain, and then future thoughts just want to follow those well worn neural pathways, and then we never change. Our spirit wants us to do something else, to reach our highest potential, and we can't do that if we just fall into step with the same old thoughts and don't let ourselves grow.

Three: people don't actively go after the goals that their inner voice has led them to because they aren't practiced at being self-directed. We spend half our lives being told what to do by others—our boss, the IRS, the meter maid, the class teacher. That's not really a problem; it's just the way it is. The problem only comes when we forget how to tune into our deepest self also. We cannot let ourselves become automatons and just fall into lockstep with the rest of the culture. We have to *fit in*, but we don't have to lose ourselves. Sometimes we tune out from our inner voice because we have, in the past, felt betrayed by authority and don't want to listen to *anyone* anymore: we don't believe they have our best interests at heart. But then we also tune out the one authority that is really on our side and wants us to be happy, the voice of our highest self. We hear an inner voice telling us how to get back on track but don't follow it. I call that putting God on hold. God calls us on the phone and we say, "Excuse me Lord, but I've got another call coming in. Can I put you on hold?" Then you put the receiver down. Permanently.

EXCUSES, LAMENTS, PROTESTS... AND AN ANTIDOTE

Before closing out this chapter, let's look at some other ways people resist setting goals and staying focused. It's important to cover every angle of resistance because resistance is the one thing that can stop you cold. You can have the best intentions in the world, but you will find yourself dead in the water if you don't examine what's getting in your way. I've met many people with big dreams and I run into them years later and they're still stuck in the same job. They haven't lifted a finger to reach their goals. I'm here to help you spot the roadblocks so you can maneuver around them. I am going over every possible act of resistance so you can recognize yourself in here somewhere.

You Can't Make Me

As I mentioned above, we human beings get told what to do a lot, and many of us have a natural resistance to it. Obeying is for dogs, not for us. When my friend Megan tells her spirited 2-year-old not to eat another cookie, little Jenny turns right around and does it anyway. But when Megan tells their dog J.J. to come here, he is at her feet in a second. Dogs are supposed to obey. People sitting in an exam room trying to stay focused don't realize that they resent being treated like a dog. "Sit! Stay! Fill in blanks!" What's their response? "You can't make me!" Whenever I hear people complain that they can't concentrate, I notice that they usually blame something or someone outside themselves—a noise in the yard, a parent who expects a lot, or a teacher who didn't speak their language. Their real problem is that they haven't learned how to listen to their inner authority, the voice of their own spirit.

The most important thing you're being told to do when you're taking a test is to concentrate. The very word *concentrate* conjures up a stern, gnarly schoolteacher straight out of a Dickens novel who's going to whack you on the knuckles if your mind wanders. This is why I use the word *focus* instead. When you concentrate, you are forcing your mind to do something it probably doesn't want to do. The truth is that it is not in the mind's nature to concentrate. Typically, it wanders all over the place, from a fragment of a song, to what you had for breakfast, to criticism over some flimsy comeback in an argument, to a fantasy about the upcoming weekend. Keeping your mind on one track is like walking a pack of dogs that all want to run in different directions. The moment you pull one into line, another one runs off. Holding them together is hard work and eventually it wears you out. You can keep yelling at the dogs, of course, but after a while they'll stop listening to you. It's better to encourage them gently to cooperate.

Contrast concentrating, which is harsh, to focusing, which is nurturing. When you try to concentrate, you feel as if you're forcing yourself to do something that somebody else expects of you. When you focus, however, your actions are self-directed. You are cooperating with yourself. You know that your goal is important and it has arisen from your spirit. The word *focus* comes from the Latin root that means "hearth" or "fireplace." The hearth is the center of the home, a gathering place of warmth and light and sustenance. In our model, focus has these qualities. To succeed in the exam room, your goals have to come from *your* center, the fireplace of your being, your spirit. When you stay focused, you are feeding and sustaining the fire, which generates energy and nourishment.

I teach students to focus because it is a supportive way of working toward a goal. Unfortunately, what most of us have learned in the school system is to concentrate, which is coercive. So ask yourself, what kind of relationship do you want with yourself? Do you want your inner world to feel like—excuse the pun—a prison? Or do you want to feel empowered and energized? Do you want to crack the whip and force your mind to stay on track, or do you want to support yourself through a process of growth? Concentrating is oppressive; focusing promotes fulfillment. And an added benefit is that staying focused is actually a lot easier once you learn to do it.

Even if achieving a higher grade is your own goal, and not someone else telling you what to do, it might still be hard to stay focused. That's because there is another kind of authority that we all have to submit to, not a person but a process. Any path that is fraught with difficulties and inconveniences (and tests), even when you really want that goal yourself, will be met with some resistance. Whenever you focus, you have to submit to a process. It is the goal itself that dictates what actions have to be taken, not you. If it were up to you, you'd make it all as easy as possible. For example, let's say you want to learn the butterfly stroke in swimming. You have to become skilled at the chain of movements with your legs, arms and torso. You can't just wing it and only work with your legs. If you want to achieve excellence at the butterfly stroke, the goal itself spells out the process, one that has its own rules. Honoring those rules takes focus. It doesn't matter if you feel like it or not. If you don't stay focused, the whole enterprise falls apart.

Whatever the reason for the lack of focus, test taking is the one situation in which you cannot afford to let your attention wander all over the place because almost every test is timed. The clock is ticking and you have to prove what you know before the examiner tells you to put your pencil down. If your attention is wandering, you will lose valuable time, time that you cannot make up later. Consequently, resistance to paying attention only hurts your performance. Listening to and following the authority of your own spirit will help you enormously, especially if you practice it during study time because not only are you building your fund of information for the test, but you are training yourself to focus in the right way and to use time efficiently. This will be particularly important during the difficult parts of the test when your attention really has to be pinpointed. The more you learned to stay focused during the preparation period, the easier it will be to do when it really counts.

Great athletes are one-pointed when they compete. That focus comes from practice, practice, practice.

"I Don't Want to Work for It"

It takes work to be able to stay focused, and these days most people don't want to—work—at anything. They want success handed to them. If the first problem was a resistance to authority, the second major problem many people have with staying focused is that they want easy results without a lot of effort.

Children are far more apt to be truthful about this. By the time we reach adulthood, however, we realize how silly the attitude is—and yet somewhere in the back of our minds we entertain it anyway. If you want to know whether this applies to you, examine your goals and the actions they inspire. Do you consistently work toward your goals or do you imagine you can cross the finish line without running the race? The problem with fantasizing that it should all be easy is that whenever you hit a speed bump, you will back off. "I'm not having fun. Where's the pleasure in this?" Then you start wondering, "Am I on the right track? I didn't think this would be so hard. If it is this hard now, does that mean I haven't got the stamina to stay the course? And if I do go through all this, will the rewards really justify all this work?"

If you have ever found yourself thinking like this, don't be too hard on yourself. You are surrounded by a culture that is obsessed with quick success. "Earn your first million before you turn twenty-five." It doesn't ask what you will do to earn that million or if the job will be rewarding along the way. The culture is goal-oriented, but in all the wrong ways. It is completely preoccupied with the end product, and not focused on the path to the product. We strive for our high school diploma to attend a good college, rush through the undergraduate years to move on to graduate school. Then we send out CV's and land a job and then...and then...and then...

Why is it that we never appreciate the whole process? Studying and taking classes and learning the material and performing on tests—all this represents growth *in and of itself*. Because we aren't taught to value work for its own sake, we just plain miss the entire journey. In other words, we aren't in school for the love of learning, but for the ultimate paycheck.

But growth occurs along the way, not the moment we cross the finish line. As we meet and face the challenges—all the tests of life—we grow stronger and smarter. Remember the seed packet? The seed grows because you attend to it; you don't just drop it in the ground then up pops a prize-winning flower. The same is true for any area of life. If you want to build tight abs you can't just renew your subscription to *Muscle* magazine and end up with a six-pack. You have to lift weights three times a week for months. Of course, rippling muscles are a great reward, but it's the *process* that counts. If you don't want to put in the effort but just yearn for the result, you are caught in an enormous cultural problem.

The roots of this problem, and why it shows up in test taking, lies in the fact that the school system, which is the first public institution we belong to, fosters a get-it-over-with mentality. It doesn't say, "Immerse yourself in the process." We move robotically through years of doing assignments, writing papers and taking tests. The material often does not interest us and we find no personal meaning in it. For many people, school is merely an irritant and very few learn what it means to connect with their spirit, to be self-initiating and self-directed. We are trained to get through the material just to pass the test at the end. A rather astounding example of this occurred recently during a talk I gave at a dental school. I showed the third-year students slides of dentists whose bad posture while working on patients had led to chronic pain. The point was simply to raise the students' awareness about their own posture so as to help them avoid debilitating consequences in the future. At the end of the talk one of the students came up to me and asked, "How much of this is going to be on the test?" It never occurred to her that I was addressing the quality of her *life*, not asking her to memorize material. I felt like saying, *"All* of it. The test is the rest of your professional career."

To succeed at tests, cultivate your ability to focus.

What goes on in schools is unfortunate because focusing *can* be taught. I believe that it is a skill that is learned under the right conditions and with the right practice. Like any skill, it can be cultivated, but it needs an educational system that values it.

When I trained as a teacher in London in the late '60s, I saw this first-hand. The progressive schools I worked in allowed children to spend their days in stimulating activities of their own choosing, thoughtfully set up by the teachers. I saw little kids sew costumes for plays which they staged, bake cookies and create a store in which to sell them, and build model boats to sail them in tubs, writing stories of their great adventures. In the course of these activities the children learned all the important cognitive skills: reading, writing and arithmetic. But the vehicle for learning wasn't slow and dull or forced down their throats. They learned to tune into their spirit, and from that place they became engaged and responsible.

It is regrettable that the American school system hasn't followed this model. The system often works against cultivating the spirit, and this failure shows up in the attitude of the students. Last year, I spent a few months observing the day-to-day life in a third-grade public school classroom and it only confirmed my worst fears. Just from simple observations of the children and the teacher (who had years of experience), I estimated that 75 percent of her time was spent asking, cajoling, and threatening the children to be quiet. And when she was attending to one child, what were the rest doing? Whenever she wasn't looking, the kids were pulling out hidden treasures in their pockets, fiddling with their clothing, passing notes back and forth, and whispering to their neighbors. As soon as the teacher glanced in their direction, they sprang back to the task at hand. What were they learning? How to fool the teacher, how to hide their real interests, and how to time their actions so they wouldn't get caught. A large number weren't doing any work at all and didn't seem to understand that they were there to learn something. One little girl pleaded with me secretly in a tiny whisper, "Tell me the answers, *please.*"

We train these little kids, sometimes by default, not to follow an inner directive, but to do what they're told, to do whatever is necessary to get approval, to give the right answer, to receive a passing grade, to be awarded a degree, and finally, to get *out*. With billions of dollars being spent on education, how much attention do most students pay to what is being taught? And how does "learning" in the third-grade classroom play out at the other end of the educational system? To answer this I've sat in the back of university lecture halls and observed what students are actually doing during lectures. Here are just some of the things I've seen:

* Texting or tweeting each other or someone outside of class

* Checking messages on cell phones

* Going over bills

* Doing e-mail on iPhones phones and Blackberrys

* Amending day planners

* Reviewing for quizzes and taking practice exams

* Eating

* Talking (not even whispering)

* Braiding hair

* Playing Scrabble on a handheld device (with three other people!)

* Daydreaming

* Manipulating an iPod

* Working on a crossword puzzle

* Picking teeth

* Spreading and reading the newspaper in full view of the lecturer

* Manicuring and polishing nails

* Sleeping

* Asking a question for which they already know the answer to make it look like they did the assignment

* Asking a question not related to the subject so that the professor won't call on them to answer a question about the subject at hand

* Updating my Facebook wall

It is worth noting that some of these graduate students were training to be healthcare professionals, which means that when they miss out on crucial information because they're checking cell phones or texting a friend during a lecture or twittering, later on someone in their care might die. They need to learn to pay attention, *now*.

By the time most of these students have reached university level, they've figured out how to ace the system, how to do the least amount of work at the last possible moment, and how to spit back the required information again and again until they escape. So little of what they're doing is related to what's inside them; it's as if the educational system has told their spirit to take a hike. No wonder you often hear graduates say they need to "find themselves"—they've been lost for fifteen years.

When a person's goals are cut off from her spirit, she ends up disliking the whole process of working; this is what ultimately causes disconnection and alienation in the workplace. And it all starts in school where she was taught to cram and get through. The cost is incalculable, not only to the individual, but to society.

Cram-and-get-through has a profoundly negative effect on taking tests because we have been conditioned for years to focus on the end product, not the moment we're in. To be successful on a test, you have to be present in the moment, to be committed and fully engaged in the task at hand. What is *this* question asking of me? This—and no other. Most students have had no real training at this, and suddenly they are expected to be riveted to the material when the test is thrust in front of them. No wonder there is so much anxiety at test time. Obsessing about the goal line causes anxiety because the person isn't thinking about the question in front of him, but is entertaining catastrophic thoughts about what will happen after the test if his answers are wrong. These students just never learned how to focus. They are disconnected.

SEE YOURSELF AS YOU CAN BE

Guided imagery is like a strong, sturdy ship. It will carry you through storms.

To cap off this chapter I am going to lead you through a sophisticated and powerful exercise that will help you stay connected to your highest purpose. It's called the **Three-Way Mirror**. Read through it and then close your eyes and do the exercise. Or you can have a friend read the exercise to you as you work through it step by step. Take your time with each instruction before you move on to the next one. To remind you not to rush through the exercises, I have placed three symbols (⊛ ⊛ ⊛) at periodic intervals. This exercise will take about fifteen minutes. Find a quiet place. Turn off your telephone, cell phone, pager and laptop. Feed the cat. Put a *Do Not Disturb* sign on the door.

 EXERCISE: Three-Way Mirror, Part I

Sit comfortably in a chair. Make sure your back is well supported and that you aren't slouching. You should be sitting up straight but not rigidly. Uncross your arms and legs. Put your feet flat on the floor and rest a palm on each thigh.

Breathe naturally, feeling your breath go in and out. Breathe as deeply down to your belly as you can without forcing the breath.

Close your eyes and continue breathing naturally.

Feel yourself supported by the chair you are sitting on. The chair is solid, yet comfortable beneath you. Now, feel the floor supporting the chair. Let yourself be fully supported by the chair and the floor.

Breathe deeply, into your belly. Release the breath on a long exhale.

Breathe in deeply and exhale slowly three times.

⇨

Now, we are going to extend this process. Keeping your eyes closed, imagine yourself looking at a large numeral 3, written on a blackboard in front of you.

Once you have seen it, let it dissolve. As you breathe out naturally, let it go.

Now see the numeral 2 written on the board. Again, see it clearly.

Now let it dissolve. As you breathe out, let it go.

And now see the numeral 1. It is big and bright and bold. See it in front of you, facing you, reflecting you. Feel yourself as big, as bright, and as bold as the numeral 1.

Once you've done this, breathe out naturally, and let it the image dissolve.

Now see the numeral 0. Imagine yourself floating through the center of the 0, and emerging into a field of light, sky blue.

As you breathe in, imagine this light blue color flowing into you and gently filling your whole body. Breathe it in deeply, letting it go to every corner of your whole body.

Now see yourself in front of a three-way mirror. You've probably seen one in a clothing store. There is a panel on your right, one in front of you and one on your left.

Continue breathing naturally as you turn your attention to the mirror on the left.

The reflection there is what you look like when you feel defeated. The sentences you say to yourself start with *I can't… I don't… I'm not… I can't do well… I don't have what it takes… I'm not good enough.*

What does your image look like? Notice its posture. It is probably hunched over or slouching. What does this image feel like? Likely unhappy or discouraged. Get a clear experience of the image in the left-hand mirror.

Breathe in and out and let this image dissolve. Now leave that side and turn your attention to the mirror on the right.

This reflection is what you look like when you are self-assured. The sentences you say start with *I can... I do...* and I am... I can *succeed, I do know what I need for this test, I am sufficient just as I am.* This is the image of your highest self.

Get a good sense of what the image on the right looks and feels like to you. Again, notice its posture. Is it upright and ready for action? Positive? Enthusiastic? Get a clear experience of *I can, I do, I am.*

Now, turn your attention to your breath again. Breathe in and out a few times and let the image dissolve.

Open your eyes.

This ends the first part of the exercise.

Before going on to Part II of the exercise, let's take stock of what you just did. Like everyone else, you carry around two images of yourself. As you saw and experienced, there is a dramatic difference between the images in the left and right mirrors. The one on the left is deflated, lacks energy and is generally discouraged. The one on the right is motivated, determined and hopeful. It is the image of your highest potential.

Most people don't realize that they carry these inner mirrors with them all the time. Moreover, they don't know that their actions—what they do in the course of their daily lives—are actually reflections of these images. If we act in ways that are productive, positive and full of zest, chances are we are under the influence of an "inner image" of ourselves in the right mirror. Conversely, if we tend to act in ways that are discouraged, defeated and disconnected, we are being influenced by the image in the left mirror.

The key is for you to *strengthen your connection to the mirror on the right.* Here's where the third mirror comes in, the one in the middle.

Get ready to begin again. You might want to get up and take a brief stretch and then have a glass of water to refresh yourself before starting the second part of the exercise. Now, let's move on and see how to establish a solid, steady, working relationship with the mirror on the right.

EXERCISE: Three-Way Mirror, Part II

Sit comfortably upright in the chair. Uncross your arms and legs.

Place your feet flat on the floor, one palm on each thigh.

Breathe naturally, in and out, and close your eyes.

See again the image on the left, and then the image on the right.

Now turn your attention to the mirror in the center.

The image in this mirror is you, just as you are right now.

Ask yourself this question: "Do I want to be like the image in the left mirror or like that in the right mirror?"

Make the conscious choice, right now, to turn to the mirror on your right and align yourself with that image of being vital, positive and full of energy. See yourself being focused, achieving your goals and being successful. See yourself being just like the image on the right.

Now, let's strengthen your connection with the image on the right in two easy steps.

First, see the image on the right giving you positive coaching and encouragement. It may say something to you like, "You can do it. You've got what it takes. You are definitely capable." What is your image saying to you? Listen. What personal message does it have for you?

Sense and feel yourself accepting that message, taking it in, assimilating it. Let the message become part of you.

Next, you are going to create a bond with the image on the right. You can create a bond by *words* ("I promise to stay connected with you"), a *physical gesture* (you and the image are shaking hands or embracing one another) or a *feeling* (of closeness or love).

What kind of bond do you want to create with your image on the right?

Whatever it might be, create that bond right now.

Once you have created the bond, repeat to yourself,

*It is my **intention** to keep my connection to this mirror.*

*It is my **responsibility** to reflect this mirror in my thoughts, speech and actions.*

*It is my **determination** to make my life a reflection of this image.*

See yourself, in your daily life, focusing on the image in the right hand mirror and living your life in the ways that keep your connection to it.

When you are *studying* for a test, see yourself connecting to the image in the mirror on the right.

When you are *taking* the test, see yourself always connecting with the mirror on the right.

After the test is over, see yourself staying connected with the mirror on the right.

Breathe deeply, in and out, one more time and then open your eyes.

This is the end of the exercise.

Practice the Three-Way Mirror once a day, especially before a test. By continually choosing to connect with the mirror on your right, and reflecting it in your daily actions, you are going to act in ways that are consistent with achieving your goals. In other words, you are going to be focused.

USING THE FOCUS TOOLS

While You Are Studying

While you are studying is a good time to train yourself to stay focused and not be derailed by distraction. Follow these guidelines and your study time will be effective practice time for using the Focus tools. This will help ensure the tools are there for you when you take a test.

Set a study goal for yourself and make it SMART. Review that section of the chapter if you haven't absorbed it.

Clear your space of distraction: phones off, e-mail off, TV off, music off (unless music really helps you stay focused).

Set your timer for 30-40 minutes and then study, study, study. Take a short break (five minutes: no big distractions!). Do another round of studying. Take a short break. Repeat the cycle one more time and then take a longer break.

If you become distracted during your study time use the tools: *Stop* the distraction (if it's a thought, or something you are doing, or someone who has come into your space). Know that this thought, activity or person is not helping you to your goal. *Listen* to your inner voice. It will tell you exactly what you need to do to reconnect to your studying. *Fulfill* the direction of the voice: do it!

When you practice using the Focus tools while studying, you are ensuring they will work for you when you take the test.

While You Are Taking a Test

When you take a test your job is to take the test. This may sound like a "Duh!" to you, but think about it. How often, when you've been taking a test, do you become distracted by other people's movements or your own thoughts or the cramps in your belly?

If you have used the Focus tools when you were studying you are much more aware of the ways you become distracted. The most common distractions while people take tests are:

Be one-pointed, then distraction cannot derail you.

✳ Unpleasant physical sensations. *My heart is pumping so hard. I can't breathe!*

✳ Negative thoughts. *I can't handle this! I'm going to fail.*

✳ Watching other people and thinking about what they are doing. *I bet she understands every question. I wonder how far along he is?*

✳ Your attention needs to be on the question in front of you and nothing else.

If you have trained yourself to use the Calm and Confidence tools you can get yourself right back on track when your body or your mind starts disconnecting. You will recognize the unpleasant physical sensations or the negative thinking, and you will apply the tools.

Consider that disconnection in your body and in your mind are actually distractions. Now use the Focus tools: **Stop** the distraction. **Listen** to the voice (*"Get back to the question"*). **Fulfill** it by taking action (work on the question and answer in a step-by-step fashion).

In other words, use the Focus tools to stay in the present and answer the questions. The best performers in any field know how to stay focused. Now you do too. Put it all into play.

SUMMING UP, MOVING ON

Focusing takes time, determination and energy. But the payoff is big. You strengthen yourself in the process and you make your dreams come true. The Focus tools will serve you well past your time in school. My youngest brother, Richard, a superb opera singer, is a case in point. After his training he set a goal to sing at the Metropolitan Opera in New York City before he was thirty years old. That image was his mirror on the right. It was his polestar, his focus. Every action he took was directed to his goal and nothing distracted him from it. His higher spirit was calling to him and he listened to it every step of the way. When the best vocal coach in New York City was too busy to work with him, he kept telephoning daily until a space opened up. When he couldn't get an audition he found a way to convince other important people to hear him. Every roadblock served to strengthen his fortitude and determination even more because he had a clear image of the picture on his seed packet, of who he really was. This took years of hard work and many tests of faith, but he stuck with it, and we all rooted for him.

Two months after his twenty-ninth birthday our family proudly sat in the audience at the Metropolitan Opera house, awaiting his entrance as Zuniga, the captain, in Act I of *Carmen*. When he boldly strode onto the stage to make his impressive debut we had to contain ourselves from crying out *Bravo! You did it!* even before he sang a note. As the curtain finally came down we stood up and cheered. He had made his dream into a reality.

When you learn to focus—when your actions are in line with your goals and your goals come from your spirit—you can successfully face any test, and you will fulfill your highest potential. The great American philosopher Henry David Thoreau said it passionately, "Go confidently in the direction of your dreams. Live the life you imagined."

Claim your birthright.

As it says in an ancient, sacred text, "If not now, when?"

QUICK CHECK: Focus

When you are studying for a test…

❏ Define your goal (make sure it's yours!).

❏ Specify the action steps you need to take to reach the goal.

Become aware

❏ Are you becoming distracted into activities other than studying?

Use the tools

❏ **Stop** and look at what you are doing. Ask yourself, "Is this action getting me to my goal?" Admit that you are distracted.

❏ **Listen** to the inner voice. What specific direction is it giving you?

❏ **Fulfill** your spirit by taking the action that leads you back to your purpose, to studying.

When you are taking a test…

Become aware

❏ Notice that your attention is starting to wander.

Use the tools

❏ **Stop** and look at what you are doing. Admit that you are distracted. Ask yourself, "Is this helping me reach my goal of completing the test?"

❏ **Listen** to the inner voice. What specific direction is it giving you?

❏ **Fulfill** your spirit and take the action that leads you to reconnect with the test and doing what is necessary to accomplish your goal.

See yourself in the mirror on the right.
Hear its message and bond with that image.
Then take action.

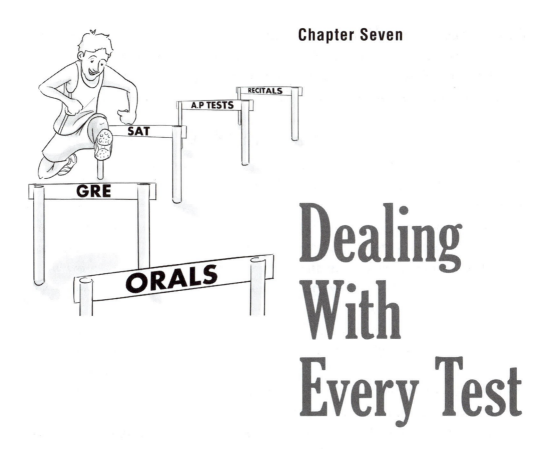

Chapter Seven

Dealing With Every Test

When I was a freshman in college I joined the cross-country running team. I wasn't into athletics, but I was required to join a team so I chose cross-country. Before our first interscholastic meet the coach drew a map of the trail, which wound its way around the eighteen holes of a local golf course. He warned us about the sudden twists and turns through the woods. Figuring that I could just keep my eyes on the runner in front of me, I didn't pay close attention to what the coach was saying. After the race started, I soon fell behind and after twenty minutes of running, to my surprise I found that there was no one in front of me. I was totally lost. I ran around in circles through the woods and onto the greens. By the time I found my way to the finish line everyone was on the bus impatiently waiting to go home.

The moral: pay attention to your coach's advice about what lies ahead.

In this chapter we'll look at the different kinds of tests you might face and how to apply what you've learned so far.

PAPER-AND-PEN TESTS

This is the largest category and includes school tests, quizzes, midterms, finals, writing samples and standardized tests. They all have the same set-up: you sit at a desk, questions are handed out along with an exam booklet or answer sheet, and you have a limited time to answer the questions and complete the test (I bet even *reading* this makes some people nervous). To ensure a higher score follow these steps.

1. Use the Tools

Create a secure platform for your performance by calming yourself immediately when you sit down in the exam room. Write the word BREATHE somewhere on the exam book or answer sheet, since it will prompt you to remember to keep breathing. Watch how you are sitting and keep grounding yourself. Sit up straight and put both your feet on the floor. I've seen people tie themselves up like pretzels—hunched over, feet twisted around chair legs, foreheads scrunched, jaws clenched. None of this feeds performance. Sit up in your chair. Release the tension in your body. Let gravity work.

Before you enter the exam room breathe deeply down to your belly and feel your feet on the floor.

Preview the test by looking it over so you know what's coming. If you start feeling or saying something negative about yourself—*I can't, I don't, I'm not*—then immediately apply the tools for keeping yourself confident. Go to the mirror, confide in your confidant, get the positive reflection about yourself, and envision yourself taking small, manageable steps. You will see each step you need to take—read the question again, underline important points, and so forth.

As you read this you might be thinking, "But Dr. B, I don't have *time* for all of this on the test!" This is a common concern, but it's not valid. If you've practiced the tools in the last three chapters, then by the time you arrive at the test you'll know how to use them quickly and efficiently. They take a lot longer to describe than to do. You are much more likely to waste time becoming anxious and fretting if you *don't* use these tools. Remember, fretting and anxiety are signs of disconnection. You want to connect to yourself again as soon as you can. If you practice using the tools when you are studying, you can count on them when you take the test.

2. Take Breaks

During a test it's essential that you refresh your system periodically by taking mini-breaks. There are a few different ways to do this during an exam without losing a lot of time. Every fifteen minutes rest your eyes for only a few seconds. Gently cup your hands over your eyes, without touching them. Open them in the darkness you've created. Stay in this position, with your hands cupped over your eyes, for about ten seconds. This is called "palming" and is very restful to your vision and your nervous system.

You can alternate palming with opening your peripheral vision. (We did this in Chapter Three.) Keep your head still and roll your eyes slowly in every direction. This takes you out of your sympathetic nervous system (fight-or-flight) and gives you a beneficial dip into your parasympathetic nervous system (calming you down).

Stretching your body is also beneficial. You can stretch in your chair without even getting up. Bend down, head between your legs, and touch the floor with your hands. This restores blood to your head and forces you to breathe. If you're allowed to, stand up, bend over, and touch the floor. Then stand on your tiptoes and bounce up and down on your heels for a few seconds, gently shaking out your arms and hands.

If you take these little stretch breaks quietly you won't disturb anyone around you. I recommend you take a sitting stretch break every half-hour and a standing one every hour.

Remember that you are refreshing your body, reminding it that you know it's there, that you haven't forgotten it. Remember, all of you is involved in the test.

3. Drink Enough Water, Have a Snack

Dehydration is often a problem for test takers. They forget to drink and get dried out, which makes them feel tired. If you can, bring some bottled water into the room. Take small sips regularly. Sometimes exam rooms have a table with pitchers of ice water. I don't recommend drinking ice water; it doesn't have the settling effect on your system that room temperature or warm water does. Also, avoid soft drinks. They are loaded with sugar. If the exam is longer than an hour bring a piece of fruit or health bar in with you. Becoming too hungry and having a drop in blood sugar and energy levels can cause you to lose your attention. You need some fuel in your tank. If you're not allowed to bring food into the exam room (check this a few days before), then have a nourishing breakfast or lunch: favor proteins over carbs and go easy on the coffee.

Nourish your body properly and it will support you.

4. Keep Using the Tools

As the test proceeds continue using the Calm tools: **breathing, grounding and sensing.** If you come across items that are tricky or that you don't immediately know, remember: tests are meant to prompt your thinking as well as your memory, so use the Confidence tools: **confide**, **reflect**, and **envision** small, manageable steps. Often what appears to be an unanswerable question may just be a knot that has to be patiently teased apart until it's unraveled. Breathe. Give yourself the message that you can figure it out, that you *are* figuring it out. If your mind starts wandering or you find yourself engaged in some other activity (biting your nails, playing with your hair, looking around the room), use the Focus tools: **stop** and pay attention to what you're doing, **listen** to your inner voice, and **fulfill** its direction. (You may also need a little stretch or a sip of water.)

5. Keep Your Attention Focused on Yourself

When you are in a room with a lot of other people and you're all taking a test, it's natural to glance around. *What's everyone else doing? Do they think this is easy? Am I the only one here who's nervous? Are they working faster and finishing sooner than I am?* The problem is that all these questions are nibbling away at your concentration on the task at hand. Nothing that anyone else is doing is going to help *you* pass the test.

Think of yourself as sitting inside your own "bubble" with your attention focused on yourself alone. (See the "Circle of Light" exercise at the end of this chapter.) Once a client described an experience that unnerved her. She looked up from her test to see another student handing in his exam booklet after just a half-hour. She thought, *My god, how can he be finished so quickly when I'm only half way through?* This thought made her so anxious that she could barely answer the rest of the questions; she had simply lost faith in herself in the face of someone else's expertise. Only later did she come to find that this person who was so quick was suffering from food poisoning and was forced to leave.

Comparison causes stress. Hold your attention on your own performance.

Whatever you see others doing, let it go. It has nothing to do with you. Focus on what *you* need to do perform at your best.

6. Be Conscious of the Time

Time is a big element of test taking, and you need to be aware of it; budget it wisely so you can finish without feeling rushed. Some programs and schools offer the opportunity to practice taking sample tests. This is particularly helpful with long standardized tests. Every bookstore has volumes of past SATs, GREs, LSATs and the like. Practicing old tests will not only help you understand the content and the way the test is structured, but you'll also understand how to apportion your time. Having a clock or stopwatch is usually helpful, although I have seen that work against people. They become overly fixated on watching their timepiece instead of answering the questions.

7. Deal with the Difficult Questions Skillfully

When you see a question that really does look too difficult at that moment *do not waste time struggling with it*. Figure out what you can, circle the question, and move on. With a paper-and-pencil test, you can always come back to an item later on. Sometimes the mind needs to sit with something before the answer is illuminated. And later questions might shed light on earlier ones. Having a fresh perspective helps. When you do this in combination with using the nine tools, you are setting yourself up to win rather than fail.

LeToya, a bright 16-year-old girl, said, "When I come to a difficult item I feel really nervous, like I'm going forget everything. Then it's really hard to go on." When we analyzed this experience in light of the model, LeToya saw that the feelings in her body crashed with the negativity in her mind. *I get really nervous* collided with *I feel like I'm going to forget everything*. She's telling herself she can't do this and her body is reinforcing the message.

Through the coaching, LeToya learned that when she saw a hard question, the first thing she had to do was to regulate her breathing so her body wouldn't affect her mind. Next, she had to give herself positive, helpful messages. "You can figure this out. You do have experience with items like this." Then she will have the confidence to keep her focus on the question and not be derailed by images of failing. She also learned the value of coming back to the item later. After applying these lessons to two more tests, LeToya's "panic attacks" became nothing more than a distant memory.

COMPUTER TESTS

An increasingly common option for some tests—particularly standardized ones—is to take them on a computer. At the appointed time you report to the test center and you are seated in a cubicle with a computer monitor and the test is administered on the screen. Though the guidelines I've given so far in this chapter are applicable to computer tests, I'll add three things here: (1) Take at least one practice exam on the computer before you take the actual test. How you sit and orient yourself to a computer screen is different from how you work with a piece of paper laying flat on a desk. Practice sitting up, looking at the screen straight ahead of you, operating a mouse, and sitting in a cubicle. (2) Find out before you take the test if you will be able to return to previous questions to reconsider or change answers. On many computer-given tests you are not given that opportunity. On some, the questions get harder or easier depending on your answer to the previous question. Knowing beforehand how the test is structured will eliminate any stress-producing surprises on the day of the exam. (3) Be aware of your *posture*. It's all too easy to slump in the chair or hunch over and lean into the screen, or to sit cross-legged. These restrictive positions aren't conducive to thinking or being responsive. You're not watching TV or playing a video game so don't sit as if you are. Keep your back and neck upright yet not rigid, and have your feet resting on the floor. It's also essential that you rest your eyes on a regular basis. Computer screens are very taxing on the vision.

ORAL EXAMS

Oral exams present their own unique set of challenges. On paper-and-pen and computer tests you are responding to written questions. Someone you may never know or see (or perhaps a computer) scores your answers. With oral exams, on the other hand, you face the examiners in person and you have to speak directly to them; they are grading your performance as you speak, which can be nerve-wracking. For many people just *being seen* turns them into a rag doll. Having to think on the spot and speaking in an articulate manner pushes them to the limit. Quietly sitting alone at a desk with an answer sheet in front of them seems like a piece of cake in comparison.

Oral examiners certainly want to hear how you handle the content, but they also want to see how you present yourself. What happens when you don't have a ready answer? How do you respond when an examiner is impatient, harsh or critical? What do you do when you realize that you've misspoken and need to correct yourself?

Here are my coaching guidelines for oral examinations.

1. Use the Tools and Get Your Bearings

As you enter the exam room and take your seat, immediately use the tools for calming yourself down: **breathe** deeply down to your belly; **ground** yourself in the chair; take in, through your **sense** of sight, what the surrounding room looks like, what the examiners are wearing, and any other details that you pick up. You are staying connected. The *Circle of Light* exercise that closes this chapter will be particularly helpful. Feel yourself sitting in the center of the circle of light. Breathe.

2. Make Sure You Understand the Question

Sometimes questions on oral exams are unclear. Occasionally this is by design —purposely prompting you to ask for clarification. Don't be afraid to say, "Could you restate (or rephrase) the question?" or "Are you asking…" If you are not sure what the question is about it's much better that you ask for clarification than stumble through an answer that may be off the mark.

On some oral exams, the examiners are not allowed to say anything, so asking them a question prompts a blank, sometimes cold stare in reply. This can be very disturbing if you're not prepared for it. Find out before you go into the exam if you can ask for clarification on a question. You can read through the exam guidelines or call or e-mail someone at the exam board. You should always know the ground rules ahead of time. If you are asked a question you are not sure you understand and the examiners aren't allowed to clarify it, it's advisable that you to say, "I think the question is asking…" so the examiners appreciate how you are interpreting it. Sometimes doing this leads you to a better understanding of the question, so don't be afraid of the process. Jump in the pool and start swimming. You *will* get to the other side.

3. Use the Formula that Works: Breathe, Think, then Speak

Oral exams are not just about giving the right answer. They measure how well you think and respond on your feet. Don't be too quick to be "right." Take a few moments after you hear the question—you can always say, "I need a moment to collect my thoughts"—and then breathe. Think about what you want to say before you start speaking. You might pause after you reach the end of a thought so you can think about what to say next. Breathe. When people have trouble on oral exams, invariably they are reversing the process: they speak, think and then gasp for breath. Reverse the process and do it the right way: breathe, think and *then* speak.

Also, you need to be comfortable with the silence while you're thinking the question over. On an oral examination, how you develop your thinking may also be part of what examiners are listening for. All the more reason to be calm, confident and focused. There is no need to rush.

4. Practice, Practice, Practice

If you are preparing for an oral exam, you must practice every question out loud in front of someone else because you have to experience what it's like to develop your thoughts by speaking them. You'll also develop a sense of what the right length is for an answer. One of the big pitfalls of oral exams is giving answers that are either too short or too long. Candidates can become contracted and don't give enough information to show how much they know, or they feel like they have to include everything and go on way too long. Practice with a study buddy, a colleague or a coach. Ask them to give you specific feedback on the following points: Was your answer clear, organized and easy to follow? Did you cover the material? Did you say too little or too much? Did you stay connected to the examiner?

Above all, practice breathing while you're thinking and speaking. Practice staying in your body using the Calming tools. Practice staying in touch with what you know and who you are by using the Confidence and Focus tools. Remember that most exams, by nature, tend to disembody and disempower people. With oral exams, you're in a one-down position sitting in front of people who have power over you. They know the questions and you probably don't. You're in a room with other people who can all see how well or poorly you are doing. So more than ever, you need to practice staying embodied and empowered.

5. Engage the Examiners: Don't Act Like a Trained Seal

Remember, you're just talking to another *person* (or other people) not to a god or goddess. Train yourself to see your examiners as people, or better, colleagues. If you start feeling like you're performing (acting, playing someone other than who you are, trying to pull a positive reaction from them), as if you have to impress someone who is larger than life, you will disconnect from yourself and you're bound to start feeling uncomfortable and anxious. Use the tools to calm yourself down, and to re-establish your confidence and focus.

6. Be Real

You are not expected to know everything and you should not burden yourself with that expectation. Sometimes oral exams are constructed to purposely force you to say, "I don't know," "I'm not sure," or "I'd have to get some consultation on this." If you portray yourself as a know-it-all, a stand-alone authority on everything, you are not presenting a realistic picture of yourself (and you may well be running head-on into the narcissism of the examiners who think *they* know everything!). If you don't know something, admit it, otherwise you lose credibility even on the matters you do know.

You also may find yourself remembering something later in the exam that you couldn't think of earlier. At that point you can say, "There is something I'd like to add to my previous answer..." Though some oral exams don't allow for this, I always coach people to try it anyway because examiners sometimes stretch the rules.

7. Don't Be Afraid to Correct an Answer

Sometimes you start speaking and only then do you realize that you've just said something *wrong*. If this happens, don't keep going. Stop right where you are. I call this "driving up onto the curb" (mentioned in the last chapter), because it basically keeps a car from careening out of control. Just say, "I'd like to correct what I'm saying," or "I'd like to start again." Sometimes examinees, out of nervousness, keep going and try to patch up or worse, *cover up* a mistake. I call this "driving up onto the curb and into the living room of the house." Stop! It's all right to correct yourself. People make mistakes; that doesn't make you stupid or inept. You're a person.

8. Sip Water

Many people suffer from dry mouth after they talk continuously even for a few minutes. Have a glass of water ready on the table (if there is a table) in front of you. If there isn't a table or the examiners don't offer you any water, bring in a small plastic bottle of water into the exam room. Excuse yourself while you take a sip. Sipping occasionally not only relieves dry mouth, but it also gives you a chance to take a very helpful pause when you have to slow down and think about what you want to say. Drinking the water slowly will help you to remember to breathe.

9. Deal with Weird Examiner Behavior

How the examiners act as you're answering questions is the big bugaboo of oral exams. Notice I didn't say, "how they act toward you," because I want you to understand from the get-go, that whatever the examiners do or say is not *necessarily* a reflection of what they think of you or your performance. It is often just their style, or they have been instructed to be impassive, not to show emotion or response. This is usually a misguided effort to standardize the exam—examiner behavior should not intrude as a variable that might affect the candidate's responses. In other words, a smile might encourage a student to go on with the right answer, whereas a frown will do the opposite. The students who receive more prompts are presumed to be getting more help. However, these controls are misguided because all too often examiners don't have the best control over their behavior. They can be as bored, hungry, tired, and even irritated as anyone else, especially when they don't like the questions or agree with the answers. So much for standardization! Some oral examiners have their own strange ideas of what acting like an examiner means, often based on an examiner they had in the past, which may have been someone they liked or hated. Now it's *their* turn. They may also be having a bad hair day or gas pains.

Here's how to prepare for weird examiner behavior.

EXERCISE: Weird Examiner Behavior, Part 1

Ask a colleague or friend to sit opposite you and listen as you tell them the story of something that happened to you today. Their instructions are to make faces at you when you're talking. Sometimes they should smile and show agreement and at other times, frown, grimace or smirk at you in a haughty way and show displeasure. Occasionally, they should act like they're falling asleep. Your job is to keep talking and not be derailed by anything they're doing.

If you're like most people you'll start laughing as soon as they start acting weird. It's not a real exam so you can see the behavior for what it is, but with a real exam this kind of examiner behavior is exactly what makes people nervous and throws off their answers. They start interpreting the examiner's behavior as if it means something significant. *He's smiling at me. Great! That must mean I'm doing a good job*, or *Oh no! She's shaking her head. I'm screwing up!* Based on these interpretations examinees start to change their behavior, trying to make the examiner act approvingly. The examinee loses focus and is no longer putting the attention where it needs to go: on the questions and the answers. Your job is to answer the question, not to elicit a sign of approval from the examiner.

 EXERCISE: Weird Examiner Behavior, Part 2

You can ask the same colleague or friend to act as an examiner. Tell them another story (or better, actually practice answering a sample exam question). As in Part 1, they should make all sorts of faces—good and bad—at you when you're talking, but this time, instead of laughing at them or adjusting your behavior to their reaction do one or all of the following:

Simply describe to yourself silently their physical actions without interpreting their meaning. Example: If they start smiling, you say to yourself, "The right and left corners of her mouth are going in an upward direction," rather than thinking, "She likes me," which is an interpretation. When you break down what they are doing into discreet, describable physical actions without any evaluative component, the way the examiner "looks" loses its emotional charge because you're not projecting onto the person. Keep this up. You'll see how well it works.

> Put them behind an "invisible screen." As you're talking, create in your imagination a clear, impervious screen that surrounds the examiner. This means that anything they do or think cannot pass through this barrier. It's as if they're contained in their own bubble, just where they should be, and you cannot be affected.
>
> Penetrate their mask. Every examiner is also a human being. Whatever they are doing during the exam is simply a mask they're creating; it comes out of their idea of how to play their examiner role. As you talk to them, penetrate the mask by seeing that that's all it is. Instead of talking *to* it, talk *through* it, so you see your thoughts and words reaching the human being behind the mask.

10. *Your Appearance and What to Wear*

This issue can be bothersome for many people taking an oral exam since all kinds of theories, mostly unfounded, start flying around about the effect—positive or negative—an examinee's physical appearance may have on examiners. I have known candidates to dye their hair, choose a certain color tie or wear a particularly tight dress for an oral exam in order to sway the examiners in their favor. Forget it! Worrying about your appearance diverts your attention to the wrong place.

On the other hand, you do want to be appropriate, so follow these guidelines: wear something that is comfortable and that you feel you look good in. Choose clothing you would wear to a professional interview. Avoid flashy clothes or anything that makes a "statement" (like "I'm cool"). You don't need to make a statement; you need to pass the exam. I usually recommend that women use a minimum of makeup and jewelry and that men wear a jacket and tie. Minimize piercings and obvious tattoos. One or two earrings are usually OK, but you may be pushing it with nose rings and tongue studs. Examiners are not always as liberal or hip as we would like them to be.

I tell everyone to *avoid fragrances* of any kind—this includes cologne, perfume, after-shave lotion, powders and hair sprays. Exam rooms can be tight, stuffy and hot. Fragrances, no matter how expensive, alluring or exotic, might antagonize someone who is allergic to them. I have even heard of an instance where the examinee's cologne reminded the examiner of a former lover—and it didn't end well! Don't take that chance.

PRACTICAL EXAMS AND PHYSICAL PERFORMANCES

From clinical boards to driving tests, and from musical recitals to acting auditions, practical exams and performances are also done in the presence of other people—an examiner, auditioner or jury. This is especially challenging because you have to perform the activity while someone is watching you, and the tests are often timed, creating even more pressure.

1. Practice, Practice, and Yes, Practice

Since these tests and performances involve a set of physical skills that have to be demonstrated, the only way to pull them off is if you've practiced thoroughly beforehand. There is no substitute for this. Go through the routine over and over again. Break the actions into small, manageable steps (the third tool for building confidence). Simulate the conditions of the exam or performance as much as possible. Don't skim or rush over anything. I knew a brilliant clarinetist who had trouble with one short passage in a piece he was going to use when he auditioned. The dreaded passage was only a couple of measures long but he described it as "going through a tunnel of hell" and he dealt with it by closing his eyes, just *knowing* it would be over soon. It didn't work. He had tried auditioning this way and it was disaster. We ended up breaking the passage down note-by-note until he finally mastered it, one note and one phrase at a time. He auditioned again and he got the job.

2. Anticipate Potential Problems

If you think through what kinds of problems might arise in a practical exam or performance, they won't catch you off guard. Dentists taking their clinical state boards and performing a root canal need to take into consideration that the patient might have to go to the bathroom during the exam, thus interrupting the procedure and taking time as well. Talk to people who have taken the exam recently and find out what experiences they had. They can alert you to the unexpected. If you're taking a driving test, simulate it by going out on a busy thoroughfare.

3. Stay Calm

No matter how well you prepare, unexpected events will come up. Count on it. During one musical audition, the power went out and the stage went dark. During a driving test, the examiner started coughing uncontrollably. In the midst of a chef's try-out in a well-known restaurant, there was a gas explosion. Any of these things will throw you off if you aren't grounded. Sometimes a practical exam purposely presents a situation different than what you're used to. Your first job in the midst of any unusual, or potentially traumatic occurrence is to *stay calm*. Just by regularizing your breath you will get through—or wait out—the unexpected event.

4. See the Examiner as a Colleague

With most practical exams, the examiner's job is to determine if you are safe and competent to practice the skill or trade in question. Let the examiner do his or her job while you do yours. This means putting your focus on what *you* are doing, not what the examiner is doing. The Focus tools are particularly helpful here. If you start drifting out of yourself and into the mind of the examiner, *stop!* Listen to your inner voice about what you need to do next, visualize the direction, and then do it. Keep calm. See and feel your own body. Breathe. You and the examiner are colleagues, not adversaries. By staying focused on your work, you respect the examiners and elicit his or her respect and attention.

MEMORIZING

Memorizing long lists of names, dates and the like can be very daunting. I don't know of a one-size-fits all system for memorizing. What I can tell you is that "just" memorizing doesn't work well. At some level, you need to understand the material you are memorizing, otherwise there's nothing for it to "stick" to. There's an old Chinese proverb that says, "I hear and I forget, I see and I remember, I do and I understand." Usually students try to memorize by just hearing (the lecture) and seeing (what they read). To really learn something, which will make it easier to commit to memory, you have to *do* something with the material. As a way to memorize material, students often re-write their notes or make flash cards. This may be moderately helpful, since they *are* doing something, yet the method still mostly relies on hearing and seeing. The "doing" part comes from going over the notes and materials, speaking the words out loud perhaps. What is even more useful is explaining the material to someone else, like teaching it. When you do this, you have to find the words and the links and the meaning in what you are studying. This could be an effective way to work with a study buddy.

STUDY BUDDIES

Having a study buddy is helpful for some people and a nightmare for others. The main advantages of having a person to study with are: (1) Together you can create a schedule for preparation which both of you commit to. (2) You can fill in for the each other when one doesn't understand the material. (3) You can practice teaching it to one another (see above). (4) You can commiserate together when you're at your wit's end.

However, the same advantages can become pitfalls when: (1) One person keeps the schedule but the other doesn't (this puts the first person in the position of being a nag). (2) One person really understands the material while the other does not (or does not do the work it would take to understand it). (3) Communication styles don't match. (4) The study time is used for complaining instead of working (or one person does this and keeps dragging the other down).

If you are thinking of taking on a study buddy I suggest you meet one another first and see if you share the same goals and ideas for how to go about the process of studying. You also have to find out if your personalities mesh or clash. Once it appears that it might work, try it out for a week or two, then evaluate. Is it working for each person? Are you learning the material? Are you getting the work done? Be honest. Your job is to prepare for a test, not buffer someone's feelings or rescue him. This applies to studying in pairs or in groups.

TEST PREP BOOKS AND COACHING COMPANIES

Go to any bookstore and you'll see whole cases filled with test-prep manuals and guides. Open the Yellow Pages and you'll see scores of listings for test-prep services. If you're thinking of spending money on a book or service, here are two words of advice: *Caveat emptor!* Translation: Buyer beware!

1. Make Sure the Book or Service Provides What You Need

Books are useful for familiarizing you with a test's content. Courses generally offer strategies for answering questions and let you practice taking the test and receiving feedback. Before you spend your money on an expensive course, look through available books to see if they have what you need. But remember, book and courses can't diagnose an individual's particular problems or needs; they only offer general help. Clients have come to me very discouraged, saying a course or book piled too much on, making it harder, not easier, to prepare. "I can't learn everything, not in that way" is the familiar refrain. No one was there to help them discern what was most important to grasp, how to adjust the material to their learning style, or to respond to other personal issues and needs. Most books or courses pay only lip service to all of the issues we have been dealing with in this book: how to keep yourself calm, confident and focused while studying and during the test itself. They don't actually show you how.

2. Respect Your Own Process

Books and courses are constructed to be appealing and be useful to a general audience. For one state oral examination in which candidates are given seven minutes to make notes before answering questions, each test-prep company recommends its own elaborate way to structure these notes. Many people become hung-up because they can't take notes in the specific way proscribed by their book or course. Instead, they should be encouraged to think for themselves and respect their own reasoning and method of preparation. If a book or a course suggests a strategy, don't accept it until you have tried it out, understood it and adjusted it to your own way of thinking and processing. It's fine even to change it radically, because the best course is the one that works for you.

If you only "do as you're told" you are not going to hone your confidence and skills as a test taker. You'll just fall back into the "I'll-just-do-the-right-thing and-get-through-this" model. It may or may not work. Learn to cultivate and trust your own process. Use books and courses and resources to do this.

PERSONAL COACHES

The number of coaches on the test-prep scene is mushrooming. Again, be cautious about where you invest your time, energy and money.

A good coach will personalize the process for you by diagnosing your particular needs and figuring out how to guide you through the test preparation period. While a course is geared to a group of people, personal coaching is geared to you. Costs for personal coaching are always higher than group coaching, and your relationship with the coach is more direct and probably more intense. Because you are putting so much faith in the expertise and knowledge of one person, it's important to select the right one. Here are some guidelines.

When choosing a personal coach ask yourself, "What do I need from a coach?"

1. Is the Coach Up-to-Date?

Once when I was preparing for an oral exam, I was advised to seek out a private coach. When I met with him, I was quickly discouraged to find that this man was at least two years behind in his knowledge of the exam. All of his practice questions were old. I didn't go back and I felt I had wasted my money on the consultation. A single phone call beforehand will tell you if the coach is up-to-date. If you meet the coach and realize you have been misled, don't go back.

2. Does the Coach Offer Precisely What You Need?

Different coaches offer different services. Before you engage one, consider your actual needs. Do you need help with deciphering test content? Do you need strategies for answering questions? Do you need coaching to deal with test anxiety? Find out if the coach offers a particular area of expertise and does that suit what you need? This can be determined by talking with the person before you pay him or her or by checking out their website.

3. Does the Coach Appreciate and Utilize Your Strengths?

When you're preparing for an exam you are very vulnerable. If you're not secure in your skills and knowledge, you will be on shaky ground and you want to know what's getting in your way. Are you just not smart enough or competent enough? You might be worried that you don't have what it takes. The last thing you need is a coach who focuses solely on the negative because it will only disempower you more. Instead, you want someone who will pick up on your strengths, your positive characteristics, even if they're subtle, such as your real interest in the subject, your drive to reach your goal, and how successful you've been at other things in your life. All of these can help you in your preparation and performance. Beware of any coach who puts you down! This person may be operating more from his or her ego rather than out of a genuine and skillful ability to see what you have to offer and capitalize on that.

4. Is the Coach Available?

When you're preparing for a test you are engaged in a process. Usually, you will be working with a coach at intervals during this process. What happens if you have a question between coaching sessions? Can you e-mail the coach and get an immediate response? Does he or she allow for a phone check-in without cost? I once went to a coach who charged for me for every minute I had him on the phone. This was excessive and expensive. Most check-in or problem-solving phone calls are just a couple of minutes long. When people come to work with me our agreement is that there's no charge for an occasional phone call under ten minutes. If it goes over that, I charge a prorated fee for the time we spend together. Almost always, these phone calls take only three to five minutes.

5. Does the Coach Have Good References?

Don't be afraid to ask for references. After all, you're about to make a big commitment and you have a right to know what you're getting into. Talk to people who have worked with this coach before and ask them questions: When did you work with this person? How was he or she helpful to you? What was not helpful? What should you watch out for? If the coach expresses any reluctance in providing you with several references, *find another coach*. It may well mean they have something to hide.

6. Does the Coach Offer Debriefing and Feedback?

Once you have finished taking your test, you may want to debrief and receive feedback. Find out if the coach offers that. I do, as a matter of routine, and I don't charge my clients for this. We always schedule time to talk—on the phone or in person—so I can hear about their experience on the test. I also want their feedback about my coaching. I want to know what worked and what didn't. Are there any suggestions for my work with future clients? They appreciate my follow-up and concern about how the process worked for them, and I have received tremendous value from their feedback.

If a person did not score at the level they desired, the feedback session offers the chance to express disappointment, as well as to analyze what happened and strategize for the next test.

In the case of people who are preparing for a performance (musical, dramatic or athletic), I actually attend the performances when I can. This gives the client more support and we are both afforded the satisfaction of seeing our work come to fruition. Since this is not possible with clients who are taking paper-and-pen tests or oral exams, I find out where their test is and what time it's being administered, and I spend some time quietly visualizing my client, seeing her or him having a successful outcome. I tell them that I will be doing this and they have all reported how supportive that has felt.

AN EXERCISE FOR EVERY TEST

As I promised earlier, I am going to give you an exercise that can help you with every test. It's called the "Circle of Light" and is my version of one taught to me by Catherine Shainberg, one of my great teachers. Dr. Shainberg's School of Images in New York City is an outstanding resource for learning to use the wellspring of one's inner world of imagery as the vehicle for action and transformation in daily life.

EXERCISE: Circle of Light

Sit comfortably in a chair, feet and arms uncrossed.

Close your eyes.

Feel yourself supported by the chair.

Breathe deeply down, knowing that when you breathe whatever is in disorder tends to return to order.

Inhale and exhale. Repeat this three times.

Sense, see and feel your right arm extending above your head.

Your arm grows longer and longer as you reach above your head.

You arm extends through the ceiling and the roof.

It grows longer and longer as it extends up into the sky and up into the heavens.

You reach and reach and reach until you reach the place of the light.

Gather the light with your right hand and bring it down.

Bring it down and down and down, right to where you are sitting.

Create a circle of white light, with you sitting in the center of it.

This light nourishes, clarifies and protects you.

Everything you need is in this circle: all your study materials, all your practicing, your intelligence, experience and sensitivity. All of your coaching and all of your supports—family, friends, colleagues, and spiritual supports—are within this circle.

At any time you can call upon anything or anyone within the circle to help you.

All you have to do is ask and the help is there for you. You will get just what you need when you ask for it.

Breathe out.

See yourself studying and practicing for your test, always within the circle of light.

This light nourishes, clarifies and protects you.

Everything you need is within this circle.

You can call upon anything within the circle to help you.

All you have to do is ask and the help is there for you.

You will get just what you need when you ask for it.

Breathe out.

Now see yourself on the day of the exam, always within the circle of light.

This light nourishes, clarifies and protects you.

Everything you need is within this circle.

See yourself at the exam, always within the circle of light.

The exam questions and answer sheet are in front of you [substitute examiners if it is an oral or practical exam].

You are always within the circle of light.

Exhale.

See yourself answering each question adequately and with excellence.

See the examiners receiving your answers.

You are always within the circle of light.

Everything you need is within this circle.

You can call upon anything within the circle to help you.

All you have to do is ask and the help is there for you.

You will get just what you need when you ask for it.

⇨

Breathe out.

See yourself answering all the questions and finishing the test in a timely manner.

See yourself passing the test.

See yourself leaving the exam room.

[The first time you do this exercise add this:] See yourself receiving your score. What is it? See it with crystalline clarity.

Breathe out.

Open your eyes and see all of this with open eyes.

This is a wonderful and powerful exercise. I usually teach it to people a week before they take the test. It's a good exercise to do once each day before the date. Even though you repeat the exercise every day, you only see the score once, the first time you do the exercise. Why? Because the first time you plant the seed. By repeating the exercise, you nourish the seed and you don't need to plant it again.

SOME FINAL GUIDELINES

Just as I give the "Circle of Light" to all my clients to practice for any test, I also give them the following six guidelines. These apply to whatever test you are facing.

1. Eat Right

When you're preparing for a test it's good to be mindful of your diet. The old saw "You are what you eat," does have its reality. Eating a good daily selection of healthy, grounding foods will help stabilize your energy and your thinking. Habits like dumping caffeine into your system, inhaling junk food or having sugar with everything, are all bound to send your energy spiraling out of control or down into the ditch of exhaustion. When you're preparing for an exam it is not the time to start some big weight-loss program or new-food regime. It is the time to adjust your diet to take in what will help you to be more balanced.

2. Be Well-Rested

Know how much rest you need on a daily basis to keep your thinking clear and energy bright. Everyone differs in how much sleep they need. What do you need? Find times to rest during study periods. Efficiency can go down dramatically if you try to do too much at once.

3. Remember: Some "Nerves" Are Helpful

Every performer, no matter how talented, no matter how advanced, no matter how many times he or she has gone out on stage or on the ball field, feels a charge before performing. And as a test taker, so will you. Remember the Yerkes-Dodson curve at the beginning of the book? Some amount of stress is actually helpful for performance. I call this kind of stress "energy." It juices you up, gets you ready, sharpens your whole system for the event to come. Don't think something is wrong with you because you feel this charge before a test. It's helpful, and as your coach, I'd actually be more concerned if you didn't feel it. Think of it as your jets starting to fire as you are on the runway. You need the energy to take off. Now you know how to keep the energy at the right level. If you start feeling over-charged, use the tools.

> It's natural to feel a bit amped up before a test. Keep using the tools. Stay calm, confident and focused.

4. Let It Go

This is the best thing to do after an exam. You've done the work and it's over. Let it go. You will likely find yourself going over questions you answered and are wondering if your answers were right. You may start worrying that they were wrong. At this point it doesn't matter. The exam is over. You can't change your answers. After exams I often receive calls from clients. Some are *sure* they failed and start crying or go into panic mode. Others are elated by what they believe was a stellar performance. Later we often find out that the people who were sure they failed ended up passing and the ones who were sure they did very well barely squeaked by. The moral here is that one's memory of an exam is usually faulty. Don't trust it. Many people compare their answers with others who have taken the exam. I don't recommend it. Everyone's memory of an exam, even one just completed, is spotty. If you must continue focusing on the exam—and sometimes it's hard not to—spend the time in prayer that you passed and in thanks that it's over.

5. Do Something Special for Yourself

You've worked hard. You need to reward yourself. Go out to dinner with a friend. Treat yourself to a day spa. Go shopping. Sleep late. Watch a few movies. Go for a walk in the woods. Don't neglect this step. You've earned the chance to do something pleasurable for yourself. Take a break and take it easy.

6. Celebrate or Strategize

When you receive your exam results either celebrate or strategize. Celebrate if you passed, strategize if you didn't. Not passing, or achieving your desired result, means that there are things you still need to learn. Find out what they are. It may be more content, it may be a better understanding about how the test is structured, or of how to take the test (using the tools in this book). Analyze yourself. Talk to your teacher, professor, advisor or coach. Be determined to structure your time and energies in a way to accomplish what you need to do to do better next time. You will. Once, when I failed an oral exam I was able to listen to the tape recording of the exam. I could hear that I was providing way too much information and probably came across to the examiners as a know-it-all. The next time around I practiced giving shorter, more precise answers. I passed. Sometimes people need to simply have the experience of taking the test so they can see what it's like. They may not do well or they may fail, but once they know what to expect they know how to better prepare.

Remember: whatever happens in your life is an opportunity to learn what you need to grow.

Though I've addressed a number of different issues and situations that come up in tests and performances, maybe you have had an experience that I haven't addressed. Please let me know about it so I can add it to future editions of this book and to my website resource. My e-mail information is in the last section on *Resources*.

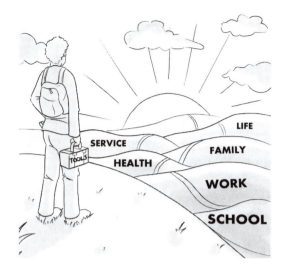

Chapter Eight

Working the Model

As this book is about to come to a close, I remember my honored teacher, Viola Spolin, who created a wonderful theater game called *Begin and End*. In it, the end of every action is the beginning of a new one. And so it is here. Throughout the book we have put our attention on using the three-legged stool model to reduce your test stress and improve your performance. You now have the chance to carry forward what you have learned about classroom performance to all the tests that life will throw your way.

Have you ever wondered, *what's the purpose of life?* I certainly have. This question is one of the biggest mysteries we human beings face and I don't pretend to know The Answer. But I am going to offer up what I believe, which is this: *The purpose of life is to face every challenge, every test, as an opportunity to be and to become the person you are meant to be, your highest self, so you can make your own unique contribution to the world we live in.*

We each have a part to play in life, which is a continuous series of tests and the object is to play one's part well, often interacting with others. In another marvelous Spolin theater game called *Part of the Whole*, each person in the group becomes a living, moving breathing part of a much larger organism. For example, someone stands up and moves like a plant spreading its leaves. Then another person joins in and sprouts like flower on that plant. Each person plays off the others. All the parts are interdependent, each contributing to the whole. This is emblematic for what life is all about. In our world community each and every one of us has a specific role to play and function to serve.

We are all destined to be something. One person is meant to be a mechanic, another a politician, another a doctor. Others are meant to be priests, moms, athletes, fathers, teachers, police officers, sanitation workers, artists or lawyers. As I am writing this sentence and crafting this book, I am playing my part as a psychologist and teacher. My close friend Joe is a carpenter, a husband and a parent. His wife Jen is running a bamboo farm and mothering their beautiful daughter, Zoë, who right now is perfectly playing her part as a child. My wife, Suk Wah, is in her study writing a novel. Think of life on this earth as a big production and each of us is a character in it, almost as if our parts were written just for us. As Shakespeare said, "All the world's a stage." And we, *mere players*, are performing our roles all the time. But the stage is life itself. No matter what you are doing in your daily life, you are part of this huge production, and the better you perform your part—the more you contribute your talents, energy, resources and time—the more likely it is that this production will be a success and serve everyone.

A playwright's imagination creates the parts that each character takes on. On the stage of life the parts we are each playing are coming out of some much bigger imagination. I would call it "God's." Others might say it comes from "Spirit," "Soul," "Goddess," "Higher Power" or "the Tao." If you don't usually think in these terms, or are afraid we're veering off into la-la land, don't worry. All you need to envision is that there is order to all this chaos, this endless drama. This will motivate you to think about yourself in a bigger way, to understand that everything you do matters in the grand scheme.

How do tests figure in? No drama—no real story—is without trials for its characters. Without the tests of life, no one would become stronger, more skillful or more experienced. Think of the sword that has to be thrust in the fire and then pounded into shape before it can become perfect. Without going through this process, it is merely a hunk of metal. The fire and the work help it to become what it is meant to be. None of us comes out of the box already formed. It is our experiences and the way we deal with them that shape us into what we are. In life, we have to perform every day, and every test—whether it is in school or in your daily routine—is a chance to strengthen yourself, to perform at your best and to grow. Tests are the stuff that actually help us become and be who we are meant to be.

Everyone's part comes with challenges. For the student these are tests.

As I was writing this chapter, Bobby Ives, one of my college roommates in the mid '60s, faced a severe test. For the past thirty years he and his wife Ruth, both ministers, operated a boat-building workshop on the coast of Maine. There they trained troubled young people to become highly skilled boat builders. The very discipline of it changed their lives. Called The Carpenter's Boatshop, the name's metaphorical significance is, quite literally, built in, as Bobby and Ruth's ministry. Operating mostly on unwavering faith, The Boatshop produced not only exquisite sailing vessels, but exquisite people. Over this time, the tests for Bobby and Ruth were enormous and constant: lack of funding, difficult students, raising a family of three children in the midst of an active, always changing environment. Yet these two flourished, making an outstanding contribution to their community and to the lives of everyone touched by their ministry.

Then Ruth was diagnosed with aggressive and inoperable brain cancer. When the doctor delivered the diagnosis he predicted she would live only four more months and said, "It's going to be an uphill battle." Without flinching, Ruth replied, "Well, we'll just have to walk uphill." So she wore her mountain hiking boots to every radiation treatment and had people all over the world (the network who knew her was widespread) cheering her on and praying for her.

And the cancer subsided. For three years.

But it came back with a vengeance, and Ruth passed away in a matter of months.

Bobby and his children were profoundly shaken, as were the thousands of people whose lives were touched by this amazing woman. But Bobby, in his role as husband, father, teacher and minister, *faced the test*. He mourned his wife and he still misses her every single day, but he continues to grow wiser and stronger as well as make his contribution running The Boatshop. "I have to keep going," he says. In his eyes you can see the smile deep in his soul, even as they well with tears.

I bring in these two people as an example for a few reasons. Everyone's life at some time or other involves extreme tests of loss, illness, physical and mental disorders, material hardship, financial reversals and unfulfilled expectations. Yet life goes on nevertheless and each of us must go on playing the parts we are destined for.

As I said in the first chapter, we don't choose all of the tests in life, but we do choose how we are going to face them. Are we going to have a miserable experience, crumble under the pressure, run away, or avoid challenges altogether? Or are we going to find the strength and inner resources to rise to them and fully actualize our potential? It was a friend who communicated Ruth's words, "We'll just have to walk up hill," to her many supporters around the world. He closed his e-mail by writing, "We will all join them on that path."

Because that's what life is—a path that runs up hills and down, with tests popping up around every turn. We can't possibly know what they will be, but each and every one challenges us to grow so that we can fully be, individually and collectively, the people we are meant to be and support each other to do so along the way.

How do *you* face tests? Can you accept them as opportunities to grow?

Video games are a huge phenomenon of modern culture, but even though they're only make believe, in a strange way they are a reflection of life. Have you ever wondered about their huge, worldwide appeal? Their origin is in the arcade games of the '50s, where you slid into a darkened booth, dropped your dime into the coin slot, and sat behind a steering wheel. A movie would come onto a small screen and suddenly you were steering a car on a road that became, by turns, easy and perilous, relaxed and eventful, exhilarating and scary. How you dealt with the bumps and potholes, the incursions and intrusions, determined your score. Every current video game is based on this model and to some degree they simulate life. We are racing around curves and meeting the expected and unexpected on a daily basis. Your ability to be a "winner" in the game of life is determined by how you maneuver the turns and deal with the surprises. Are you prepared? Do you have confidence? Do you have the strength and courage to take on whatever comes?

It's one thing to be at home manipulating your little joystick through the twists and turns on a video screen. It's quite another to stay in control when your wife is dying, or your child is autistic, or you just lost your job, or you are addicted to drugs.

Whether your tests are horrifically large, or mundanely small (your car doesn't start, the dog crapped on your rug, you can't find your keys), they are ongoing. No one can avoid life's tests. Rich or poor, wise or naïve, happy or sad, we are all constant and inevitable test takers.

In a moment I'm going to ask you to close your eyes and think about all the tests you have faced in the last twenty-four hours. For example, here is the list of the tests I've been facing in the last day, starting with what I'm doing right now and working backwards:

* Coming back to my desk to put in the time writing

* Tennis practice with a tough opponent

* Writing a difficult email

* Eating a healthy lunch when I'd rather have a cheeseburger

* Talking with my wife about a challenging financial issue

* Meeting clients who are oppositional

* Getting out of bed when the alarm goes off and I don't feel rested

Now you do it.

EXERCISE: The Tests We Face.

Close your eyes, and work backwards through your day.

Remember each test you faced today.

See each one in detail.

What was the test? How did you respond?

When you've gone back as far as you can, open your eyes.

You see, there's no way of escaping tests. They are part of the fabric of our lives. But you don't have to do it on your own or unequipped. The three-legged stool is your platform to face any test that comes your way. It works because it's a comprehensive model that accounts for your whole being—your body, your mind and your spirit—since every part of you is actually involved in every test

But the model works for a more fundamental reason. Let's analyze it a little.

There are three domains, each with their "best state": body/calm; mind/confident; and spirit/focused. And there are nine tools, three in each domain.

Here is a chart of the model:

Domain	Best state	Tools
Body	Calm	1. Breathe 2. Ground 3. Sense
Mind	Confident	4. Confide 5. Reflect 6. Envision
Spirit	Focused	7. Stop 8. Listen 9. Fulfill

Looking at the tools above, we can see that a similar pattern runs through all three groups:

* The first tool in each domain (tools 1, 4 and 7) *interrupt* an old habit of disconnection.

* The second tool in each domain (tools 2, 5 and 8) ***redirect the energy.***

* And the third tool in each domain (tools 3, 6 and 9) are all about ***moving on,*** in a forward direction.

Now look at in this way:

In this diagram the bull's-eye is the *present moment*. The only time you can ever move is in the present. It continuously affords you the chance to proceed in a new, productive and successful way. Every test takes place in the present. To succeed, you have to interrupt and redirect any old habit that keeps you disconnected and takes you out of the present and put a new habit in its place. Only then can you move ahead. Instead of staying stuck, you have a chance, whenever you choose, to actually change your life as long as you are calm, confident and focused.

Recently I conducted a retreat for the staff of a university and after I drew this diagram one of the participants called out, "Yes, but this is the *ideal*!" as if to say "We can't possibly succeed every time."

And this is how I answered him: "Yes, it is the ideal. And that's what we're striving for. Don't dumb down your ambitions just to play it safe. Of course you can't achieve perfection all at once, but don't let that stop you. The goal is whatever you are striving for; it is also your inspiration."

Every end is a new beginning. Every moment is a chance to excel. You come closer and closer to your ideal self when you are fully connected in your body, mind and spirit, when you face any test being calm, confident and focused.

You can do it.

Step up to the plate.

Chapter Nine

Help for Parents

T his chapter is for parents of high-school students who are frequently in distress over test taking and who consistently perform poorly on tests when you know they could do better.

If your child hates tests, life is hard for your child and for you. You worry along with them when they become severely anxious for any reason. You are frustrated when they won't study. You believe you have failed as a parent when their test scores are lower than their peers'. You might be intensely angry at the school system—if not the whole culture—for putting so much weight on testing. It shouldn't make your child suffer or put you in the position of worrying for them.

As the stress rises and your child's performance worsens, you probably feel hopeless and helpless. You want to do something to make it all easier, but all you can do is shrug your shoulders. You need to learn how to help your child and this book provides you with a method.

Even if your kids are in college and supposedly out of your hands, they might still need some assistance from you if they continue to struggle with test issues. The information in this chapter will help you understand their long-standing problems. If your child is in primary or middle school, your sensitivity to the issues and knowing how to resolve them can make a big difference now and in the years to come. By using the tools in this book you can be proactive in preventing debilitating test stress.

WHAT CAUSES POOR SCORES?

Based on my thirty years of working with test performance issues, I have seen that there are four causes of poor scores:

* **Trouble with the content.** The student does not thoroughly understand the material being tested or has trouble memorizing.

* **Physical tension.** The student is highly anxious and can't settle down and concentrate while studying and during the test itself.

* **Issues of self-doubt.** The student does not trust his or her own thinking and reasoning process in answering questions.

* **Difficulty staying on task.** The student continually becomes distracted while preparing for tests and when taking them.

Any or all of these could be the culprit for why your child is underperforming in school.

When you and I were growing up, we were basically told that taking tests was a matter of absorbing information and then spitting it out on the test. If you managed to remember any of what you learned afterwards, all well and good, but the important thing was the test score. It was what I call the "regurgitative model" of education. We were made to accept it since it was the only model we were presented with. Over the last forty years, however, we've learned a lot about learning. We now know that test performance can be greatly improved by paying attention to the state the person is in when he or she prepares for and takes tests. Students still have to "absorb" information, but how well they do depends on a number of issues, and they are all addressed in this book. Is the person calm, confident and focused? If she is, she will have a tremendous advantage over her fellow students. She doesn't have to stay stuck with dismal scores. She now has the tools to rise to the occasion.

UNDERSTANDING YOUR CHILD

To determine how stress is negatively affecting your child's test performance, please complete the following checklist based on your observations.

Check all that apply.

My child...

❏ 1. is extremely nervous while studying for a test, talking about the test, taking the test, or waiting for results

❑ 2. is very worried he/she will fail

❑ 3. refuses to study

❑ 4. can't grasp the material

❑ 5. is highly irritable before tests and/or when the results have arrived

❑ 6. continually compares him/herself unfavorably with others

❑ 7. is habitually disorganized around studying

❑ 8. continually struggles with difficult concepts

❑ 9. can't sit still when studying and when taking a test

❑ 10. seems to understand the material but doesn't trust him/herself on the test

❑ 11. can't see the relevance of the subject

❑ 12. tries to memorize material without understanding it

❑ 13. does poorly on the test itself even though he/she has studied hard

❑ 14. may be reacting to stress that I myself am causing with my own worry

Let's analyze what you checked so you can refer to the appropriate sections of this book:

If you checked

items ...	this is an issue of...	go to...
4, 8 or 12	Understanding the content. Your child needs to learn **how to prepare.**	See "Trouble with Content" on page 167.

| 1, 5 or 9 | Tension and anxiety. Your child needs to learn to **calm down.** | **Chapter Four: How to Calm Down** on page 35. See section on "Calming Down" on page168. |

⇨

2, 6 or 10	Self-doubt. Your child needs to learn how to be **confident.**	**Chapter Five: How to Be Confident** on page 59. See section below on "If Your Child is plagued by Self-Doubt" on page 169.
3, 7, 11 or 13	Not having goals and/or becoming distracted. Your child needs to learn how to stay **focused.**	**Chapter Six: How to Stay Focused** on page 87. See "If Your Child Has Difficulty Staying Focused" on page 170.
14	You may be negatively influencing your child. You need to learn ways to reduce your own stress about the results of their tests.	See below, "Are You Causing More Stress for Your Child?" on page 171.

USE THE PERFORMANCE INVENTORY

A good way to talk with your child about how stress is negatively impacting his or her performance is to ask them to complete the self-diagnostic inventory (the BPI) in Chapter Three on page 30, and then discuss the results together. The BPI can be a helpful tool if they are willing to talk with you openly about what is admittedly a difficult problem. Many teenagers won't choose this option because they are embarrassed that they're struggling, or they wish the problem would go away without having to deal with it at all, or they want you to mind your own business in general about everything.

It's difficult watching your child have a painful time with tests.

If they refuse to discuss this issue or do anything to resolve it, you will continue to see the end result—poor test scores and emotional pain. Diagnosing the problem will be more difficult without their cooperation, but not impossible. Sometimes I have to start with the fact that the parents don't see their child clearly. I've had many of them tell me, "But my son studies so much," and the child repeats that refrain. Then we come to discover that the studying is fraught with anxiety, self-doubt and distraction. Just because a kid looks like he's studying doesn't mean he's taking in information. He may well be hiding underlying fears and self-doubt that are blocking absorption. Whenever we go over their study habits objectively, we uncover the true obstacles, but they won't see them if they don't look. If your child is not forthcoming or easy to "read," suggest that you consult with particular teachers, an advisor, or one of the school's guidance counselors. And finally, if you don't find specific answers to your questions or concerns here, you can write to me about them on my website: http://www. WorkbookForTestSuccess.com

If your child is showing signs of stress—poor scores, anxiety, loss of self-confidence, loss of focus—you need to take action. You *can* work to resolve these issues. All you need is to be patient with yourself and with your child.

Let's look into the different areas of difficulty and what you can do about them.

TROUBLE WITH CONTENT

Understanding the material is the first and the most key issue. You can always take your chances on a multiple-choice test and hope to beat the odds, but your results will be tepid at best. If you want to score big, you have to actually *know* the answers because you've mastered the material. The automatic assumption is that the child isn't studying enough, but that isn't always the case. Talk with her to determine, *from her perspective*, what is causing the trouble, what is the root cause of the issue. Ask the following questions:

* ✳ "Is there something in the material you specifically don't understand?"

* ✳ "Do you feel like this material is just too difficult for you?

* ✳ "What doesn't make sense to you?"

* ✳ "Are you having trouble memorizing?"

* ✳ "Are you just bored with this material?" *(Caution: when a child says something is "boring" what they might mean is that they don't understand it or like it.)*

Here are some suggestions:

❏ **You, the parent, can ask the teacher to shed light on the situation.** Sometimes a child can't pinpoint her difficulties and, if she's too embarrassed, shy or resistant to talk with the teacher, she may need you to do so on her behalf. The teacher is a good resource because he may be more familiar than you are with your child's learning style, so ask for his observations. Also, see if he can explain the material to you. Do the explanations seem clear? In other words, is the teacher part of the problem? Can the teacher show you a way to help your child?

❏ **Consider arranging for a tutor to work with your child.** A tutor may be helpful to your child by providing close personal attention. Tutorial resources are increasingly available and don't have to be costly. There are many possibilities that are free or very inexpensive: peer tutors (fellow students) in the school, after school programs that include a homework component, and college students looking for extra income. You can always go online, especially to Craigslist (www.craigslist.com) and advertise for a tutor (Jobs Available) or see who is advertising their services (Jobs Wanted). Tutors are also available through my website. See the *Resources* section at the end of this book.

CALMING DOWN

Jitters and tension make it hard for anyone to concentrate. A bad case of nerves can seriously undermine a student's test performance because it robs them of their concentration. This checklist will help you to help your child when nervousness or agitation appears to be in the way of a better test experience.

❏ **Read Chapter Four: How to Calm Down**. Make sure you understand the tools and are using them yourself.

❏ **Review the three Calming tools with your child:**
Breathing, grounding and sensing.

❏ **Explore what kind of prompts may work** to help him to remember to use the tools if you see that he forgets. My CD, "Dr. B's Gentle Prompts for Calming Down" can also be helpful here. (see *Resources* on page 198).

❏ **Is your child getting enough regular physical exercise?** Bike riding, working out at the gym, running and swimming are all tension-releasing activities that give her the opportunity to let off steam and "restart" her system. Watching TV, talking on the phone and playing video games are not aerobic. All too often kids try to study after long hours of these activities and their energy is already zapped.

❑ **Is your child getting enough sleep?** Is he going to bed too late? Does he have a hard time getting out of bed in the morning and does he look tired? Does he appear tired at other times of the day, like after school? Children need a lot more sleep than adults do, at least nine to ten hours a night and anything less can severely hamper their school performance because their tired minds aren't paying attention. Recent research shows that inadequate sleep can cause problems that look like attention deficit.

❑ **Review your child's diet.** A daily intake high in carbs, sugars and caffeinated drinks, is, unfortunately, all too common in our culture. While these foods and "energy drinks" appear to keep the engine stoked, they are actually wearing your child down. A balanced diet keeps glucose levels from roller-coasting and has a positive effect on metabolism, energy levels and brain function.

❑ **Learn to calm down yourself.** As a parent, it is very easy to pick up on what your child feels and start feeling the same way yourself. (Also, of course, you have your own adult problems to cope with.) If your child is anxious, or sad, or angry you may quickly begin feeling the same thing even if you were feeling quite calm just moments before. In psychology we call this the "induced reaction"—you are induced into your child's state. This is a very human response, especially with people who are close with one another like parent and child. You increase your chances of reducing your child's stress if you learn how to keep yourself calm no matter what is going on with them. The material in **Chapter Four: How to Calm Down**, (page 35) will show you how to do this.

> As a parent, learn how to calm yourself down. It's a must. Use the tools.

IF YOUR CHILD IS PLAGUED BY SELF-DOUBT

First, read **Chapter Five: How to Be Confident**. Make sure you understand the tools and are using them yourself. Then use this checklist:

❑ **Are you the right person to be your child's confidant?** As you will see, she has to be able to confide her lack of self-confidence to someone (Confidence Tool #1). You might think of yourself as her best friend but you may not be the person-of-choice for her as a confidant. Sometimes kids don't want to look insufficient in front of their parents (or just about anybody). You have to give up the idea that your child *should* confide in you. Think of someone else she can talk with: a teacher she respects; an advisor or counselor at school she trusts; a clergy member connected with your church, mosque or synagogue; one of her close friends who is a responsible individual. Encourage her to share her deepest thoughts with that person.

❑ **Make supportive, positive, but accurate statements to your child.** "You work hard." "You've taken on big challenges before and succeeded." "You can do it." "I believe in you." "I know you've got what it takes." You'll notice that these are specific.

Saying things like, "You're the best kid in the world!" may be a loving sentiment (and you might really feel that way), but at that moment your child feels anything but the best. It's also vague. Avoid over-generalizing and hyperbolizing. Just reflect back to your child something accurate and positive about him. This is Confidence Tool #2.

❑ **Break up tasks into small, manageable steps**. Confidence problems spring up quickly when a task looks overwhelming. Help your child to see that the task can be broken down into small, manageable steps, each of which she can imagine herself taking successfully. Each time she completes one step, it will increase her belief in herself. This is Confidence Tool #3.

❑ **Be confident yourself.** Your child's self-doubt might induce you into thinking you haven't done a good job as a parent. Not necessarily true! Everyone has issues, but don't confuse yours with your child's. She is a separate entity. You will be a better resource for her if you work on keeping your own self-confidence strong. Using the tools in Chapter Five will help you do that.

IF YOUR CHILD HAS DIFFICULTY STAYING FOCUSED

Trouble staying on task often points to a lack of motivation. The child who isn't self-motivated presents a difficult problem for the parent and teacher. How hard can you push without encountering resistance and possible breakdown? What if your child cannot see that every human being has the innate desire to realize his or her potential? If a child doesn't feel motivated, it doesn't mean he has no internal motivation to excel. He has it because it's part of being human, but something is blocking it. Once the blocks are cleared his natural desire to excel will shine through.

If your child has difficulty becoming motivated, find out what is getting in his way. Is it an overall sense of helplessness that even if he tries, he won't get anywhere? Perhaps he has taken on tasks in the past that were too immense for him and he was bound to fail. Now he doesn't want to take on anything. Perhaps he's just never felt the thrill of achievement and needs one good experience to give him a taste for it. Perhaps he is the youngest in the family and his siblings always, always outshine him. In this case, make sure he spends more time with kids his own age so he has a fair chance to succeed. Sometimes children have parents who are over-achievers and expect too much of them. They go along with coercion for years, but at some point they want to be their own person and so they rebel. Youngsters often know only one way to rebel: do the opposite of what mom and dad want. You need to be honest with yourself about whether you've been pushing too hard and have turned *achievement* into a negative word.

Whatever the cause, lack of motivation will most certainly affect the ability to stay focused. First read **Chapter Six: How to Stay Focused**. Now ask the following questions:

☐ **Whose goal is it that your child succeeds?** Of course you want her to do well, but if she doesn't have that goal herself, you are going to be in an uphill battle that you might never win. Talk with your child about this. A straightforward discussion about her goals can go a long way toward clarifying why she needs to work harder. Sometimes you can frame an issue in a way that helps her see that she really does want to pursue a certain goal. The first part of the Focus chapter (on setting goals, page 90) will be helpful in clarifying these issues and taking proper action.

☐ **In what ways does your child becomes distracted?** Does she stay on the phone, clock onto the web or e-mail, play video games, watch TV, eat—all in place of doing her homework? Can you help her set realistic working periods with breaks for "treats" and distractions? Consider getting a timer (see page 98) as a tool so she can focus better and more consistently. Because children these days often have very short attention spans, start with short study spurts (10 minutes) with a goal of working toward a 30-minute spurt with a five-minute break.

☐ **How focused are you?** If you have clear goals and minimize distraction, you can be a good role model for your child. She can see the effects for herself. The different sections of the Focus chapter can help you strengthen this part of yourself. Remember: cultivating good work habits is ultimately something children should learn to do for themselves because they see the positive results and feel good about having accomplished a goal. Though you may have to encourage and mentor them through this process, they are doing the work so that *they* can go on to lead a more fulfilling life. They can't motivate themselves to work hard just because you want them to. The long-out-of-favor proverb "Virtue is its own reward" needs to return.

ARE YOU CAUSING MORE STRESS FOR YOUR CHILD?

In the last section we looked at "kid" factors, things your child is doing that cause his stress to grow and test performance to suffer. There are also "parent" factors—things you may be doing that ratchet up his stress. Fair warning: in this section I am going to ask you some challenging personal questions. You can help your child, and yourself, greatly by honest self-reflection as you read through the next few pages.

There are basically four categories of what I call unhelpful parent behavior. As you look at the list below, see if there are any you identify with right away. You can go directly to that subsection (below the chart) or continue reading through.

Comparison	Do you compare your child's performance to a sibling's ("Your sister never had trouble with this"), or to yourself ("When I was in school I loved math")?
Unrealistic expectations	Do you think your child is an unrecognized genius, or much smarter than everyone else seems to think or believe?
Your self-esteem is affected by your child's performance	Do you think your child's test performance is a reflection of your parenting? Is your real reason for wanting him to do well because it means other people will think you are a good parent? Do you want your child to be successful because you underachieved as a child and don't want her to repeat your story?
You micro-manage your child	Do you believe the only way your child will stay on track is if you are constantly hovering over them making sure every "t" is crossed and every "i" is dotted? Do you "helicopter" over your child, intervening on his behalf with teachers, coaches and other kids.
You have a "suck it up" attitude.	Do you believe life is hard and we are meant to suffer?

Are You Comparing Your Child to Others?

Do you ever say to your child, "I don't understand why you find chemistry so hard. Your brother sailed right through this stuff," or "Your friend Robert doesn't seem to have any problems with spelling," or "I *loved* geometry when I was in high school, what's the matter with you?" If you do, he is going to feel belittled and humiliated. Comparisons like these send a message that you don't understand *him* or really care about *him*. You are making a situation that is already emotional even worse.

Comparing him to a sibling, a classmate, or yourself just makes him feel as if he's naturally stupid and inept and no matter how hard he tries, he'll never be able to do anything about it. What else can he conclude when you tell him it was easy for others? As I state in Chapter Five (How to Be Confident, page 59), comparison is a trap, ensnaring you in an emotional tangle. The comparison takes the attention off the actual stress-producing aspect of the test, and onto issues of self-esteem and love, so the child cannot address the real obstacle. The best thing to do is to focus on what is going on with him and what *he* needs, not on what anyone else is doing or has done. Go out of your way to ask your child questions so you can understand his needs.

Do You Have Unrealistic Expectations for Your Child?

Sometimes parents idealize their children and see them as mini super-heroes capable of doing just about anything. But what happens if yours doesn't show an aptitude for a subject you think she should excel in, or if she doesn't like a subject that you think she should enjoy? What do you do when she under-performs?

Some parents start blaming the teacher or the material or the test because it is hard for them to see their child as anything less than a little genius. This mentality gets in the way of seeing her for who she is. It is hard to see that she may not be the star in the way that you want her to be. Every parent wants the best for his or her child. And so should you. You are her greatest advocate and most enduring source of support. But you cannot be genuinely helpful unless you encourage her in a realistic way by recognizing her true strengths *and* weaknesses. You have to acknowledge and—this is harder—accept the things she likes and the things she doesn't, and be honest about her possibilities *and* limitations.

Focus on your child's needs. Not on yours.

Do You Think Your Child's Performance Is a Reflection of Your Parenting?

Some parents believe that when their child fails a test or receives a bad report card, it makes it look as if the parents aren't doing their job. "What kind of parents let their child fail? Don't they make them study? Aren't they paying attention?" On the other hand, a straight-A report card seem to broadcast that the parent is doing a sterling job. In either case, you are tying your child's performance to your own self-esteem. This type of thinking isn't helpful to either of you.

If your child performs poorly on a test it doesn't necessarily mean you have done a bad job as a mother or a father. It could just mean your child needs some help—either with the content or with performance issues. If you confuse your child's performance with *your* self-esteem you are making the issue personal and emotionally charged, which only inflates the stress levels. This is further complicated when the parent performed poorly in school and now has unresolved issues of shame, anger or guilt. If you have difficulty separating out your child's performance from your own self-esteem or from your own performance as a child, you can avail yourself of different forms of support such as parenting books, online help, peer counseling (talking with other parents), or professional therapy. The section on *Resources* will point you in the right direction. You can also use the "Parents' Corner" of my website.

Are You Micro-Managing Your Child?

Sometimes a well-meaning parent, wanting their child to succeed, will always be hovering close by to make sure everything is done, and done right.

This can extend to constant intervening with people who work with the child: the teacher, coach, parents of the child's friends. The term "helicopter parent" is a recent addition to the lexicon of child rearing. While it is natural to want the best for your child, the very best is to give your child room to grow. It's hard to watch him make a mistake, or make the wrong choice, but true learning and growth come only from personal action. If you micro-manage your child and those around him you are acting like permanently affixed training wheels to your kid's bicycle. He will become dependent on you, and will never learn how to find and maintain his own balance and move ahead.

If your tendency is to over-intervene with your child or on her behalf, I would recommend you read again **Chapter Six: How to Stay Focused**. First, clarify your goal as a parent. I suggest it is to provide a safe and healthy environment where your child can learn by doing, and grow in their own, unique way. Become aware when you feel the urge to jump in and take over for your child. At that moment use the tools: **Stop!** Ask yourself, "Is my intervening here supporting my goal?" **Listen** to your inner voice, which will direct you to take actions consistent with your goal (*Calm down. Let your child take responsibility for himself*). And finally, **fulfill** the direction of the voice by giving your child the space he needs. Stand back, observe, and, if it helps you, pray.

Do You Have a "Suck It Up" Attitude Toward Challenges?

Often parents think that kids today have it way easier than they should. I've heard people say, "When I took the SAT, they didn't let *me* in the exam room with a calculator." They seem to think the calculator ought to alleviate all their child's woes and he should now skate to success. When a kid is stressed out over a test, some parents just don't understand it and they don't offer a lot of empathy. "I had to suck it up, so should Billy." The problem with this attitude is that it might have floated in your day but times have changed. When you were your child's age you probably did what you were told ("suck it up"). Kids today are more aware of stress. While we all—children included—have many challenges to face, telling your child to just "suck it up" painfully disregards the very real struggle he is having and ought to be learning to deal with. If you support him instead of demeaning his struggle, not only will you help him with the test he's about to take, but you'll give him the tools to handle other stressful situations in life.

FINAL POINTERS

If you have read this book and worked through the checklists in this chapter you've already gone a long way toward helping your child reduce the stress of test taking and learn concrete skills to improve test scores.

Here are some final pointers.

❏ **Pay attention to the study environment at home.** There are some basics about creating a healthy study environment at home that will help your child study more effectively.

   ❏ If you can, find a consistent place for him to do homework or study for tests. That way, when he gets there, even though his mind isn't happy about having to study, his body knows he has to buckle down.

   ❏ Have all the materials they need at hand (books, paper, calculator, pens and pencils). Remember: ten minutes searching for a pencil sharpener doesn't count as "study time"!

   ❏ If you have more than one child, or space is so limited that having a separate desk or table is not a viable option, give each child her own basket with everything she needs in it, and then store the basket in the same place at the end of the study time.

❏ **Understand and appreciate the stresses your child is facing on a daily basis.** Are you aware of the different requirements in all of your child's classes? Try saying this to your child: "Help me understand what you're finding so difficult in math." This lets her know that you are there for her.

❏ **Don't judge your child and don't interpret his behavior.** Judging your child means saying something to him that sounds critical: "You are not good at math because you don't use your head and think logically." Interpreting sounds like you are his therapist: "I think the reason you're not doing well is that you expect people to do everything for you." (This is also judgmental) These approaches don't work. Judgments and interpretations are triggers that make children turn off to their parents.

❑ **Determine whether your child is as confident as he appears.** Do you ever have the feeling that he is always trying to put up a good "front"—that he wants it to appear as if everything is all right when it really isn't? If you suspect this, acknowledge his desire to do well, and also affirm that sometimes having a few doubts is normal. It's better to bring them to the light of day and see what they are than to pretend they don't exist because ultimately the self-doubt will undermine his self-confidence.

❑ **If your child is under-performing on tests, does she express an interest in improving?** Ask her if she would like to work with a program (like the one presented in this book or on my website). Would she like to work with a coach or tutor?

❑ **Look out for increasing disconnection and possibly depression.** Listen to what your child is saying about particular subjects or about school in general. If he is complaining a lot, is mostly dissatisfied and is rarely happy when he comes home from school, it is likely a sign that he is growing more and more disengaged and is possibly even depressed. There might be something that he does enjoy at school, but overlooks. If you find out what that is you may begin to understand what fires him up. Could it be certain subject matter? A particular teacher? Answering these questions will also give you a clue as to why your child is disconnecting in other subjects. If he seems to have lost all interest in school and in other parts of his life, he may be depressed and need a different level of support, such as professional counseling.

❑ **Get help and consultation.** Sometimes performance issues point to an underlying anxiety or depression that needs professional attention. Talk with the school counselor about what services are available in the school or ask the counselor to make a referral to a professional outside the system. Review the Resource List at the end of this book and on my website: **www.WorkbookForTestSuccess.com**

Without a doubt, tests are challenging. They are also here to stay. Better to give kids what they need so they can handle them successfully than watch them suffer and sink. Remember, the common misconception is that doing well on tests is only a matter of mastering the content (subject matter). As we have seen, that is only one part of the picture. The more enduring, important part is the test taker and how calm, confident and focused he learns to be through the process of studying and taking the test.

Of course, you want your child to be successful on the many tests he will have to face in school and in life. But being successful doesn't merely mean garnering a high score. It means growing in body, mind and spirit. It means being calm, confident and focused so that he can handle whatever challenge life places in his path.

Chapter Ten

For Teachers

I t is my fervent hope that if you are a teacher, a school administrator, or an educational policymaker, you have found the material in this workbook to be useful and provocative.

Teaching is arguably one of the most challenging professions in the world. It demands ongoing attention to an ever-changing flux of variables—from an individual student's cognitive and emotional growth to dynamic group factors, from highly charged cultural and political issues to rapid advances in technology and information processing. Keeping a finger on the pulse of all of this is a full-time, virtually nonstop, excruciatingly difficult job, and yet that's what you're expected to do as a teacher. The dedicated teacher has to be wide-awake and ready to meet the challenges of an ever-evolving system.

Earlier in the workbook I mentioned sitting in for a few months on a third-grade class in a public school near our home. All day, I charted what the teacher and children did. My findings were grim: 75 percent of the teacher's actions were directed to getting the children to be quiet. Almost 50 percent of the children's activities had to do with spitting back material the teacher told them to "learn." The other 50 percent was spent fooling around, sneaking food, writing, passing notes, and so on. The children were variously bored, agitated, minimally engaged and noisy. The teacher had to keep quieting them down. The kids would stay hushed for a little while, then they would regurgitate more stuff, then become bored and rowdy, and then the teacher struggled to quiet them down again. And so the cycle kept repeating. At the university level it's no better. Many students are engaged in diversion activities instead of paying attention to the lecture.

There are big disconnections here, which unfortunately are more the rule than the exception. The teacher is misled about what is happening and what the students are actually doing; there's a disconnect between what the teachers are providing and what the students are really learning. This is a huge waste of time, energy, and personal and public resources. Let me be clear: I am not criticizing hard-working and well-meaning teachers. As I will discuss later in this chapter, the roots of this disconnection are not about teachers being misguided.

Each of us who work in schools has to answer fundamental questions. *What is education for? What am I actually doing with these human beings in my care? Is the whole purpose to give students experiences that inspire them? Or is it to train them to regurgitate, on demand, more and more information without digesting and assimilating it? Is it to guide students in accepting the moral responsibility to self and others or is it to scare them into being obedient? Is it to favor competition or foster contribution?*

As an educator you must always ask, "Am I serving my students' best interests?"

Because we are caught up in the day-to-day tussle of government mandates, curricular requirements and student needs, sometimes we understandably lose touch with our fundamental purpose: to give the student what he or she needs to live a life that is healthy, productive and fulfilled. Our true role is to inspire our students to live connected, meaningful lives and to give them the tools to achieve that. Our students face tests, small and large, every single day, and we need to know how to best prepare them for these challenges and support them through the process.

HOW TO USE THIS WORKBOOK

In the first chapter I introduced this workbook as a tool box. It is meant to equip students—high school, college, graduate—with the nine tools for being calm, confident and focused on any test—the qualities necessary for success in performance situations. The nine tools make up the model of the three-legged stool, which encompasses body, mind and spirit.

This is a model you too can use. Teachers who are calm, confident and focused are less stressed and more successful in their role in the classroom. They are also more exemplary as role models for their students.

If, on opening this workbook, you happened to turn directly to this chapter, I urge you to start from Chapter One and read the book in its entirety, for two reasons. One, you will gain considerable insight and valuable techniques to help your students achieve better results on a test, as well as have a better experience. Two, doing this will give you the opportunity to reflect on how you, as a teacher, embody the three essential qualities yourself. In other words, how calm, confident and focused are you? We can only teach what we are. Your subject matter (whether it is math, literature, history, science or language) is secondary to you, the person. If you are calm, confident and focused, you will reflect those qualities to your pupils. Following your example, it will be easier for them to be calm, confident and focused. It's really hard to teach/tell/emphasize the importance of being these qualities if you're standing there a nervous wreck.

As I was writing this chapter I had the rare opportunity to observe the teaching and learning in a brain anatomy lab for first year medical students. One afternoon I watched, in awe, a phenomenal performance by a neuroscientist as he cajoled, prompted, challenged and above all, inspired the students *to want to* understand and learn the complicated nerve pathways from the brain to the rest of the body. He lit a fire in those students, and even though I understood very few of the seemingly hundreds of technical terms that were flying around, I was completely caught up in the excitement he generated about *how things work*. He was supremely focused, strongly confident, and in his own, highly animated manner, very calm with these students as each of them struggled to learn in his or her own way. His confidence in them was apparent, and that too came across strongly. I would have to say that man was the living embodiment of what I'm striving to teach in this workbook.

My ardent hope is that you will be able to become the same—or close to it. Trust me, it is doable. Read the chapters. Do the exercises. Cultivate your awareness. Use the tools. Reflect on your experience. Employ the material with your students. Use this workbook as *your* tool box. The expression, "You are really teaching when you are learning," is truly applicable here.

THE THREE-LEGGED STOOL

Here, in brief, are some guidelines on how you, the teacher, can use the model of the three-legged stool in the classroom. Since life is a journey of learning, you may also want to use if for yourself. Before reading on, though, make sure you have completed the performance inventory (BPI) on page 30. What do your scores tell you about yourself? Which of the three legs is weak and needs work? Which is strong? Be honest with yourself. Depending on your responses, you will want to re-read the chapter on the leg you need to strengthen. In addition, you will also want to cultivate your awareness of when you are becoming disconnected; then practice using the tools to reconnect and get back in "the zone."

Calm

When do you lose it? Are you triggered by unruly student behavior, demanding administrators, irate parents, endless requirements on your "free time," school and government standards for student test performance which you know don't really work? The list goes on. It is essential that you recognize your particular triggers. What are your bodily signs that you're off—heart racing, face reddening, stomach tightening? Was the trigger a thought, or was it something another person did or said? (*If that father screams at me one more time I'm going haul off and whack him!*). It is very easy to be induced into someone else's tension and anxiety. They are all hyped up and suddenly so are you. You must find your own way to stay connected to yourself no matter what happens. Don't be dragged into what others are feeling. You can be empathetic with the other person without being seduced into the same feeling state, the same negative emotions. Besides the fact that you protect yourself from the other person's storm, you will also give yourself a much greater chance to effect change when you remain calm.

Use the tools. Once you become aware of your triggers, and you recognize your own signs of physical disconnection, use the tools to reduce your stress before it escalates. Breathe deeply and steadily. Ground yourself. Even if an emotional tempest is raging in the other person, you still have the capacity to feel your feet supported by the floor and you can still release any tension in your face, neck, shoulders and gut. Sense the space all around you and around the anxious or angry person facing you. By connecting to the bigger picture you are actually tapping into your parasympathetic nervous system, which, as I explained in Chapter Four, calms you down.

To improve your performance as a teacher, learn to be calm, confident and focused.

Confidence

Every teacher knows that some percentage of the students in her classroom are going to provoke and test her. Either they are bored and trying to entertain themselves, or they're trying to show off to their friends. They'll interrupt by talking to a classmate or erupt with some other antics. Sometimes it's just irritating and it can be written off, but at other times, it challenges the teacher's confidence in herself. She's not sure she's strong enough to hold her students' attention. It might make her doubt whether they respect her. Suddenly, she doesn't know if she's good enough. Moments like these can soon turn to quicksand if you let yourself be dragged down by them because once you lose your grip, you begin to sink fast. With awareness and the tools, you can quickly regain your footing, turn the negativity around and find yourself on firm ground again.

What are your negative self-statements? When a student challenges you, sometimes in a rude, obnoxious way, it can trouble you deeply if it triggers a negative self-statement, the kind that has attacked your sense of worth your whole life. Teaching, especially good teaching, repeatedly tests your confidence. Why? Because as a teacher, by challenging your students, you are constantly putting yourself on the line. You wonder every day "Am I getting through?" You are forever feeling the push-back from students who are resistant, lazy, angry or tired. A student doesn't understand something, or can't see its relevance, or just isn't interested. Instead of becoming negative about yourself (*I'm not a competent teacher*), how do you ignite their interest, engage them and teach in a way so they "get it"?

Also, your self-worth is constantly being tested. Students, especially late teens and early adults are themselves struggling intensely with issues of self-worth and they will find infinite ways to challenge yours. You will know this happening when you feel besieged by a feeling of vulnerability and you worry, "Do they like me?" Your self-confidence needs to be cultivated and strong as you are being buffeted by the trials and tribulations that are part and parcel of being a good teacher: struggling daily with budding individuals who need to be inspired to grow and may be afraid to and not want to.

Learn to become aware of when you start thinking "I can't... I don't.... I'm not" about your own performance. *(I can't handle this. I'm not good enough. I don't have what it takes).* This kind of negative thinking disconnects you from your positive, determined self that wants to do a good job, and can.

Use the tools. As soon as you notice your confidence is slipping, learn to confide in your inner confidant—your highest self, your spirit. You may call this your God, Goddess or Higher Power. It is also the fully realized image of yourself as you are meant to be. Tell your confidant the kind of negative thoughts that are getting under your skin. Usually you'll see you're expecting yourself to be *perfect*. Well, no one is. Try to let go of unreasonably high standards and give yourself a break. Release the hold the negative thoughts have on you or they will fester and grow. Naturally these thoughts will arise automatically when you're in the type of situation that triggers them, but that doesn't mean you have to feed them. Let them come, and let them go. They don't have to run your life.

Next, let the confidant, your highest self, reflect back to you something positive and accurate about you so you can counter the negativity. It will say something like: *"You have taken on many challenging situations before; you are certainly capable of dealing with this one."* Receive this message and take it in so that it influences your belief in yourself.

Lastly, envision successfully taking a series of small, manageable steps to correct the negativity (*What do these kids* like *to do? Well, I could brainstorm with them and poll their different interests. Then I'll engage one of them each day to help me plan the next day's lesson*). By seeing yourself taking these "outer" steps, you are actually correcting course on the *inner* level. Any negative thoughts you have about yourself will reverse direction as you engage your imagination in seeing yourself being successful.

As a teacher you are going to be challenged every day in many ways. Tests, for the students and for you, are ingrained in the woodwork of this profession. Accept that reality. By showing your students how you take on challenging situations in a calm and focused way, you are modeling for them how confidence is actually built. Your ability to do this rests on your belief in yourself and on how well you can move ahead, in challenging times, one firm step at a time.

Focus

The focus leg of the stool—the one representing spirit—is the most important of the three for sustained success. Paradoxically, in education, it is the least appreciated. The word *success* comes from the Latin root that means "happy outcome." Until very recently "happy outcome" in our culture meant "lots of money." The 2009 world financial crisis certainly revealed the pitfalls of that belief system. To me, "happy outcome" means that the product of your hard work is happiness and satisfaction, whether that translates into a fat paycheck or not. All the world's spiritual traditions teach this one message in different ways: happiness doesn't come from *things*, it springs from *being*. When you are focused, in the way that I use the word in this workbook, you act in accord with your highest, best self. You also contribute to the lives of others for their well being. This, the saints and sages say, is the road to true happiness.

How does this translate to your focus as a teacher? As we saw in Chapter Six, when you are focused you have a goal and you take actions that lead you to the goal. The first question to ask yourself is, "What is my goal as a teacher?"

I think that a teacher's daily requirements are so demanding that they end up becoming goals in themselves and one loses sight of the other, higher goals like inspiring and empowering your students, awakening their curiosity, cultivating a passion for learning, giving them the experience of community, and showing them, by being a committed partner in their learning, what it means to be responsible to self and others.

When are you distracted? Become aware when your actions are disconnected from your greater goal. This is what I call distraction. In my experience, a distraction for many teachers is complaining about the system and all its wrongs. Sure, there's a lot that doesn't work, a lot you would like to see changed—from the volumes of required record-keeping, to syllabi that are outmoded, to the seemingly countless tests your students have to take. If you allow yourself to be caught up in the complaining mode you will have little energy and interest to achieve the goals I just talked about. In addition, your negative feelings about the system can easily lead to taking out your frustrations on students. If *they* only acted better your life would be easier. You carp on insignificant (albeit sometimes obnoxious) student behavior. You start ragging on students when you know there must be a better way of handling your frustration. You know you have lost focus and drifted off course when you address them in a harsh, demeaning manner.

> **Empower your students. Inspire them to be focused.**

Use the tools. When you become distracted by negative thinking and action and you start veering off track, use the three Focus tools to reconnect to your spirit. As soon as you catch yourself disconnecting—say you are being overly hard on a student—use the first tool. Stop. Ask yourself, "Is the way I am thinking or acting leading me to my goal?" The answer will be no. Next, listen to your highest self and receive its specific direction for reconnecting with your spirit. Take a deep breath, calm down and approach the student directly and respectfully, even though you don't like how he is behaving. And finally, fulfill the direction of the voice and reconnect to your spirit by taking actions that lead to your goal. For instance, look directly at the student and tell him, in a calm, confident and focused way what you expect of him and the ways in which he is missing the mark. But you have to be focused when you're doing this because you are a model for your students; you're not just uttering words. And remember that you are preparing students for *living*, not just remembering facts. There is a deeper purpose to your actions than teaching algebra, so your actions must be aligned with the common good.

WHAT ARE OUR STUDENTS REALLY LEARNING?

While this workbook is focused on test performance, any thoughtful reader will have recognized my higher goal: to address the fundamental issues that contribute to test stress and poor scores, and how these issues point to what is lacking in the way we educate our youth. In graduate school, when I studied the philosophy and techniques of family therapy, I learned an interesting thing—that the "trouble maker" in the family (usually a child or teenager), was actually not the real problem. His or her disturbance pointed to something else in the larger family system that nobody was recognizing, let alone addressing. So it is in our schools: students who are not performing well can give us valuable clues as to what needs to be transformed in the school system as a whole.

This workbook is a toolbox to help repair what's broken, both individually and systemically. It is meant to give test takers what they need to become empowered to perform at their top level during a test. It is also meant to give you, the teacher, the awareness and tools you need to equip yourself and your students for the tests we all face.

Having worked at every level of the educational system for the last forty years— from Head Start nursery school programs in 1969, to professional graduate healthcare training in 2009, I've had many opportunities to reflect on the larger question of just what is it that we are actually teaching in American education. What I have observed is that generally what students learn in their early schooling doesn't match up with what they actually need later in life. The following table is meant to stimulate your thinking and provoke discussion amongst teachers and educational policy makers. As you will see, there is a mismatch between the habits of thinking and action that students develop in school and what is required of them in day-to-day living. I hope this helps makes the case for teaching the skills of being calm, confident and focused as necessary for life, not just the classroom.

What are students actually learning in school?	What do they need in life?
Least/last When preparing for tests, many students procrastinate and cram. They learn how to handle tests by doing the least amount at the last possible moment. They're always behind eight-ball, always playing catch-up. This becomes a stressed-out style for dealing with tests in life.	**To be well prepared** Since life presents new tests at every turn, we need to be prepared to deal with whatever comes our way. By knowing how to calm down, be confident and stay focused we can take on any challenge. Instead of feeling overwhelmed we are empowered.
Give the right answer Schooling and testing reward correct answers. It doesn't matter what level of thinking goes into the answer. Too often that thinking is spotty or faulty.	**To think critically** Life is messy, and the "right answer" to a particular issue is often not readily apparent. We need to cultivate the ability to think critically about what is facing us and consider our options for action.
Self-serving Competition, the cornerstone of our educational system, too often pits students against one another. They learn to think only about themselves *(How can I get ahead?),* often to the exclusion and sometimes to the detriment of others who may not have the same gifts and privileges.	**To serve others** We are each part of a worldwide social fabric. We exist not only for ourselves, but for each other and the common good. When you are part of a community you reflect, *How can I contribute?* You appreciate that everyone has a unique part to play, and each is valued for his or her contribution.
Get in to get out Students do what's necessary to get to the next step. Their attention is trained on the result. On every student's mind is, "Will this be on the exam?" This attitude avoids the present and focuses on a nebulous, scary future.	**To be present** Life is an ever-flowing stream of present moments. By teaching students to be calm, confident and focused we train them to be in the moment and to take full advantage of the countless opportunities to learn and grow individually and together, right now.

THE FIVE STEPPING STONES TO GREAT TEACHING

To close out this workbook I offer what I view as the five stepping stones to great teaching. In my own journey I have had the honor and privilege of being taught by some extraordinary teachers—passionate about their subject of inquiry, devoted to their students, and committed to creating a better world. I strive to emulate their example. Here is my attempt to sum up what I have learned about the art of teaching and how it translates to facing tests.

1. Enjoy What You Are Doing

When you are passionate about your work—the material you teach and the act of being a teacher—your enthusiasm translates directly to your students. It inspires them to be passionate about learning, about what they will eventually commit themselves to, and how they will handle life's tests. Conversely, if you are bored, your students will be resistant and won't want to learn. School—and life—will become a chore for everyone involved, a necessary hurdle to jump over.. You can't fake passion, of course. If you don't have it for what you are teaching, find it, talk to someone else who does have it and can help you, or seek work that really turns you on.

2. Model Respect

"Respect" means to "hold in esteem or honor." You can model it by respecting the differences and contributions each student makes to your class and after that, to society. Everyone has something to offer, and your job is to honor that. Remember, your students are watching you. When you show them respect you are sending the message that this is the way to act towards themselves and towards each other. Respect doesn't mean wholesale acceptance. Individual differences exist, and should be appreciated. Respect also doesn't require you to be warm and fuzzy. That is a matter of individual personality and style. Case in point: in junior high school I had a lot of trouble with elementary algebra. All those x's and y's—I just couldn't get it. I had a "strict" algebra teacher: assignments had to be handed in on time, classes couldn't be cut, and grading was according to the precision of one's thinking and answers. Though I was clearly struggling, the teacher never once made me feel dumb or inadequate. Rather, he respected that I was having difficulty and that algebra was not "my thing." He encouraged me to work hard, he helped me break down the material into small, manageable steps, and he introduced me to older students who served as tutors. Though he never smiled—that was not his style—I had no doubt

> Great teachers are passionate. Be passionate in your own way.

that he respected me, and that respect actually urged me on to learn the material, although I had to do it in a way that made sense to *me*. I went from failing the initial quizzes to receiving a B- on the final. This was a big achievement and great source of pride for me. By being respected, students learn to respect themselves and their own process when they study for and take tests. They take themselves seriously.

3. Accept Reality

Life often unfolds differently than the way we would like it to, or hoped it would. You have a few options when this happens, which is more or less every day. You can complain (to whomever will listen), you can sulk, you can become angry, you can be disappointed, or you can curl up in a fetal position and long for the womb. But there is another approach: you can step into the flow of life and accept things just as they are. You can work with what is.

For teachers this is a daily challenge—so many things happen day in and day out that we don't like or want. (After all, we're usually working with kids and teenagers). So what? The sooner you realize that you are not really controlling *anything,* the more you will accept what is and work with it, which means you're not fighting it. This includes all of the demands placed on you by testing and the unpredictability of student performance. Accept reality. Stop wishing it were different or thinking things like, "If I were God, I never would have made such a mess of it. The world could be run so much better." This kind of thinking is stress-producing because it disconnects you from dealing with what *is*.

At one talk I gave recently, I projected the Serenity Prayer onto the screen. During the break someone approached me saying she had a different version she thought I might like. I did like it, and I offer it to you:

> *God, grant me the serenity*
> *To accept **the people** I cannot change,*
> *The courage to change **the one I can**,*
> *And the wisdom to know **that's me.***

If you're really going to accept reality, it means you have to accept your own flaws and foibles, and accept your students for who they are. From you they learn to stop fighting with themselves.

4. Question the Staus Quo

Does it seem strange that I just made a case for accepting reality, and now I'm encouraging you to question the status quo? Let me put this together: while we do need to accept that we live in an imperfect world, we can also strive to make it better. As I said above, wishing or wanting things to be different only causes more stress. Instead of wishing things were different, understand that it is what it is, but certain things *can* change if you approach them the right way. As regards testing, complaining about it won't get you very far. Testing is here to stay. Better to work vigorously to make tests more culture-fair and more reflective of the subjects they test. Just by using this workbook, you can make the testing experience far less excruciating by training your students to be calm, confident and focused.

5. Be Responsible

When a student in your charge has difficulty learning, or difficulty with tests, who is responsible? In the London schools I was trained in, if a child wasn't grasping the material, it was up to the teacher to find a different, better way to teach that child. That was the teacher's *job*. It wasn't just dumped into the lap of the student.

Unfortunately, in most American schools, everyone starts blaming and finger-pointing all over the place when a student is failing: at the parents, the culture, the curriculum and so on. And who suffers? The student. Labels, diagnoses and medications are all too frequently easy outs. And they can have terrible, long-term consequences. The name-calling of the label sticks around through adult life, and drug side-effects can create a whole new nest of problems. Okay, so whose fault is it?

One of my great teachers, Viola Spolin, suggested that we define *responsibility* as "the ability to respond." (Notice the word *blame* isn't in there anywhere.) Yes, perhaps it sometimes can be helpful to identify when someone is clearly dropping the ball, but what we really need to do is address the problems, to continuously cultivate our ability to respond to our students' needs. In order to do this well and with integrity, I believe we need first to learn to take responsibility for ourselves, to cultivate the best in who *we* are so that we can be healthy, productive contributors to a safe, supportive world community. It starts with you, the teacher. You have a sacred role to play, a contribution to make that is uniquely yours. By being responsible, you are training your students to emulate you as they grow and to handle life's challenges in a way that increases happiness and decreases suffering. You can teach them responsibility by cultivating your ability to respond, rather than pointing the finger at something or someone else.

THE CHALLENGE OF TESTS

Significant at this time in our history is the rampant rise of testing across America and its negative impact on students, teachers and the culture of schooling. We are obsessed with numbers—test scores and percentile rankings—to which we hinge teacher's salaries and school funding. We relentlessly continue to push tests that are unfair, outdated, culturally biased, anxiety provoking and that don't really test what they are supposed to be testing. Does this sound like a supportive, nurturing environment where youngsters can learn about their world and explore who they are? Where they can develop the cognitive and social skills necessary for successful living? No. It sounds like we're failing.

As educators, we must continually ask ourselves, "Whose needs are we serving?" I see too many teachers exercising their own need for control and their own not-so-hidden agenda to "get by" and "score high" at the terrible expense of their students. These teachers, themselves the victims of policies and curricula that need extensive re-thinking and overhaul, are not only hurting their students, but are sacrificing their own precious opportunity to offer something of immense value—their own humanity and the wisdom, accumulated over the years, of what it means to live in a meaningful and connected way.

Let us prepare our students for the lives they will lead outside of school by teaching them how to face any test. By our own example, let us show them what it means to be calm, confident and focused in the midst of life's challenges. In this way we can all face the enormous test of living together interdependently, supporting and nurturing one another.

In ancient scriptures a story is told of "The Thirty-Six." It is said that at any one time there are thirty-six divinely chosen souls embodied as humans, placed on this planet, and for them the Creator keeps the earth alive and thriving. There's one hitch: no one knows the identity of The Thirty-Six, not even The Thirty-Six themselves. One of them could be your six month old child, or the person sitting next to you on the bus, or your physician, or your mail carrier, or your sister. One could be a student in your class. And one could be you, yourself.

Our real test is to create a world in which we all live together in peace.

Since the identity of The Thirty-Six is hidden, let us strive to treat one another, and ourselves, as if each of us *is* that crucial person. May our thoughts, speech and actions honor this possibility. And may we empower every one of our students to make a valuable contribution to our world community and to spark that empowerment and responsibility for connection in everyone they meet.

I look forward to meeting you along this path.

AWARENESS LOG: CALM

Use this sheet to help track and increase your awareness of your body when you are not calm. Recording what you were doing and what tool you used.

Awareness is the first step to changing old habits. Once you become aware that you are disconnecting in your body you can use the three tools for calming down: **breathing, grounding, and sensing.**

Fill in the columns below with the date, where you were disconnecting in your body, and which tool you found particularly helpful.

You can photocopy this sheet and carry it with you through your day.

Example:

Date	Where are you disconnecting in your body?	Tool(s)
7/02/09	My shoulders were all tensed up	Breathing, grounding

Date	Where are you disconnecting in your body?	Tool(s)

AWARENESS LOG: CONFIDENCE

Use this sheet to help track and increase your awareness when your confidence starts slipping, and how to turn that around.

Fill in the columns below with the date, what you were saying negatively about yourself, and which tool you found particularly helpful. Remember: the three tools for regaining your confidence are **confide, reflect, envision**.

You can photocopy this sheet and carry it with you through your day.

Example:

Date	Negative self-statement	Tool(s)
7/13/09	"I can't succeed at calculus."	Envisioning small steps

Date	Negative self-statement	Tool(s)

AWARENESS LOG: FOCUS

Use this sheet to help track and increase your awareness of when you lose focus and how you put yourself back on track.

Fill in the columns below with the date, the distraction you engaged in, and which of the focus tools were most helpful. The three tools for staying focused are: **stop, listen, and fulfill.**

You can photocopy this sheet and carry the log with you throughout your day.

Example:

Date	Distraction	Tool(s)
4/25/09	Kept checking e-mail	Stop!

Date	Distraction	Tool(s)

THE BERNSTEIN PERFORMANCE MODEL (BPM)
SUMMARY OF THEORY AND PRACTICE

Theory

An optimal level of stress stimulates optimal performance.
When stress is too high or too low, performance suffers.

Stress is a function of disconnection.
Feeling stressed means you are disconnected in one or more of the three domains: spirit, mind and body.

Reduce stress and improve performance through connection.
Keep focused in your spirit.
Remain confident in your mind.
Stay calm in your body.

Practice

To reduce stress: 1. *Cultivate your* **awareness** *of disconnection.*
                        2. *Use the following core* **tools** *to reconnect.*

FOCUS   **Stop** *and ask, "Is this distraction taking me to my goal?*
                 Listen *to your inner voice for the next step.*
                 Fulfill *your purpose. Get yourself back on track.*

CONFIDENCE   **Confide** *in your confidant. Let go of the negativity.*
                 Reflect *back something accurate and positive.*
                 Envision *taking small, manageable steps.*

CALM   **Breathe** *deeply down to your belly.*
                 Ground *yourself. Feel the floor. Release tension.*
                 Sense *your surroundings through your five senses.*

RESOURCES

Following is a list of resources for test takers, educators and parents. In addition, talk with fellow students about resources they have found particularly helpful. You can also explore the web and consult with a school advisor or counselor. When you come across a book, service or network you find personally helpful please consider sharing it for future editions of this workbook by writing to DrB@WorkbookForTestSuccess. com

Questions or comments
If this workbook has prompted questions and comments please send them to the email address above.

Website
Please explore the website connected with this Workbook. The url is: http://www. WorkbookForTestSuccess.com. On the website you will find webinars, opportunities to connect with other test takers, resources for teachers and parents, as well as Dr. B's blog.

Aides
Additional aides are also available on the website and are in development. These include: CDs and downloadable mp3s including *Dr. B's Gentle Prompts for Calming Down.*

Individual coaching
Individual coaching is conducted via Skype, chat, e-mail and phone. For details of programs and fees please send an e-mail to Coaching@WorkbookForTestSuccess. com

Group coaching
Coaching for groups is conducted by teleconferences, bulletin boards and social networking. Coaching can designed for already existing groups within a school (whole classes, after-school clubs), or between schools. Group coaching is also available for teacher and parent associations. Please request information via email.

Training
If you are interested in being trained as a coach in the Bernstein Performance Model (BPM), please write to Training@WorkbookForTestSuccess.com

Speeches and Seminars
Dr. Bernstein is a national speaker and workshop leader on the subject of stress and performance. For a selection of titles and booking information please see the website.

Referrals
A national network of educational specialists, tutors and psychotherapists is in development. On the Workbook website you will find the appropriate link.

Local Networks
Explore local parent and teacher list-servs. An excellent example is the Berkeley Parents Network, http://parents.berkeley.edu.

Books
Following is a small selection of publications that you might find helpful:

College admissions
Sandra and Ian Griffin, **Step Into College** booklet series. **118 Tips on Succeeding in Standardized Tests** and **110 Tips for Getting into the College of Your Choice**. Contact: http://www.stepintocollege.com

Elizabeth Wissner-Gross. **What Colleges Don't Tell You (and Other Parents Don't Want You to Know)**. Hudson Street Press.

Connection to the natural world
David Abrams. **The Spell of the Sensuous.** Vintage Books.

Education
Deborah Meier. **In Schools We Trust.** Beacon Press.

Parenting
Michael Riera. **Staying Connected to Your Teenager.** DaCapo Press.

Stress
Robert M. Sapolsky. **Why Zebras Don't Get Ulcers.** W.H. Freeman & Co.

Guided imagery
Catherine Shainberg. **Kabbalah and the Power of Dreaming.** Inner Traditions.

Your stories, questions and comments are welcome.
Please write to DrB@WorkbookForTestSuccess.com

WITH THANKS

This work is a product of my lifetime as a student, a performer, a teacher and a psychologist. Many people have assisted and guided me along the path. To everyone mentioned here, please accept this work as an expression of my appreciation and gratitude.

First, to my school teachers: Miss Hardy, who in the sixth grade at P.S. 193 in Brooklyn, taught me the meaning of 'personal integrity'; Chester Miller, who made junior high school fun; Mssrs. Grebanier, Blatt and Chagrin and Miss Isaccson at Midwood High School for being such stimulating individuals; my college teachers Louis Cox and Herbert Ross Brown, who challenged me to think and write clearly, and Richard Hornby who encouraged my creativity as an actor and director; graduate school mentors John Weiser, Cliff Christensen, Ed Sullivan and Les McLean, who supported my work. And above all, to David E. Hunt, my dissertation supervisor, who listened and encouraged me to speak in my own voice.

The next group of teachers were outside the school system and had a profound influence on my development: theatrical visionary Viola Spolin, who taught me what it means to get out of the way and let it happen; Ronald Watkins, Shakespeare scholar, who showed me how passion translates into art; to Collette Aboulker-Muscat, who gave her life to exploring the mysteries of the inner landscape; and to Catherine Shainberg, Collette's protégé and great spirit, for her unflagging support. And to Sidney Zakarin, my indomitable Boy Scout leader, Troop 221 in Brooklyn.

My first professional colleagues in education: Wendla Kernig and Moira McKenzie, headmistresses of infant schools in London, and the teachers, students and parents at those schools, who taught me the necessity of action, the importance of spirit, and that community is the foundation for learning. Ruth M. Beard at the University of London, clarified the meaning and uses of Piaget's psychology; and Lillian Weber, Vivian Windley, Herb Mack, Ann Cook and Deborah Meier, who blazed a trail starting in New York schools to make them more active, community-based, responsible places.

To my mentors and colleagues in the field of psychology: Jon M. Plapp, my first supervisor and life-long friend; Edward C. Whitmont, Sylvia Brinton Perera, John Conger, Lisby Mayer, Mel McGraw, Gilbert Newman, Claude Steiner, Eric Maisel, Ruth Cohn and especially Beverley Zabriskie, who encouraged me to be the psychologist and performance coach I am today. I am particularly grateful to William F. Riess, for his ongoing and generous support of my work and this project.

To my colleagues in education: Catherine Hunter, head of San Francisco Friends School and Sharon Cravanas, college advisor, for providing me the opportunities to do the first research studies of my work, and to Paul Chapman, head of Head-Royce School, where the work was done. My professional colleagues in health care across the country: Dean Charles N. Bertolami of the NYU School of Dentistry for his genuine enthusiasm and for recognizing the value of this work; my friends and colleagues at UCSF: Troy E. Daniels, Jennifer Williams, for introducing me to the School of Dentistry; Richard McKenzie, Maureen Conway, Linda Centore, Dorothy Perry and David Hand. Also to Charles J. Alexander, Karl Haden and Linda Keating for the opportunities they gave me to share my work with educators, students. and practitioners. To Deans Jack Clinton, Sharon Turner, Huw Thomas, Terri Dolan and Rowland Hutchinson. Professional colleagues at American Dental Association: Barkley Payne, Marsha Steigel, Jacqueline White, Tina Martinez, Marcia McKinney, Drs. Hal Fair, and John Drumm; and to the many dentists, hygienists, assistants and office managers across the country who have attended my seminars on stress and performance. To Ann Battrell and her colleagues at the ADHA, Nancy Hunnicutt and the students at the American Student Dental Association, and to Dan Lowenstein and the faculty and students of "Training the Mind" at UCSF School of Medicine for the exceptional opportunity to review some of this material as the book was in the final stages of editing. And to Lee S. Shulman, President Emeritus of the Carnegie Foundation for the Advancement of Teaching, for providing the inspiration of the "lamed vov" story that closes the book.

To my colleagues in music: Daisy Newman and the staff and students of the Young Musician's Program in Berkeley, for participating so fully in the coaching process and enjoying the results; Kathryn Cathcart, for our close collaboration over many years, allowing me to bring this work into opera through The Singer's Gym. To Sheri Greenawald, Director of the San Francisco Opera Center for inviting me to work with the Adler Fellows; to Robert Hughes, for his interest and support, and to Ron Herder, who encouraged me to follow the inner voice.

To those who assisted in bringing this work into book form: Ellen Griffin for her initial encouragement, Amanita Rosenbush, for her expert, undaunted editing, Dorothy Wall, for helping me clarify the first proposal for the book, Susan Page, for her continuing enthusiasm and encouragement, and to Margaret Miller for her copyediting. To Dave Innis and Adam Burleigh, the talented graphic and visual artists whose work is part of this book; and to Wilma Wyss, for her astute, creative eye and skill as the book's designer. To literary agents Faith Hamlin, Joe Spieler and Amy Rennert, who guided me through the process of thinking through this Workbook in its early stages. To those who read the manuscript at different times and offered valuable feedback: Kymberly Smith, Scott McComas, Tony Barreca, Amelia Wilcox, Elizabeth Wissner-Gross and Alexandra Zabriskie. To my colleagues in the National Speaker's Association, most particularly Rebecca Morgan, and the Front Burner Club: Janet Bailey, Ian Griffin, Jeanne K. Smith. To members of the California Center for Sport Psychology, all for encouraging, and in some cases, challenging me to complete the manuscript. To Beth Diamond for urging me to attend the lunchtime seminar on test anxiety at UCSF, which kicked off this whole project. To a new friend and colleague, Rebecca Weller Brown, for her clear and direct feedback. And to Dr. Thomas Phelan for his generosity in being a mentor to me in the publishing process. To Rabbi Michael Lerner, who has taught me the value of Torah and the meaning of Shabbat, and to Judy Rosenfeld and Neil Gozan for their belief in me. I am grateful to the Hineni Foundation and particularly to the Hebrew Free Loan Association in San Francisco, for its dedication to individuals like myself who are ardently making their dreams a reality.

To friends who have supported me in so many ways over the years: Jay Zimmerman, Peter Shore, Leslie Sanders, Jonathan Mitchell, Marina Harris, Lynnia Milliun, Alexandra Chalif, Jesse Falk-Finley, Mary Ann Brandt, Joe Silvera, Frank Blau, Mel Konner and Ann Kruger, Howard and Christina Rovics, and Nancy Quinn. Special mention to Joe Ruffatto, whose friendship has been like a strong, steady anchor in a sometimes stormy sea; to David Martin, and Donald Sosin, soul brothers; and Pat Singer and Suzin Green, soul sisters. My life-long friends Harry and Judy Warren, Bobby and Ruth Ives, Virgil H. Logan, Jr., Marc David Block, Lewis C. Johnson and Candace Falk. To Gilbert and Monique Gaytan, for their extraordinary creativity and for challenging me to always go further. And to Andrea I. Jepson, whose generous and unflagging support has seen me and this project through many phases.

My family has been an ongoing source of encouragement in every way. My sister Didi Conn and brother-in-law David Shire have given me and my wife much more than I can possibly thank them for; my parents, Beverly Shmerling and Leonard Bernstein, for believing in all of their children; my talented, hard-working brothers Andrew and Richard and their families; to Hildy Bernstein, Marjori Bernstein, my aunts and uncles Charlotte, Julie and Gerry Bernstein; Tina Boardman; and my amazing aunt Rachel R. Lehmann, who, God willing, will be a healthy 106 years old when this book is published. When I asked Rachel her secret of such robust longevity she smiled, with a twinkle in her eyes, and said one word: "Love."

To my students, for the many, many opportunities they have given me to learn and to grow: from the young children in Brunswick Park Infants' School in London to the dental and medical students at UCSF, and all of the singers who attend The Singer's Gym.

To my clients, for their openness and commitment. It is impossible to say how much I have learned from them, about the material in this book and about myself in the deepest ways, and how grateful I am to them for their trust and hard work, proving again and again that transformation is possible.

To my wife, Suk Wah. Our life together gives me the opportunity every day to live what I have written about in this workbook. No one knows me better. My appreciation for her strength, determination, humor, sweetness, beauty and dedication to her own growth, is unbounded. We met at a single's dance the night after I had a dream about finding a wife. How fortunate that I learned to pay attention to my dreams!

And to my spiritual teachers for their lives of service, teaching and guidance.

If I am not for myself, then who will be for me?
If I am only for myself, what am I?
And if not now, when?

Rabbi Hillel
1st Century CE

About the Author

Ben Bernstein, Ph.D., is a psychologist and educator specializing in performance enhancement. He coaches Academy Award, Tony Award and Pulitzer Prize winners and his client list includes dentists, athletes, attorneys, physicians, business executives, opera singers, students and actors. A graduate of Bowdoin College, Bernstein received his doctorate from the University of Toronto and holds a master's degree in music composition from Mills College.

An educator for the last 40 years, Dr. Bernstein has taught at every level of the educational system. Originally trained in the progressive British infant schools in the late '60s, he has received major grants from the American and Canadian governments for his work. He currently lectures on peak performance nationwide. He is a master teacher at the San Francisco Opera, the founder of *The Singer's Gym*, and an award winning composer.

Dubbed by American Theater Magazine as "the imagination masseur," Bernstein was the first director of improvisation at Robert Redford's Sundance Institute in Utah, and has directed theater at The Juilliard School in New York and the National Academy of Dramatic Art in Sydney. He created and produced original musicals and films with psychiatric patients in the US and Australia. He is presently a member of the creative team for the new animated children's television series *Didi Lightful*.

Bernstein coaches his three younger siblings in their successful artistic careers: sister Didi Conn, Frenchy in *Grease*; brother Andrew, head photographer for the NBA; and youngest brother Richard, in leading roles at the Metropolitan Opera. His wife, Suk Wah, is a novelist. The couple live in the Bay Area, California.

Spark Avenue® is a web-based boulevard for individual growth and mutual success.

On Spark Avenue you will find a worldwide network of educators, artists, healthcare practitioners, social entrepreneurs and other humanitarians making a creative contribution to healing and transforming the world.

Divisions of Spark Avenue include: Publishing; Products; Services; Training and Consulting.

If you would like to set up your business on Spark Avenue or if you have a book, a DVD, a product, a service, or an idea that sparks creativity, contribution and connection, please contact us at: NewSparks@SparkAvenue.com

We welcome your inquiry.